Media Policy and Music Activity

How do people make music – and how does this activity relate to the policies of governments and the music industry? What is the relationship between live music and music we hear on radio, or in music videos? How has the digital revolution affected music-making in industrialized and in developing nations?

In *Media Policy and Music Activity*, Krister Malm and Roger Wallis look in depth at the relationships between policies governing the output of the music media and music activity in society. Investigating musical activity in six smaller nations – Jamaica, Trinidad, Kenya, Tanzania, Sweden and Wales — their study includes interviews with a broad range of musicians, policy makers, and with media and music industry employees. They discover that, all too often, media policies designed to encourage local cultural industries flounder on the rocks of non-implementation. Despite this, music activity continues to thrive on a local level, often in direct conflict with pressures from the international music industry.

The book provides an introduction to media policy and its relation to cultural production. A practical base in case study material is combined with a broad theoretical framework for understanding the music media, making *Media Policy and Music Activity* ideal reading not only for students and researchers, but also for policy makers, media practitioners and anyone interested in the role music plays in our everyday lives.

Krister Malm is Director of Musikmuseet in Stockholm, and Associate Professor of Musicology at Gothenburg University. **Roger Wallis** is BBC Correspondent in Sweden. Their pioneering research into the workings of the music industry was first published in the book *Big Sounds from Small Peoples* (Constable, 1984). Roger Wallis is the co-author, with Stanley Baran, of *The Known World of Broadcast News* (Routledge, 1990), an analysis of the broadcast news industry.

Media Policy and Music Activity

Krister Malm and Roger Wallis

London and New York

First published 1992
by Routledge
11 New Fetter Lane, London EC4P 4EE

Simultaneously published in the USA and Canada
by Routledge
29 West 35th Street, New York, NY 10001

© 1992 Krister Malm and Roger Wallis

Typeset in 10/12 pt Times by
Florencetype Ltd, Kewstoke, Avon
Printed in Great Britain by
Butler & Tanner Ltd, Frome

All rights reserved. No part of this book may be reprinted
or reproduced or utilized in any form or by any electronic,
mechanical, or other means, now known or hereafter
invented, including photocopying and recording, or in any
information storage or retrieval system, without permission
in writing from the publishers.

Publication has been facilitated by a grant from the Swedish Council for
Research in the Humanities and Social Sciences. This volume is also
Report 23 Musikmuseets Skrifter, Stockholm.

British Library Cataloguing in Publication Data

A CIP catalogue record for this book is available from the British Library.

Library of Congress Cataloging in Publication Data

Malm, Krister
　Media policy and music activity / Krister Malm and Roger Wallis.
　　p.　cm.
　Includes bibliographical references and index.
　1. Mass media and music.　I. Wallis, Roger.　II. Title.
ML3849.M27　1992
780'.0302--dc20　　　　　　　　　　　　　　　　　　92-13299

ISBN 0 415 050197
　　　0 415 050200 (pbk)

Contents

List of tables	vii
List of plates and figures	ix
List of abbreviations	xii
Preface	xiii
1 The music industry and music media – an introduction	1
2 Concepts, postulates, constraints and methods	21
3 Case study: Jamaica	38
4 Case study: Trinidad	65
5 Case study: Kenya	84
6 Case study: Tanzania	108
7 Case study: Cymru – Wales	125
8 Case study: Sweden	156
9 Conclusions	196
References	257
Index	264

Tables

1.1	Sales and releases of phonograms in the US market	13
1.2	Radio listening and radio output in Sweden	14
3.1	Consumer electronics in Jamaica	39
3.2	Survey of programme content on Jamaican radio, 7 July 1986	48
3.3	Survey of programme content on Jamaican radio, 27 May 1987	49
3.4	Survey of programme content on Jamaican radio, 13 December 1988	50
4.1	Survey of programme content on Trinidadian radio, 3–4 June 1987	70
4.2	Survey of programme content on Trinidadian radio, 4 and 6 February 1988	71
4.3	Survey of programme content on Trinidadian radio, 13 November 1989	72
5.1	Survey of programme content on Voice of Kenya, 21 and 25 April 1988	90
6.1	Survey of programme content on Tanzanian radio, 11–13 April 1988	114
8.1	Audio hardware in Sweden as % ownership amongst 9–79 age group	159
8.2	Percentage of Swedish music on P3	162
8.3	Music output of Swedish local radio stations, comparing music off phonograms/live recordings and total output	163
8.4	Sales of pre-recorded music, 1991	178
8.5	Phonogram industry statistics in Sweden, 1965–91	179
8.6	Market shares for different companies and groups of phonogram producers in Sweden	180
8.7	New releases of international/Swedish phonograms in LP format, and market shares for different groups of producers	182
8.8	Releases of phonograms with Swedish recordings, by style	182

8.9	Estimate of secondary incomes to Swedish phonogram industry, 1990	185
8.10	Distribution of subsidized phonograms (applications, grants in numbers and percentages)	189
9.1	Comparison of investment and variable costs for AM and FM radio (US$)	201
9.2	The development of Neighbourhood Radio in Sweden during the 1980s: transmission time and distribution of licences by major categories	217
9.3	A comparison of state support for arts and music in Wales and Sweden	230
9.4	Music output of Swedish national radio, P3, by country of origin and music genre	233
9.5	Average share of music content on the radio for music of different origins in six sample nations	240

Plates and figures

Plates

1.1	Quote from Time-Warner boss.	9
1.2	Bringing international culture to the local level. Television House, the headquarters of Trinidad and Tobago Television, with its large dish guaranteeing access to MTV and other satellite channels for re-broadcasting locally.	10
3.1	The colourful mural outside one of Jamaica's many record manufacturing plants. Bob Marley financed this one through his Tuff Gong Records Company.	40
3.2	No CDs! Singles are still popular sound carriers in Jamaica. The inside of Randy's Record Store in downtown Kingston – a visit here is a must for many a Western reggae pilgrim.	41
3.3	'Your work turns up on any number of records' – Jamaican saxophonist Dean Fraser checking out a local record store.	46
3.4	'On key, not just playing a fast one.' Jamaica's leading DJ, Barry G, in the JBC studio.	51
3.5	'We don't use instruments – we just settle 'pon a riddem.' Local music activity in the absence of financial resources.	55
3.6	'Have you seen me dish? Where me dish gone?' Satellite dishes moving down the socio-economic scale. A 'spider's web' in a poorer suburb of Kingston.	58
3.7	'Very little happens by policy – things happen when everything's in place.' In place here, Jamaican film director, Perry Hensell.	63
4.1	The Trinidad Carnival providing an outlet for all manner of creative images.	73
4.2	Loudspeakers replacing live steelbands in Trinidad.	77
4.3	What impact for the future of the steelband movement? Lots of girls in the school band.	81
4.4	Older and younger calypsonians. The Roaring Lion upset about soca: David Rudder claims his music definitely is calypso.	82

5.1	Joseph Kamaru's store on River Road, Nairobi.	88
5.2	The Makuyu Stars' rehearsal hut from the outside.	102
5.3	Inside the hut of the Makuyu Stars – homemade drums and a simple box guitar.	103
5.4	A lone operator: the Kahabati one-man band from Saba Saba, also available on disc.	104
5.5	'A musician's life is a . . .' Playing in the cage on the club owner's instruments.	106
5.5	While a few customers drink and dance outside.	106
6.1	Despite import restrictions and a lack of hard currency, there are plenty of cassettes for sale in Dar es Salaam.	109
6.2	An impressive notice points the way to a record pressing plant which was never completed.	111
6.3	A typical line-up of a Swahili jazz band – the now-defunct Safari Sound Band entertaining at a restaurant just outside Dar es Salaam.	112
6.4	The Tanzanites playing at Dar es Salaam's biggest hotel have fairly modern synthesizers. Many other jazz bands have to make do with amplifiers that are almost antique.	118
6.5	The Black Systems Youth at their open-air rehearsal venue, a sports ground in Dar es Salaam.	119
6.6	Ngoma shows are enjoying more and more popularity in a Tanzania without television.	122
7.1	'Trying to reflect the audience': a Radio Cymru outside broadcast unit preparing for a Saturday morning live transmission from the Town Square in Caernarfon, North Wales.	132
7.2	Meeting your target group – the SAIN stall at the annual Eisteddfod.	143
7.3	Latest communication technology spreading local music industry information. A Teletext page with record prices from Cytgord.	143
7.4	The somewhat confused entrance through a backyard to the Studio Les 16-track facility in the little slate-mining town of Bethesda, Wales.	148
7.5	The Welsh love to sing – anywhere. An impromptu gathering of folk musicians at the Eisteddfod.	154
8.1	The Swedish *nyckelharpa* (keyed fiddle): once almost extinct, it is now kept alive by enthusiasts who build their own instruments.	192
8.2	Folk music gaining ground in Sweden.	194
9.1	Digital Satellite music feeds. Not only TV but any number of music channels available in different satellite footprints.	203
9.2	The music press heralding the ASCAP assault on Europe in	

	early 1990: 'Don't discriminate against US songs on European radio or else . . .'.	205
9.3	The old and the new. Modern 'midi' technology, synthesizers and other music machines allowing one musician to do the job of ten.	244

Figures

2.1	The relationship between media policy and music activity.	23
2.2	Factors affecting the establishment and maintenance of a music industry, and its relationship to music activity in the environment.	25
2.3	Phonogram companies/broadcasters/listeners in a system.	30
9.1	An extended system including sponsors, advertisers, terrestrial and satellite TV channels.	207
9.2	Deregulation of existing monopolies, leading to new forms of ownership/format concentration.	220
9.3	The availability of cultural products on a local level changes the role of national institutions as intermediaries.	238

Abbreviations

ARTCO	(Kenya) Arts Co-operative Society
CCM	Chama Cha Mapinduzi
CCN	Caribbean Communications Network
CD	Compact Disc
CHR	Contemporary Hit Radio
COTT	Copyright Organization of Trinidad and Tobago
CPTC	Creative Production Training Centre
DAT	Digital Audio Tape
EAR	East African Records Ltd
EBU	European Broadcasting System
EBS	Educational Broadcasting Union
ICTM	International Council for Traditional Music
IFPI	International Federation of Phonogram and Video Industries
JBC	Jamaican Broadcasting Corporation
JCDC	Jamaican Cultural Development Commission
KAPI	Kenya Association of Phonogram Industries
KRPA	Kenya Record Producers' Association
MC	Music Cassette
MISC	Music Industry in Small Countries Project (see Wallis and Malm 1984)
NACC	National Action Cultural Committee
NAR	National Alliance for Reconstruction
NBS	National Broadcasting Service
NSRP	Not Suitable for Radio Play
PNM	People's National Movement
PPL	Phonogram Performance Ltd
PRS	Performing Right Society
SKAP	Swedish Association of Popular Music Composers
TI	Taped Interview
TFC	Tanzania Film Company
TTT	Trinidad and Tobago Television
VoK	Voice of Kenya
WIPO	World Intellectual Property Organization
WORM	Write Once Read Many Times

Preface

'Whenever I come into contact with radio folk from other countries it becomes very obvious that the thought processes and problems are very similar. The shame of it is that, despite this wealth of experience, few countries seem to learn from the mistakes of others.'

This quote came in a letter to us from one of Britain's most experienced radio regulators, Lin Glover. She was commenting on a July 1992 proposal from the Swedish government to deregulate radio by auctioning off frequencies to the highest bidder, without any checks or balances – this seemingly easy way out of a difficult problem has been tried and has failed in a number of nations.

Lin Glover's comments sum up very succinctly the whole point of our own research exercise, namely the use of an international comparative study to facilitate the flow of information and experience between countries and decision-makers involved in the tricky area of media policy.

Any comparative study involving a group of nations incurs considerable costs for fieldwork and creates a need for a network of favourably disposed and qualified persons in the places to be studied. The Swedish Council for Research in the Humanities and Social Sciences funded the study during a three-year period – the Council has also contributed to publication costs.

It would be impossible to thank all those who have helped us during our visits to the countries that comprised our study (Jamaica, Trinidad, Kenya, Tanzania, Wales and, of course Sweden). The following really deserve a special mention: Dermot Hussey and Olive Lewin in Jamaica, Christopher Laird in Trinidad, Godwin Kaduma and Martin Mhando in Tanzania, Arthur Kimole and Sammy Oyando in Kenya, and Huw Jones and Llyr Edwards in Cymru/Wales.

The first section of the volume represents a fairly comprehensive introduction to, and analysis of, the workings of the music industry, setting out theories as to how the industry is developing, specifically with regard to related sectors of the media such as broadcasting. This is based on Roger Wallis's 1991 doctoral dissertation at Gothenburg University on globalization and integration trends in the music industry – thanks therefore to Professors Lennart Weibull, Keith Roe and Simon Frith who all provided important input at various stages in that academic process.

An abundance of gratitude is also due to our loyal fans (?) at Routledge – Jane Armstrong who initiated the project, Rebecca Barden who took it as far as the manuscript stage, and desk editor Virginia Myers who gently but firmly forced it through the production pipeline.

Finally, thanks to our sorely tried families who have had to put up with us being far away for periods of time, usually when we were needed at home for more pressing domestic chores.

Chapter 1
The music industry and music media – an introduction

PRESENTING THE MEDIA POLICY AND MUSIC ACTIVITY PROJECT

Citizens of Kenya who woke up early on 1 August 1982 got a surprise when they turned on their radios. Instead of the normal, soothing fare of Jim Reeves and Boney M, the airwaves were full of the reverberating rhythms of East African pop. The reason; there was a coup attempt by rebels in the Air Force and one of their first actions had been to change music policy at the Voice of Kenya radio monopoly. The coup was short-lived, but the rebels did succeed, temporarily at least, where the government had failed on two occasions during the 1980s. Two separate edicts requiring far more local music to be featured on the VoK were formally issued, in 1980 and again in 1988. Neither had any substantial effect on output.

The Midsummer weekend is an important national holiday for the people of Sweden; it is the climax of a short hectic summer with long days and very little darkness. Midsummer is celebrated with many open-air festivities, including no small measure of Swedish music; a Midsummer without Swedish music is almost as unthinkable as a carnival in Trinidad without calypso or steelband. This, as one might expect, is reflected in the output of Swedish radio. In 1989 things were different. A composers' strike forced both national radio and television channels to refrain from playing almost any Swedish songs that were not in the public domain. The reason for this somewhat unusual action was growing discontent with the amount of Swedish music which could be heard in the broadcasting media. Three years earlier, in 1986, the government had even ordered the Swedish Broadcasting Corporation to take effective counteraction 'should the amount of Swedish music tend to decrease'. Three years in a row this was exactly what happened without any action being taken; composers used the legal possibilities open to them to force a change. The next year, 1990, statistics showed an increase of four percentage points in the Swedish music content of the country's national light music channel.

The above are two good examples of pressure groups coming from 'underneath' and attempting to change or merely implement media policies where governments seemed to have failed. But national policymakers have also been coming under pressure from 'above', from the international level.

In Europe, the EC spent much of the 1980s pondering over policies which could serve to increase the amount of European material in audio and audio-visual media. This involved, in effect, decreasing the amount of programming from the normal source, the USA.

The policies which were adopted, including a generous move towards general deregulation of the media, actually led to an increase of the material intended for exclusion. The US-based (if not always US-owned) film industry lobbied successfully for a watering-down of quota regulations for European audio-visual media. A growing number of European nations had also begun to consider music quotas as a means of defending local content against the flood of Anglo-American hit music emanating from the giant media conglomerates. A US response to this came from the American copyright organizations representing composers and publishers (and thus, indirectly, even the media conglomerates). They warned that protective national measures in Europe that were seen to discriminate against US music could result in the Americans cancelling their traditional reciprocal relationships with their European national counterparts. There was even a threat of starting to negotiate directly with radio stations, which could result in US music being much cheaper to play than, say, Swedish or French. Such a scenario was also being aggravated by the increase in satellite radio and TV channels (channels which do not respect national frontiers) and the emergence of bigger and bigger media conglomerates which also live a global existence, floating up above sovereign national states.

With such developments on both the local and international levels, it is not surprising that national media policymakers have been experiencing numerous difficulties. Several more examples will follow in the course of this volume as we delve more deeply into the events of the 1980s on the national and local level in six different countries, comparing these to relevant happenings on the international scene.

Some readers may be familiar with our earlier study – MISC or the Music Industry in Small Countries project – of the music industry in a number of smaller nations and its development during the 1970s. The MISC report, *Big Sounds from Small Peoples* (Wallis and Malm 1984), charted the flow of music industry technology and products to virtually every corner of the globe, observing some of the ways in which this development assisted or came into conflict with national and local cultural interests. We observed how accessibility to technology at an affordable price had enabled groups of enthusiasts to establish local music industries. Such operations, however, were rarely isolated from the world at large.

The Small lived in a strange form of symbiosis with the Big transnational giants and their subsidiaries, who were constantly expanding and controlling more and more of the available distribution and manufacturing resources.

The problems faced by cultural policymakers in the 1970s were mainly concerned with the availability of music industry technology, nationally and locally, and the uses to which it was put. The uncertainties and difficulties of the 1980s, however, tended to focus more on the broader issues of media policy. Unfortunately, awareness of the importance of this field often came too late. Action came even later, if at all. International organizations such as Unesco, the Council of Europe or the World Intellectual Property Organization (WIPO) could provide few universal patent solutions. Traditional concepts of broadcasting were under attack from those whose stated aims were to shift the emphasis from elitist control to consumer sovereignty. The concept of the 'Public Service' brief, encompassing some measure of obligation towards minority cultural interests and activities, was being declared redundant. At the same time, new communications technologies such as satellites, and the growth of huge transnational conglomerates involved in cultural industry activities, were weakening the ability of many countries to exert sovereign control over national policies in the media and cultural field. All too often, politicians seemed content to sit on the fence and 'wait and see what happens' whilst technological and economic factors enjoyed a free-for-all, mapping out new media landscapes.

This book is based on a research project that has encompassed studies throughout the 1980s in six small nations coupled with studies of international developments. Our aim has been to map out the interaction between music in the mass media and music activities in society at large in this sample of countries, all of which have been represented in our previous MISC project. The six were: Jamaica and Trinidad in the Caribbean; Kenya and Tanzania in East Africa; and Sweden and Wales in Europe. The investigation also attempted to cover the international music and media industry and its role in moulding the music life of small nations.

The type of questions we were seeking answers to were:

— How and by whom are policies formulated for music in mass media?
— What are the actual policies? What means of implementation are used?
— How dynamic are such policies? Why and how do they change?
— How have different kinds of music changed their character when incorporated into mass media (a process we previously termed 'mediaization')?
— How does the music content of mass media influence music activities on the local level?
— Which are the main factors and phenomena and who are the most

influential actors involved in the interaction between the music media and music life at large?
— What is the role in different economical/political contexts of new technologies and production modes such as digital technology (CDs), satellite and cable distribution, music video clips, etc.?
— How effective have different policy measures aimed at supporting local music been?

Several reasons lie behind the choice of the six sample nations in this study. That they were originally part of the larger sample of twelve countries in the MISC project was an important aspect; the research team was already familiar with the media structure and music life of these nations. Indeed, for a general overview of the music and media scene in the six nations, we propose to refer the reader to our 1984 report (see Malm and Wallis 1984). Other factors supporting the make-up of the sample can also be noted. Kenya, Tanzania, Jamaica and Trinidad have a common historical background. They have all been under British colonial rule and have the British legacy of public service broadcasting. Of course, this is also the case with Sweden and Wales. Jamaica and Trinidad have a long history of supplying the international music industry with source material (reggae and calypso). In recent years, there has been growing interest within the industrialized world in the musicians and sounds of countries in Africa, such as Kenya and Tanzania.

All four African and Caribbean countries are classified as developing Third World nations. There are, however, considerable differences. Kenya and Tanzania are among the poorest countries in the world. They share a similar general pre-colonial background. During the post-independence period, on the other hand, their development has been governed by different political ideologies (though within one-party political systems). While market economy principles have been applied in Kenya, Tanzania opted for an African brand of socialist planned economy.

The economies of Jamaica and especially Trinidad are in what the World Bank would term 'better health' than those of Kenya and Tanzania. Both Caribbean nations have a multi-party political system and market economies. Both share a common language with their powerful northern neighbour, the United States of America; their proximity puts them in the footprints of scores of US broadcasting satellites.

Wales and Sweden are industrialized, comparatively wealthy nations in Europe. Wales contains a minority culture within a larger country. The parallels between this situation and the situation of a small independent country like Sweden are of obvious interest.

This sample of nations clearly has enough in common to provide a foundation for meaningful comparison. At the same time, their different political and economic situations allow an assessment of how media policies and music activities develop under very different circumstances.

This volume is divided into four main parts. The first provides a general introduction to the area under scrutiny. In the second, the research framework is laid down; major concepts, postulates and methods are presented. Part three is devoted to six case studies describing developments and processes concerning media policy and local music activities in each of the sample nations. The final section sums up observable patterns and trends, and suggests conclusions that can be drawn from the previous data.

The music industry is the hub around which much of the music scene today revolves in most countries. Thus it seems logical to continue with an introduction to the workings of this industry, an introduction which will lead into a theoretical and conceptual framework for the presentation and interpretation of our practical data.

INTRODUCING THE MUSIC INDUSTRY: HARDWARE, SOFTWARE, GLOBALIZATION AND COUNTER-MOVEMENTS

The music industry is a complex animal. It encompasses all those artists, composers, individuals and organizations that are involved in the process of producing, performing, manufacturing and disseminating music for a mass audience. The industrial process most of us associate with the music industry is the production and distribution of software, the most common sound-carriers being vinyl records, CDs or audio cassettes, known collectively as phonograms. Software also includes other sound and image carriers with their recorded music and their packaging, such as videograms and films.

Phonograms and videograms can be regarded as constituting the primary music mass media which make up the better part of the music content in secondary music mass media, e.g. radio and television. An important and specific case of mass media software is the content of live broadcasts (where the broadcaster is responsible for the synchronization of the sound on to a carrier or for direct dissemination).

Mass dissemination of information about music is also closely linked to the music industry. Here the software embraces books, papers, magazines, posters and so on, as well as radio and TV programmes where music forms the basis of speech content.

A prerequisite for phonogram activities, of course, is the production and distribution of related hardware. The hardware sector of the music industry provides music consumers with machines that play their phonograms and videograms, either directly or via dissemination from secondary music mass media. Another hardware activity involves designing and manufacturing for musicians machines that produce sounds, usually with an ever-increasing degree of dependence on electronic components. Equipment is also manufactured with various degrees of sophistication for the recording of musical performances, ranging from the most simple built-in microphone with associated circuits in a cassette recorder to the most advanced multi-channel recorders. Hardware also includes studio equipment, mass duplication equipment, transmitters, etc.

Throughout this century, the phonogram industry has alternated between being hardware- and software-led. Each time a new sound carrier has been introduced, this has required consumers to purchase new hardware, with accompanying re-releases of older recordings in the new format. Once the new carrier and associated playback equipment is widely available, then the emphasis is once again on the supply of a new range of software. Those who cannot keep up with technological developments in primary music mass media run the risk of being excluded from secondary sources; if radio stations implement a policy of using only CDs for quality reasons, then a phonogram producer who for technical or economic reasons can only produce analogue cassettes will suffer a disadvantage as regards media access.

Broadcasting has witnessed a veritable explosion during the past two decades. Most of the new programmes have been music-based. Indeed, without software from the phonogram industry, this tremendous expansion of broadcasting would have been impossible. As radio has expanded, broadcasting organizations in most countries have not increased their own music recording activities. Recordings from the commercial phonogram industry have been the main fillers of increased hours of transmission. Since the early 1980s, the audio-visual equivalent of the phonogram, the video clip, has performed a similar function for television, providing cheap programme material and comprising the prerequisite for 24-hour-a-day music video TV (e.g. the MTV satellite channel). The policies that determine the way in which such media develop and function can thus be expected to have important relevance for both music consumption and music-making in society.

The phonogram has been with us for over a century. In common with most cultural industries, the phonogram industry operates on a transnational level. From the early 1900s, a few major companies have produced phonograms for consumption in a global market, with Anglo-American material enjoying a dominant position. The parallel with the film industry, including a strong measure of mutual dependency, can be noted ever since the introduction of sound movies. Films served to publicize songs on phonograms and vice versa (Hamm 1979: 334–48; Edström 1989: 38ff.). Internationally distributed television series were later to play a similar role. The international spread of MTV-style television via satellites during the 1980s provides yet another example of global integration through the mutual dependence of the phonogram and audio-visual industries.

The music industry, like the film or television industry, also operates on national and local levels. Where markets linked to language areas are deemed sufficiently large, specific versions of international cultural products are sometimes produced. The Swedish pop-group ABBA, for instance, produced extra versions of some of their hit songs in Swedish, Spanish and even Russian during their period of global success in the 1970s, in order to facilitate marketing in relevant sales territories. Whereas most films and imported TV programmes are still dubbed or subtitled for different language markets, the general emphasis in the music industry's global marketing and distribution strategy as we enter the 1990s is on the combination of specific artists and musical material. The goal is global sales of products, featuring superstars performing particular musical works, rather than on the spread of pieces of music which are then reproduced in different national versions (unlike, say, the global market for newspaper cartoons and comic strips).

The music industry is thus at the forefront of a move towards global standardization of cultural products, further ahead than, say, the international pocket-book industry which still relies on language versions for increasing sales. A handful of global phonogram companies are constantly increasing their degree of control over manufacturing and distribution resources (even those used by smaller creative units not owned by the transnationals, so-called 'independents').

The music industry, in other words, is very much part of the future global scenario sketched out for the electronic/consumer/entertainment industries by the top management of these industries. It is a future involving a few giant organizations involved in several forms of entertainment and based on different continents. In March 1989, the new Chairman of Time-Life said after his company's merger with one of the world's five biggest phonogram companies, Warners:

> We believe there will emerge, on a worldwide basis, six, seven, eight vertically integrated media and entertainment megacompanies. At least one will be Japanese, probably two. We think two will be European. We think there will be a couple of American-led enterprises, and we think Time Inc. is going to be one.
>
> (Financial Times, 6 March 1989)

Some two years later, Time-Warner became even more international, announcing a $1bn Pacific alliance with two Japanese companies, Toshiba and the C Itoh trading company. The deal gave the Japanese companies a 12.5 per cent stake in Time-Warner's film and cable operations; in return, Time-Warner hoped to get access to Japan's fast-expanding cable business for its video/film software operations (*Time Magazine* 1991). Time-Warner's music division, however, was excluded from the deal, possibly because Toshiba already had a phonogram subsidiary together with another global phonogram company, EMI.

The economic pressures to sell the same cultural products and related hardware in as many places as possible around the globe, thus profiting from the presumed advantages of scale, have been a growing feature of the post-Second World War decades. By the late 1960s, this was triggering off a rising tide of conflict and concern amongst smaller nations and cultures. Musicians, cultural authorities, decision-makers and politicians expressed fears that their own musical culture and range of musical activities would be flooded out of existence. These were recurring themes in two major Unesco conferences: in 1972 in Helsinki and in 1977 in Lagos.

Concerns have continued to grow as the media have expanded. Several observers have noted a growing antagonism between the globalization of culture on the one hand, and the attempt to preserve cultural identity and protect national interests on the other. Many governments and institutions have pondered over the consequences of such trends, often producing an impressive array of policy rhetoric. For example, the report of the Kenyan Presidential National Music Commission noted in 1984 that:

> The part played by the media cannot be ignored. Whereas it is true . . . that, through them, cultural diversities in different parts of the world are easily made accessible to all countries, the question we nonetheless have to ask is, to what degree would these media present music that is foreign at the expense of our own music, and what guidelines can be used for the selection of the music that is presented in the media?
>
> (Omondi 1984: 3)

The worries expressed in the Kenyan report cited above are understandable. With the general availability of recording equipment in the 1970s, virtually every nation had at least its own rudimentary phonogram industry, often struggling to compete in a market of limited size with international products which were selling worldwide. The spread of cassette technology to every corner of the globe, coupled with widespread piracy of popular artists' recordings, was providing universal accessibility to the international repertoire of the transnational companies. The same technology, however, coupled with the general availability of relatively cheap yet reasonably sophisticated recording equipment, had allowed for the growth of a variety of national and locally based phonogram producers. The music they produced was not purely 'local' in a traditional sense but often represented a hybrid of globalization and indigenization, with international influences affecting the interpretation of local sounds and styles and vice versa. We have suggested the term 'transculturation' for such phenomena (Wallis and Malm 1984: 300ff.; Robinson, Buck and Cuthbert 1991: 227ff.).

The problems facing smaller national and local phonogram producers in the 1970s and early 1980s were mainly concerned with manufacturing and

Time Warner deal takes US back to the future

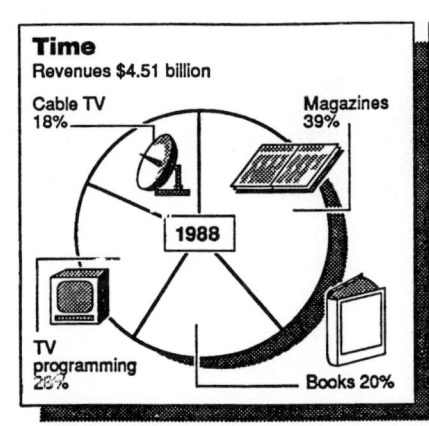

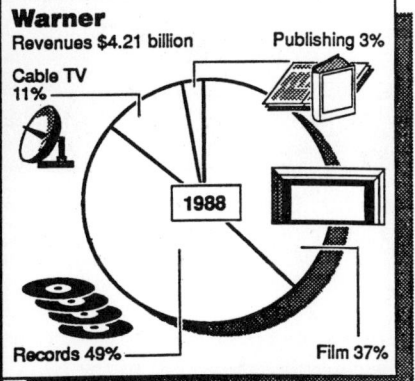

Time Revenues $4.51 billion
- Cable TV 18%
- Magazines 39%
- TV programming 23%
- Books 20%
- (1988)

Warner Revenues $4.21 billion
- Publishing 3%
- Cable TV 11%
- Records 49%
- Film 37%
- (1988)

suggested a full-blown merger.
Both had defensive reason' wanting a merger. Time ha' under takeover threat w' Ross, a man known for w' zons and high overheads, well-publicised disagr with Warner's penny-j main stockholder, Mr Siegel of Chris-Craft In (As part of yesterday's stock swap, Chris-Craft'. cent voting block will be to about 10 per cent. T. York Times reported that gel abstained at Satu Warner board meeting bt could not be confirmed.)
Both companies say the m will create a global US com} which can compete worldwic. Mr Nicholas, who will run the combined company, said: "We believe there will emerge, on a worldwide basis, six, seven, eight vertically integrated media and

Mr Nicholas, who will run the combined company, said: "We believe there will emerge, on a worldwide basis, six, seven, eight vertically integrated media and entertainment megacompanies. At least one will be Japanese, probably two. We think two will be European. We think there will be a couple of American-led enterprises, and we think Time Inc is going to be one."

In a__ __ __, īime Warner will be awesomely well-capitalised. Because the merger is in the form of a stock swap,

a cash purchase, the com-company will have no addi-debt. With potentially an $3bn in shareholders nd little more than half bt, Time Warner will be ise large capital sums tions. Mr Murdoch has nitted he had touched f his financial room to e by seeking outside o capitalise a new com-ıke acquisitions.
question facing Wall ow the combined com-be run. Only the cable ı will be combined. The g operations will be run .entralised operations, .ting to Steve if they report steve," as Mr Holmes puts it, "or to Nick and Dick, if they report to Nick and Dick." There will be only nine corporate offi-cers. Whether this arrangement works out has to be seen.

high altitude test

That 0.6 per cent price rise (0.5 per cent if you leave out food and

Plate 1.1 Quote from Time-Warner boss (*Financial Times* 1989-03-06).

Plate 1.2 Bringing international culture to the local level. Television House, the headquarters of Trinidad and Tobago Television, with its large dish guaranteeing access to MTV and other satellite channels for re-broadcasting locally.

distribution resources, as well as with difficulties of access to secondary music media, above all, to the broadcasters.

By the mid-1980s, digital technology in the form of the CD was making major inroads in the industrialized nations. By 1988, it was estimated that global manufacturing capacity for CDs had reached 800 million, equivalent to almost twice the estimated number of LP units sold worldwide (Wallis and Malm 1990: 11). Two years later, actual worldwide sales of CDs were almost up to the same 800 million figure. Traditional vinyl technology was on its way out in both richer and poorer nations, with analogue cassettes becoming standard carriers in the developing world. CD sales overtook those of the conventional LP in the USA in 1988. The same happened two years later in Sweden. In Jamaica, an important music industry but low per capita income country which has some of the most up-to-date recording equipment in its local studios, the first store offering CDs opened as late as the spring of 1991. In Kenya, in East Africa, the sole vinyl pressing plant operated by transnational Polygram closed in late 1990; the likelihood of a CD plant being established in the immediate future seems remote and cassettes are established as the standard music carrier.

The situation in the early 1990s differs, in other words, from a decade ago. We can witness a technological gap beginning to appear between the rich and the poor as regards access to local, 'state-of-the-art' mass-reproduction technology. The music from the poorer nations can still be brought to the ears of the industrialized world via the use of modern, digital lightweight portable recording equipment. Even if music-lovers in the industrialized world thus get access to various forms of 'world music', this development has hardly simplified the task of bringing independent local music industries in, say, Africa or the Caribbean up to the technological standards that have been developed in the industrialized world.

Another significant development in this context has been the growth of business conglomerates, incorporating the integration of hardware and software sectors. The spread of analogue cassette technology during the 1970s was facilitated by the fact that Asian hardware manufacturers had little concern for the software side (software piracy, in other words, did not cause them many sleepless nights). With Sony purchasing CBS records, Time-Warner joining up with Toshiba, Virgin records with Fuji, MCA with Matsushita, etc., this all changed. Digital technology was not necessarily going to be readily available for the provision of cheap pirated copies of music industry software.

THE ORIGINS OF THIS RESEARCH: OBSERVATIONS IN SMALLER COUNTRIES AND INTERNATIONAL TRENDS

The geographical starting point for our earlier MISC project was Sweden, but the focus was on comparative studies of the music industry in different smaller countries and nations. An important stimulus had been the growing international debate and somewhat scanty awareness of the relationship between cultural behaviour and socio-economic and technological developments (Bontinck 1974; Blaukopf 1976: 122). In the music field, curiosity about the role of popular culture, particularly among youth, and the question of whether or not this area should be encompassed by cultural policy in general, was bringing together researchers and practitioners representing many different disciplines and interests. This was particularly noticeable in nations 'on the receiving end' of the burgeoning international music industry, i.e. the net importers. MISC's stated aim was to study the effects of 'technological, economic and organizational changes in the music industry on music life in a sample of small nations and countries'. More specifically, MISC's aims can be described as follows:

1 To shed light on the relationships between different actors involved in and affected by the music industry on different levels (international, national/local).
2 To estimate the universality of problems facing national and local music industries with the increased influence of international activities.
3 Via a comparative study, to link up with other researchers working in this virgin territory and add to a scanty body of knowledge on the effects

of the expanding international music industry on the national/local levels.

MISC allowed us to describe the intriguing relationship of mutual dependency between the transnational music industry and the plethora of smaller, national or local music producers. Five 'majors' (SONY-CBS, Polygram, EMI, Time-Warner WEA, BMG-RCA) dominate the greater part of the global production and distribution of recorded music. The smaller 'independents' take the risks in the local market, and achieve a high degree of local competence developing artists and repertoire talent which the majors can occasionally exploit internationally. And as the radio and TV media themselves become more internationalized, through satellite transmissions or ownership changes, questions of the constraints on media policies assume ever-greater importance for the survival of local music industries.

Since the mid-1980s, local phonogram companies in smaller countries have been trying to use the video clip as a promotional tool, experiencing the problems that ensued as marketing costs rose in their small potential markets. A music video, of course, can hardly function as an advertising message without communication channels to the potential consumer, without regular television or specific 'music television' outlets where such videos are played. In 1982, a senior European broadcaster described the relationship between radio and the phonogram industry as 'a marriage of convenience . . . we are like a department store where the record industry's products are on display, but cannot be bought' (Wallis and Malm 1982: 93). With the establishment of the music video as a standard marketing and promotional tool, paid for, in principle, by the phonogram industry, television has developed a relationship with the phonogram companies which resembles that between the latter and radio. The picture is further complicated by the fact that, whilst the bonds are getting tighter between broadcasters and the rest of the music industry, other actors (notably sponsors and advertisers) are also increasing their influence (Wallis and Malm 1988).

The relationship between radio and the phonogram industry is characterized by a strange paradox. Statistics from the global phonogram industry suggest that it is responding to increased costs and demands on efficiency (i.e. sales of more copies of less products) by decreasing the number of products it releases. Available figures from the 'official' US phonogram industry show that this was the trend throughout most of the 1980s. Values of sales remained about the same, thanks mainly to the introduction of the CD attracting customers wishing to update their software. The number of new releases, of both singles and LPs, on the other hand decreased during the 1980s, if we are to believe researchers at Polygram USA.

Radio, in the wake of deregulation policies, is expanding rapidly in virtually every country; as we have noted, this is almost exclusively through

Table 1.1 Sales and releases of phonograms in the US market

Year	Phonogram sales US (million)					Value	New releases US	
	Singles	LP	MC	CD	Total	US$m	Singles	LPs
1981	147	272	174	—	593	3,636	2,315	2,810
1982	137	241	197	—	575	3,592	2,285	2,630
1983	125	240	243	1	609	3,815	2,105	2,300
1984	131	235	338	6	710	4,370	1,980	2,170
1985	120	167	339	23	649	4,389	2,200	2,360
1986	94	125	346	53	618	4,651	1,815	2,345
1987	82	107	410	102	701	5,567	1,762	2,406
1988	90	72	450	150	762	6,254	N/A	N/A
1990	82	12	442	286	768	7,541	N/A	N/A
1991	96	5	360	333	—	7,716	N/A	N/A

Sources: IFPI, London and Polygram, USA and RIAA research department, MIRO World, London

Notes: [1] Figures apply to the major companies affiliated to the Record Industry Association of America (RIAA).
[2] CD releases in the USA in 1987 totalled 3,571; it is reasonable to assume that the difference between this and the figure for LP releases is accounted for by the large number of CD re-releases of older material. The RIAA, according to their research department, stopped collecting release data after 1987.

the increased use of recorded music. If releases from the phonogram industry do not show a corresponding increase, then one can assume that more radio stations are simply playing the same selections, leading to an element of streamlining in their media policy.

Listening patterns seem to be demonstrating a similar characteristic, reaching a saturation level at some point. Between 1985 and 1990, radio output in Britain increased by 65 per cent, but the average time spent listening increased by only 17 per cent. The number of listeners who listened to the radio on an average day was 78 per cent in 1987, a figure unchanged since 1980 (PSI 1991: 49–52). Similar trends are reported elsewhere. In Sweden, for instance, average radio listenership increased from 73 per cent in 1979 (as 'Lokalradio' or county radio was introduced) and levelled out around the UK figure of 78 per cent by 1987 (the 1990 Swedish figure was indeed 78 per cent!). With deregulatory measures allowing for the introduction of small-scale, third-tier radio, programme output in Sweden increased from approximately 70,000 hours per annum in 1980 to almost 400,000 hours ten years later, an increase of over 400 per cent. The average time spent in communion with one's radio, however, according to the results of interviews carried out by Swedish radio's research department, only increased from 115 to 134 minutes, i.e. 16 per cent, once again, virtually the same as the UK figures (Carlsson and Anshelm, 1991: 166).

Fragmentation of the audience is an inevitable result of deregulatory expansion. This leads to a number of policy dilemmas, not least for traditional public service broadcasters operating national channels. Should they try to survive by competing with a similar output to those of their competitors, or should they do something entirely different? For every actor in the expanded market, the rule applies that at some point audiences can become so small as to have virtually no relevance in a mass communication context.

Table 1.2 Radio listening and radio output in Sweden

Year	Radio listening average listeners/day	Radio listening average mins/day	National radio	County radio	3rd-tier radio	Total
1981	69%	111	372	381	699	1,452
1982	68%	107	378	424	727	1,529
1983	71%	124	379	458	1,175	2,012
1984	65%	N/A	377	485	1,423	2,285
1985	73%	131	377	607	2,450	3,434
1986	74%	133	380	688	3,055	4,123
1987	77%	129	380	858	3,815	5,053
1988	76%	125	380	954	4,686	6,020
1989	77%	134	432	1,153	5,033	6,618
1990	78%	132	432	1,384	5,250	7,066
1991	N/A	N/A	430	1,500	5,700	7,630

Radio production (hrs/week) spans the National, County, 3rd-tier and Total columns.

Sources: Swedish radio's audience research dept (PUB), Neighbourhood Radio Board. Estimates of average listening figures are based on telephone interviews.

Broadcasting is devouring more and more hours of recorded music provided by a commercial phonogram industry. This industry, as we noted above, is not responding by increasing its production of new releases to the same extent. Its main preoccupation is with cutting down the inherent uncertainties of the market, concentrating sales on a smaller number of products and thus, hopefully, generating enough income to cover the increased costs of marketing, which result from publicity tools such as the video clip.

Such developments raise a multitude of policy-related questions. Many concern the changing role and importance of traditional *national* media institutions such as national radio/TV channels. Are they becoming bypassed by a joint move towards internationalization and localization? Satellite transmissions do not respond to national frontiers, and internationally available products from the cultural industries become available on the most local level. Local access to music industry technology also in theory allows for a multitude of activities with local music, even in broadcasting and cable. This, as we shall see, has forced us to question some of the earlier assumptions regarding the role of the national level of music industry operations, so central to the focus developed a decade ago in the initial MISC project. There has been a tendency to bypass national policy-making and media institutions, as Tunstall has noted from studies of Europe:

> If both the supra-national and sub-national levels of broadcasting and media have been growing stronger, does this indicate a weakening of the national level in Europe? Broadly speaking, this appears true. But the weakening is most noticeable in the smaller population countries
> (Tunstall and Palmer 1991: 4)

We shall return in detail to the role of national institutions in small countries in our concluding section, looking not only at industrialized nations in Western Europe but also at developing nations from other continents in our sample. But first let us return to the body of knowledge on which our research efforts have been based.

SOME NOTES ON OTHER RELEVANT MUSIC INDUSTRY RESEARCH

Although the phonogram has been reproducing and mechanizing music since the last decade of the previous century, as recently as the late 1970s there were remarkably few studies of the socio-economic aspects of the industrial processing of music. The reasons would seem to be threefold:

1 difficulties of choosing analysis methods;
2 business secrecy; and
3 a lack of academic interest amongst music and indeed media researchers.

By 1980, apart from Blaukopf's important study of the phonogram as a mass medium (Blaukopf 1977), there were only a few cases of musicologists concerning themselves with the popular music forms and workings of the music industry (e.g. Tagg 1977, 1979). In retrospect, one can note that much of the interest in popular music, its function and the industry that made, sold and disseminated it, came out of non-musical concerns (Frith and Goodwin 1990; Roe and Carlsson 1990) from sociologists involved with the concept of 'mass culture' or the study of youth.

Mass communication scholars, too, had not traditionally seen the phonogram as an instrument of communication, despite the many hours that millions spend in more or less active communion with recorded music each and every day. Theorists' traditional areas of interest in the mass communication field have been the press, radio, television and film. Jeremy Tunstall's pioneering volume on the media in the US (Tunstall 1977) does not include the terms 'gramophone', 'phonogram' or 'record industry' in its index, even if the importance of recorded music as a filler of airtime on US radio is stressed. The same applies to McQuail's standard introduction to mass communication theory (McQuail 1969, 1983). One had to wait until 1985 before an issue of the journal *Communications Research* was devoted to the theme of 'Music as Communication' (1985, vol. 12, no. 3), and until 1987 for the first edition of the anthology, *Popular Music and Communication* to be produced (Lull 1987). The latter represented an attempt to move a number of disciplinary approaches to popular culture closer to the field of mass communication research. Writers on broadcasting policies and deregulation in particular have rarely concerned themselves with the musical aspects. The focus has generally been on the informational role of broadcasting in enabling citizens to fulfil and enjoy their democratic obligations and rights. There has also been an emphasis on the risk that any form of government regulation can provide politicians with the means of tampering with the information flow (Holmes 1990; Stepp 1990; Curran 1991).

A somewhat disjointed body of scientific writing on the phonogram industry emerged in the 1970s and comprised three main approaches. The first involved a socio-economic look at the *production of commodified culture*, likening the phonogram company to other profit-seeking industries that manufacture goods for sale, but noting the differences. Phonograms are 'non-material' goods embodying a 'live, one-of-a-kind performance . . . and/or unique set of ideas' as opposed to goods 'serving more obvious utilitarian needs' (Hirsch 1969, 1972). Hirsch argued that this leads to uncertainties in the phonogram company's environment (what talent is available, and what the public are likely to buy), resulting in an overproduction of cultural products. Put crudely, this is what Denisoff has termed the 'chuck it on the wall and see if anything sticks' syndrome (Denisoff 1975). Denisoff's picture of the 'popular record industry' is one of everybody in the industry trying to manipulate everyone else, but never finding the manipulation formula. Hirsch's work also focused attention on the interfaces between the phonogram company and its environment. Profit maximization is sought by engaging armies of promotion people who concentrate on marketing a small selection of available phonograms, primarily via the medium of radio – this was before the days of video clips and MTV!

Some of the earliest and most influential writing in the production of culture approach came from Peterson and Berger (like Hirsch and Pearsall, also from the USA and viewing the music industry from a US perspective). Peterson and Berger see the business of popular music phonogram production as a cyclical process, following the state of competition between the large and the small companies (Peterson and Berger 1971; Burnett 1990). These authors also highlight the way in which the major companies seek to decrease uncertainty by increasing their control over sectors outside the actual phonogram company (contracting top artists, taking over merchandising and distribution operations). They introduce the notion of *integration* in this context, a concept so central to theories developed in this volume.

A second common academic approach to the music industry can be described as *interactionist*, studying relationships between and values held by different individuals and groups. Whilst writers in the first category above have concentrated on the flow process through the phonogram company (seen as distinct stages), or on a more macro level, the output of the industry and the way in which parts of it reach the consumer, those favouring an interactionist approach focus on relations between those involved in the creative process (Kealy 1979; De Coster 1976; Hennion and Vignolle 1978). A consensus framework, similar to that applied sometimes in the analysis of the functioning of news selection procedures in the print and electronic media (Cohen and Young 1981: 32, 335–40, 393ff.) has also been applied in this context.

A third approach to the phonogram industry, and indeed to the music industry as a whole, has been that favoured by sociologists, the *culture/ subculture* approach. This has focused on different groups and their use of music, particularly in relation to a function of defining/strengthening group identity (Frith 1978; Willis 1978). Such research has attempted to analyse the significance of popular music for those who consume it. These writings can be seen as an alternative to the more pessimistic views on popular culture expressed by earlier writers associated with the so-called Frankfurt School.

Theorists such as Adorno, Marcuse and Horkheimer saw the great general public as an uncritical mass when exposed to the products of cultural industries. They feared that the very process of receiving mass media served to inoculate the whole capitalist production system against subversion. Through mass reproduction, art would lose its true revolutionary role, turning critical human beings into passive consumers, happy with their lot however terrible it was, and thereby easily open to manipulation (Adorno 1941; Marcuse 1970; Horkheimer and Adorno 1972).

A dilemma for the Frankfurt School was that if art were to fulfil an oppositional function, then it must presumably reach a large section of the public (to be able to bring about change). But to reach this large audience would require the industrial resources of a mass media industry, leading to accommodation so that the art works (as media products) ultimately serve a self-negating function. Writing about popular music in 1941, though referring more specifically to jazz, Adorno proposes a rather high-brow view of popular music's predictability, distinguishing it from better forms of music; 'the complicated in popular music never functions as "itself" but only as a guise behind which the scheme can always be disguised' (Adorno 1941). Adorno, in other words, was not so concerned with the structure of industries which mechanized or mass-produced art, but more with the structure of popular culture itself, as well as the effects on society.

For those of us who closely followed the fortunes of rock-'n'-roll music in the 1960s, or the emergence of punk in the 1970s, it is easy to dismiss Adorno *et alii* as being too tied up with conspiracy theory, seeing all popular culture as a means of retaining the status quo, as a form of manipulation by those in control of capital. The Frankfurt School does seem to give very little credit to the individual's (or even groups of individuals') ability to select and make critical judgements regarding media usage. But this latter generalization has to be qualified in the light of the historical context – Adorno and his colleagues were watching the growth of fascism with horror and disbelief.

That the sentiments expressed by the Frankfurt School have continued to crop up in different guises is an indication that these theorists should not be misread or easily dismissed. Swedish observers remember well how Adorno's dilemma regarding art's role as an agent of change cropped up again during the early years of the 'Swedish Music Movement'. In 1972, a phonogram by the Hoolabandoola Band containing pop songs with political texts became the first release from one of the small, alternative Swedish companies to appear on the national Top 20 sales charts, thereby assuring them of repeated plays on national radio. Some activists saw this as a sign of success; others were more dubious. Here was a cultural 'revolutionary' movement suddenly supporting, by its presence, one of the most commercial phenomena in mass media, a chart which served to concentrate sales to a small number of popular releases (cf. Fornäs 1990). If the revolutionaries were inevitably going to be co-opted into the capitalist system by such processes, despite their stated aims of decreasing the influence of the international music industry, then Adorno's disillusionment about mass-produced popular culture becomes more understandable (Frith and Goodwin 1990: 275). The Frankfurt School, however, unlike the production of culture, the interactionist and the cultural/subcultural approaches, tells us little about the structure of the industry, nor about how specific groups use available popular music or initiate new forms of activity where music is a common bond. As Frith has pointed out, pitting art against business is not a fruitful way of analysing mass culture such as rock music.

> to reduce pop history to the struggles of musicians (or small businessman heroes) and corporate clowns is to ignore the critical issue: the music industry's strategies for market control . . . have been developed precisely because the market is one they can't control.
>
> (Frith 1981: 91)

Frith brings us thus back to the approaches practised by Hirsch, Peterson and Berger, and others for understanding the music industry. The cultural/subcultural approach highlights the user end; individuals and groups create and use popular music for their own purposes. An industry is waiting to provide services when the possibility arises. Much of the phonogram industry's relationship to the music media can only be understood in this context.

THE DEVELOPMENT OF A SYSTEMS APPROACH

A common denominator in much of the research listed above is a move towards a systems approach to understanding the music industry. An early contribution was DiMaggio and Hirsch's conceptual framework involving the application of three levels of magnitude to the study of popular culture production (DiMaggio and Hirsch 1976). The first focuses on the individual's professional role in the industrialization process (recording engineers, A&R gatekeepers, producers, etc.). The second level considers the industrial unit (e.g. a phonogram company or a radio station) as a self-contained or 'closed' system, bound together by individuals mutually dependent on one other and sharing certain values (Becker 1976). The third or macro level considers the cultural production unit as a system dependent on a larger environment. This refers to the constraints applied by such variables as ownership structure, technology, legislation, etc.

Gröndal in a study of the growth of mass media in Sweden has identified four significant 'development factors': technical, economic, organizational and market (Gröndal 1986: 31). Peterson (1982, 1985) has further specified such 'constraints' in terms of a number of categories: technology, law, industrial structure, organizational structure, market and occupational careers. In part, this is similar to the notions of equilibrium in organizational theory, whereby businesses survive through seeking a balance of demands and rewards between different interest groups (Barnard 1938; Dean 1951; Rhenman 1964; Lawrence and Lorsch 1967).

A problem with much of the literature that introduces the concept of systems is a certain lack of clarity regarding the use of the term. In particular, a discussion of 'open' and 'closed' systems can lead to confusion. It is hard to conceive any example of a truly 'closed' system, which does not exchange any physical materials or information with its environment. Even so, there has been a tendency, noted in the previous paragraph, to use the term when discussing the internal workings of the music industry.

If we regard a system as consisting of a number of components, each having certain attributes or properties, the components being connected by certain relationships (Rhenman 1964: 78), then it follows that two or more components and their relationships can be parts of different systems at the same time. An example would be two phonogram companies without their own manufacturing resources which purchase phonogram reproduction services from the same supplier and combine to purchase in bulk. In other words, in complex macro systems incorporating many subsystems, one can expect a move towards integration, with certain relationships becoming common to more than one subsystem.

This is a point made in one of mass communication theory's more important tracts, that of De Fleur and Ball-Rokeach (1989). They observe that mass media have become institutions in (US) society, and that, as such, they can be viewed as complex social systems, consisting of individuals or groups linked together by repetitive phenomena or functions (De Fleur and Ball-Rokeach 1989: 130). They produce a graphical representation of a total mass media system ('the mass communication system of the United States') which takes account of both geographical levels (national and regional/local but not international) and external conditions such as demands and contributions of financiers, advertisers and legislation. Here we can note a clear overlap with the demand–reward equilibrium concepts from organizational theory and Peterson's eight constraints mentioned above.

De Fleur and Ball-Rokeach also present some other postulates regarding the workings of media systems. They state that:

1 external conditions define media content;
2 the primary internal condition in a media system (holding it together) is a financial one; and
3 technological advances lead to media systems becoming more specialized or fragmented.

For a project that looks at the music industry's problems in smaller nations spread over the globe, such research also suffers the disadvantage of a US pedigree. The international level of operations is absent – the system stops at the national US level. But this body of knowledge has been critical for our conceptual framework which sees the music industry as a system held together by a set of demand–reward relationships, the paramaters of which are affected by a number of identifiable constraints. Three main constraints form the basis of our theoretical framework: technology (the machines and processes that are available); economy (financial resources); and organization (human and cultural resources and structures, including legislation).

Chapter 2
Concepts, postulates, constraints and methods

THE CONCEPTS OF MEDIA POLICY AND MUSIC ACTIVITY

When investigating the interaction between media, policymakers and music, one comes across phenomena and processes for which no generally accepted terms exist. In general, we have avoided coining new terms, attempting as far as possible to describe our findings using normal language. Sometimes, however, a need arises for more precision.

This book revolves around two main concepts: 'media policy' and 'music activity'. The word 'music' is central to the subject. The term 'media' in our usage covers all means of mass dissemination of music or information about music. As mentioned above, these media consist of hardware and software components.

The term 'media policy' comprises all kinds of action patterns and strategies used by states, corporations, institutions, formal or informal organizations, and individuals to influence developments within the media sector. A media policy can be more or less formal. In some cases it is founded on conscious studies, analyses and even tests and is specifically spelt out in documents. In other cases the policy can be a loose set of rules that have evolved over time out of practical experiences, opinion polls, etc.

Policies that are described in official documents might not be the ones that are actually carried out. Very often, policies that are formulated at government or company board level are interpreted in different ways or simply ignored by the individuals responsible for their enforcement. Thus it is important to differentiate between formulated and actual policies. Some actors may even implement media policies without being aware of it.

A number of parties are involved in shaping music policies for the media. Direct policymakers include governmental institutions, company boards, department directors, etc. But there are also more indirect influences through decisions in related bodies such as competing corporations, copyright organizations, musicians' unions, and through the 'cultural establishment' or lobbyists of different kinds.

Media policies can also be categorized according to their subject. The two main categories are policies for the general media environment and those for media content. The first category would include policies governing the kinds of media that can or should be introduced in a certain geographical area (and can thus be both mandatory and permissive policies). Examples are strategies formulated by a company in order to launch the compact disc in a certain country, or the decision by a government whether or not to allow satellite dishes. The second category includes all kinds of principles or rules for the selection of music content in a medium.

The design and concrete content of media policies and the relations of different sets of policy rules to each other are, of course, dependent on the context. If, for instance, a radio station decides to use a computer to select the music played over the air, then this requires a very exact set of policy rules for the music content of the programmes, otherwise the computer couldn't be programmed. Another radio station working with DJ personalities may not have any stated rules at all but leave the choice of music to the individual presenter. A station without explicit rules for music content may have an intrinsic or hidden music policy which can be revealed by content analysis.

The net result of implemented media music policies is that certain music media with a certain music content become available. The presence of these media and their content influences the music culture in the geographical area concerned. The result of this influence manifests itself in the form of changes in 'music activity', which is the second basic concept in our study.

Music activity can take place on different geographical levels. Transnational media giants record superstars; this is music activity on an international level. A symphony orchestra in a small country would often function on a national level. The term 'local' is used to denominate the level of music activity of the common man in society. This is the level below the national level of government and corporate activities. It can apply to a geographical/social area such as a household, a neighbourhood, a village, a town or a county. It can also refer to a particular ethnic group or subculture within a country. 'Local music activity' thus refers to activities involving music carried out by a local population.

Music activities can be further divided into two categories: performance and non-performance (Grandin 1989: 1–61). Performance activities include the actual playing of music in different contexts, i.e. any kind of musicmaking from the singing of a lullaby, drumming and chanting in ceremonies, to stage events and media events, live or recorded. Performance also includes music-related activities such as dancing.

Non-performance activities include every possible way of listening to and hearing music, talking about music and expressing musical values, as well as acquiring phonograms and turning on and off different music machines. Thus the same musical activity can be a performance activity to some participants and a non-performance activity to others.

Music activities can be traditional, that is, they are seen by members of local communities as belonging to the musical heritage of their society. They can also be recognized as new activities, recently introduced into the local music culture.

Figure 2.1 presents our model of the relationship between media policy and music activity in a particular music and media environment, with a particular culture, traditions and economic constraints. A policy debate can, but does not always lead to policy formulation. Similarly, formulated policies can result in actual implementation, but not necessarily. Actual media policy affects both performance and non-performance music activity. Music activity in its turn also makes its mark on the policy debate in society. Feedback from music activists to both policymaking decisions (formulation) and actual policy can be extremely weak; thus the dotted lines in the model.

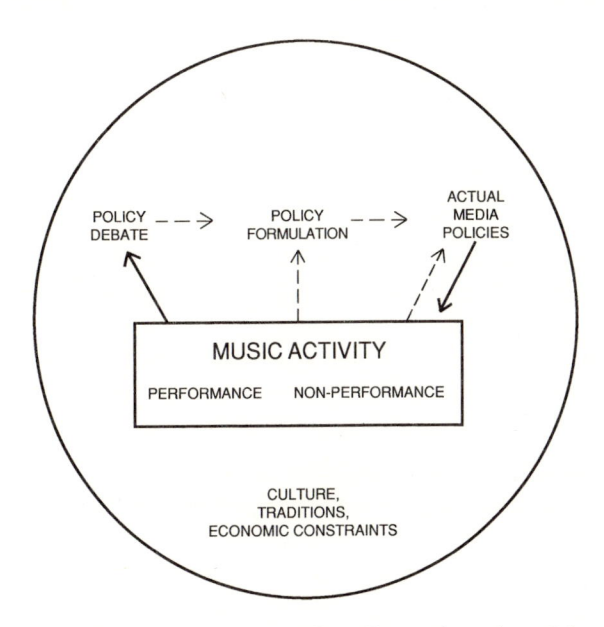

Figure 2.1 The relationship between media policy and music activity.

POSTULATES AND HYPOTHESES

Two of our basic assumptions have been that

1 The music media serve to increase the amount of non-performance activities on the local level.

2   The music media today constitute the main means of introduction of new music activities on the local level.

The results of the Music Industry in Small Countries (MISC) project show that the very presence of music mass media not only introduces new activities but also changes traditional activities and traditional music styles. The process whereby local forms of music are adapted to mass media was termed 'mediaization' in the MISC project (Wallis and Malm 1984: 278–81; Malm and Wallis 1985). The mediaization process has many aspects. For example, the recording studio is a very different environment from the live scene with its direct interaction between artist and audience. The process whereby music is fed through the 'music industry pipeline', e.g. the recording studio and a distribution system involving radio broadcasts, disc jockeys and record shops, also changes and shapes the musical traditions involved, thus giving birth to new musical styles.

The MISC project also confirmed the introduction by the media of new ways of making music. With media distribution a music, at least as a sound structure, is freed from the boundaries of time and space. This means that a certain genre of music can suddenly begin to influence what happens in a time and place very distant from its origin. It's fair to maintain that this has been an on-going process since the notation of music was invented. A sound recording, however, carries with it far more information about a music style than does notation. It can also be decoded by anyone with playback equipment without the painstaking process of learning how to read and write music. With music video clips and video documentaries often supplemented with printed matter, the amount of information that is transmitted grows.

The movement of musical sound in time and space amounts to a form of transplantation of music. The transplantation processes become more and more visible as time goes by, for a number of reasons:

1   the amount of available recorded music grows;
2   access to recording and playback facilities increases all over the world;
3   better communications nationally and internationally lead to the creation of networks between different music traditions and their exponents. Such networks can be formal, for example, in the case of subsidiaries of transnational companies, transborder broadcasting of different kinds, organizations and fan clubs. They can also be relatively informal or linked to extra-musical activities such as tourism.

The assumptions made above are very general ones. The way the media influence local music activities is dependent in each particular case on the media policies that are implemented. The changes in local music activities can also be perceived in different ways depending on the perspectives of different members of local populations. Thus the aim of this research project has been to map out precisely these different areas, noting the effects of different media policies on music activities as perceived by people with different perspectives.

THE MUSIC INDUSTRY: A SET OF SYSTEMS BOUND BY VARIOUS CONSTRAINTS

The operations of the music mass media have become more and more integrated into the operations of the music industry as a whole. Media policies formulated within the music industry – for instance, regarding which artists and styles are to be recorded and distributed – define to a considerable extent the parameters for policymaking within other sectors. Therefore a number of our postulates assume that the music industry operates on different levels, and that those operations are bound by a number of constraints.

The music industry is viewed in our context as a system or set of systems operating on different levels (local/national/international) with different types of interaction within and between actors or participant groups on each level. The operation of the system is seen as being constantly affected by a number of constraints which function in this context as independent variables. Three significant constraints are identified, namely technological, economic and organizational. Figure 2.2 illustrates the relationships under scrutiny.

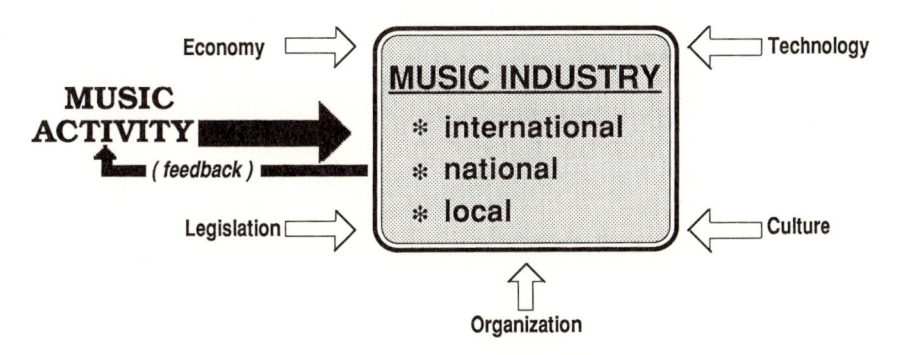

Figure 2.2 Factors affecting the establishment and maintenance of a music industry, and its relationship to music activity in the environment.

The existence of a music industry presupposes some level of music activity which can be processed via, say, phonogram technology and disseminated in different ways via different media technologies. The scale of a music industry operation can vary. On the local level, one might find the smallest 'cottage industry' with a band or a choir making its own cassettes for sale to fans, friends and relatives. On a national level, one finds a variety of institutions. The phonogram industry usually consists of subsidiaries of the transnational companies and/or nationally owned independents, working generally with a combination of international imports and some domestic artists. Broadcasting organizations can be state controlled or 'independent' companies, financed by taxes, licences or through sales of advertising time. The introduction of cable has allowed international satellite services to compete with national broadcasters. Deregulation has also allowed new local operators to enter the fray (Tunstall 1986; Mulryan 1988; Wallis 1990).

The distinction between a local and national level of activity might seem pointless when discussing, say, a small island like Jamaica. But the national level does have significance, since it is at this level that music activity operations can be matched by cultural policies of a sovereign, national government. Laws can be made, taxes can be introduced and exempted, cultural and media policies can be formulated, subsidies can be constructed aimed at increasing the music industry's activities with national and local music (as opposed to international imports). Such decisions, formulated nationally per country, or internationally via agreements between different national governments and organizations, contribute to fixing the parameters within which music industry operations within a nation can be undertaken.

On the international level, important actors for this research are the transnational cultural industries. There we find the group of international phonogram companies known as the 'majors' or the 'Big Five' (Sony-CBS, EMI/Virgin, WEA, Polygram and BMG, with MCA hovering on the perimeter). They market and distribute music recorded by international stars, aiming for profit maximization through selling the same products in as many markets as possible. They are also constantly battling against pirates who use cheap mass-reproduction equipment to make informal copies for illegal sales.

That developments in the music and media industries during the 1980s have been a result of a combination of technological, economic and political/cultural factors is hardly surprising. Much human endeavour is the result of a combination of people, resources and machines. In the MISC study, we described how the compact cassette and associated playback and recording equipment have comprised technological innovations that have been simple enough to use (and cheap enough) to allow for them to permeate into almost every society, covering a wide range of socio-economic characteristics.

Technology provides opportunities for new audio experiences; these change all the time as new sound carriers or new instruments and recording techniques are developed. It also provides some restrictions. Sound carriers and playback can only handle a limited amount of software – the 3-

minute song was a result of the limitations of the 78rpm disc. Technology also serves to establish operating norms such as those governing recording quality, frequency range, good 'sound' – in other words, 'technologically fixed aspects' which govern the production of recorded music (Etzkorn 1982: 559). The dissemination of music via broadcast and narrowcast media is also subject to technological constraints. Two radio stations cannot normally broadcast simultaneously on the same frequency; policies have to be formulated and implemented regarding the distribution of frequencies and permitted transmitter size – broadcasting can never be totally 'free' of all societal control, however much many would-be broadcasting entrepreneurs preach the message of 'free' or 'independent' radio. As Mulryan has succinctly pointed out, this is mere 'rhetoric' (Mulryan 1988: 148).

A number of technological developments are likely to cause considerable changes in both the workings of the music industry and the nature of music activity as a whole, with digital technology, as we have noted, making its most immediate impact in the developed nations.

Digital Audio Tape (DAT), allowing the consumer to record with CD quality at home, but requiring digital playback equipment, is likely to enter the market in the richer nations at a higher rate after the signing of an accord between the IFPI and the hardware manufacturers in 1989. This software/hardware agreement requires the inclusion of electronic circuits in digital recorders, circuits which limit the ability to make multiple copies from CD to DAT cassette. The recordable CD known as WORM (Write Once Read Many Times) has emerged from the laboratories and could be an important innovation for small to medium-sized phonogram producers. WORM could allow them to produce a small number of high-quality copies for use by broadcasters, even if the normal sound carrier used for dissemination was the cassette (often shunned by radio stations).

Whereas sophisticated digital editing equipment allowing for a variety of refined editing techniques is extremely expensive, the price of semi-professional video cameras and editing equipment is falling. This might allow local enthusiasts to enter the music video market rather in the way in which they started to enter the phonogram market during the 1970s.

The combination of synthesizers, computers, modems and suitable software programmes has also facilitated the growth of rudimentary home studios where amateurs can create their own orchestral, multi-track recordings. It can be predicted that this development will continue, producing more sophisticated systems for amateur or semi-professional use. Whether such equipment will carry a price affordable in the developing nations is another matter.

Electronic instruments are constantly making a greater impact on music activity. Machines that produce digitally sampled sound have an impact on the economic and human prerequisites for the retention of traditional skills of making and performing on conventional instruments. Labour-intensive musical activities, such as symphony orchestras, will almost certainly be affected in the industrialized world. Amateurs and professionals will continue to buy the latest gadgets. In some cases, professionals will be made redundant by music machines and their operators; some drummers have already been replaced in studio recording sessions by samplers and sequencers.

Not only available technology (albeit at an affordable price) but also other factors govern the transformation of music activity into music industry software, and its dissemination. *Economic* factors can also be expected to impinge on music industry activities. The notion of economic man partaking in business activities merely to maximize financial reward, a notion which was popular amongst classical scholars of organization theory (Fayol 1916; Taylor 1911), has long been superseded by a realization that individuals in organizations have more than just economic needs. In a market economy where there is more than one phonogram company, instrument manufacturer or broadcaster, for instance, one can predict that different entities within the music industry will compete for physical, cultural and economic rewards with other entities within their environment (Aldrich 1979; Lawrence and Lorsch 1967). It follows that as phonogram companies grow in the direction of a monopoly via an oligopoly, then demands of economic efficiency can be expected to take precedence over other potential rewards. At the other end of the scale, on a local level, where economic risks are less (assuming accessibility to technology at an affordable price), then potential cultural and social rewards can be expected to have a greater influence on activities than a desire to maximize economic efficiency.

The comprehensive nature of the *organizational* constraint has already been covered. The ability to create a functioning international organization has been a prerequisite for growth of the major transnational phonogram companies. The organizational culture that develops (combining musical and business activities) has a strong bearing on decision-making concerning phonogram output, as well as norms governing relationships in the industry's interfaces with the market, including related media organizations, and its music source environment.

Culture in general (and particularly music culture), as well as legal frameworks (also in a sense a cultural phenomenon), are also constraints which are regarded as present in the organizational variable. To mention but one example, the role of popular music as a medium for communication in Jamaican and Trinidadian society, it can be postulated, played a significant role in the process whereby those islands were to produce source material for the international phonogram industry.

The activities of transnational businesses on a national level in different countries can be expected to be constrained by cultural traditions in those countries. It will be harder, for instance, to introduce a functioning copyright system whereby publishers can generate income in a society where cultural norms treat music as the collective property of society, rather than as a good which is subject to individual ownership.

Legislation is an element of the organizational constraint which operates on all levels. Internationally, it can comprise international agreements and conventions. Nationally or locally, laws introduced by sovereign national or local government attempt to fix parameters within which music industry activities can be pursued.

Studies of the prerequisites for music industry activities lead to two important observations. The first is that the constraints are dynamic; they do not merely spell out minimum levels or threshold values for operations to start, values which then stay constant. They change constantly. The second conclusion is that their speed of impact varies. Technological innovations and economic factors can have an immediate impact compared to, say, the cultural factor, which is subject to some lag. Technological and economic factors, in other words, can be expected to force the pace of development in the absence of clear, workable media policies because of this same lag. We will note many examples of this in the following chapters.

STRUCTURAL CHANGE THROUGH FORMAL AND INFORMAL INTEGRATION

A prime interest for any study of the influence and continued growth of global cultural industries is the way in which systems and subsystems within these industries grow through different forms of integration, allowing for both internationalization and localization of activities. Phonogram companies can grow, for instance, through diversification and amalgamation.

Integration can be formal or informal. Formal integration is that resulting from restructuring within the business, through amalgamations, mergers, financial deals, etc. The latter occurs in different ways. The larger phonogram companies have grown primarily through horizontal integration (for example, by buying up other phonogram companies) and through vertical integration. The latter involves increasing control over different operations in the production and distribution process: for example, by purchasing music publishers, record pressing plants, distributors or even radio stations.

In recent years, the large transnational phonogram companies have themselves been bought up by other companies in the electronics and entertainments sector, as we have mentioned. In another round of company buyouts, the Big Five phonogram transnationals have themselves bought up large independents such as Chrysalis (EMI), Virgin (EMI) and Island (Polygram).

30   Media Policy and Music Activity

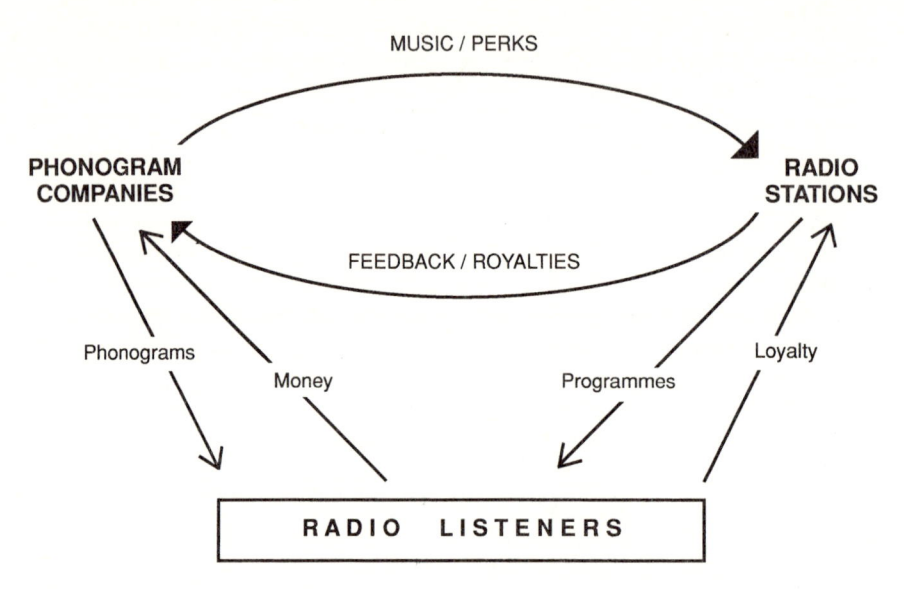

Figure 2.3   Phonogram companies/broadcasters/listeners in a system.

These examples of integration are highly significant as regards developments on a national level in different countries. Large international conglomerates and their subsidiaries are far less dependent on the wills of national legislators in different territories.

The other form of integration, informal integration, involves increased degrees of mutual dependence, through common interests rather than ownership. This is equally important from the point of view of undestanding the development of the music industry, partly because the influence of new and different actors increases in its wake. A typical example is that of the interdependency between broadcasters and phonogram companies.

If broadcasters cut down on their own recording operations, relying more on phonograms/videograms from outside, then the importance of the decision-makers at phonogram companies increases. Radio and television become more dependent on music policy decisions made by others. As public broadcasters have seen their funds dwindling, less money has been spent on recording sessions. The broadcasters' need for commercially available music has increased, thus increasing their dependence on the phonogram industry for programme material. The dependence is mutual, with the phonogram industry, in its turn, depending more on broadcasters to publicize products (as the broadcaster's role as an alternative finder of non-recorded musical talent decreases).

We have previously proposed the value of a system approach for understanding the process of informal integration (Wallis and Malm 1988: 267–84). This involves identifying systems which attempt to approach a state of equilibrium by balancing demands and reward relationships between the participants. If there is too great a discrepancy between perceived demands and rewards then the system will either act to repair the deficiency or break down. Figure 2.3 is a graphical representation of a simple system involving broadcasters, phonogram producers and the general public.

Radio stations present listeners with an output, much of which is recorded music. We presume that listeners remain loyal to a particular broadcaster as long as they like the fare that is offered and are not tempted to look for other alternative stations. Some of these listeners make a decision to purchase the phonograms they have heard, providing income for the phonogram company (so-called 'primary income'). Phonogram company income pays not only for production costs, including royalties to artists and composers, but also for the costs of providing broadcasters with programme material, including any other perks that may be involved over and above the supply of CDs and vinyl discs or tape. Perks can also involve subsidizing the costs of artists appearing in shows put on by the broadcaster. With commercial broadcasters, phonogram companies can also buy broadcasting time during advertisement slots.

Phonogram companies also get some of their income via the feedback bond from the broadcasters. The rewards can consist of valuable knowledge (regarding what sort of music goes down well with the station's gatekeepers or the audience) as well as money. In countries which have signed the Rome Convention (Britain, Germany, Sweden, etc. but not the USA) not only composers, but also phonogram companies and performers have a right to pecuniary remuneration when phonograms are played in public. These neighbouring rights give rise to a flow of 'secondary income' to the phonogram company, income which can be augmented still further if the phonogram company can get a slice of the composers' royalties via controlling publishing rights. We noted above that formal vertical integration included the buying-up of music publishing companies.

The system illustrated in this case never needs to reach a state of complete equilibrium. Indeed, it is always in a state of dynamic flux. It is not necessary, however, for each demand–reward relationship, or pair of bonds in the diagram, to be perceived to be in some form of economic balance. Each actor will continue to stay in the system as long as net rewards from all bond relationships relating to the same actor are perceived to be sufficient for satisfying conditions of survival. In other words, phonogram companies do not automatically leave the system (e.g. through closing down) if record sales fall. They try to compensate by increasing their net reward from the other relationship they are involved in, that with the broadcasters. Thus we can witness a conscious attempt to shift the source of phonogram company income from primary to secondary sources. Trade and copyright organizations step up the pressure on broadcasters to pay more for the music they use to fill programmes. In Sweden, as we shall see later, secondary income for the phonogram industry has reached almost the same level as incomes from sales of phonograms in the market. Such developments can affect decision-making in the broadcasting industry. Dues to the phonogram industry can be cut by playing older recordings or rereleases on CDs of music that is 'out of copyright', or by playing phonograms produced in countries that have not signed the Rome Convention (primarily US recordings). At some point in time it might even become cheaper for a radio station to record its own music or at least play syndicated material recorded by and for broadcasters but not for release on commercially available phonograms, rather than having to pay Rome dues (known variously as PPL, Gramex or IFPI fees).

The phonogram industry's global integration with other industries is occurring both directly, via business fusions, and indirectly, as a result of informal integration between different sectors of the entertainment and consumer industries. As radio and television have expanded, encouraged by the deregulation fervour which has spread from the USA to Europe, competition in broadcasting has toughened. Stations need not only audio and audio-visual products from the music industry to fill their programmes, but also seek more and more support from advertisers and sponsors. Even licence-financed public broadcasters are turning more frequently to sponsors to fill up holes in their coffers. The intricacy of such resulting systems forces us to move further and further away from the notion of the music industry as a set of loosely coupled subsystems (Burnett and Weber 1987) to one where ties become much stronger.

DATA COLLECTION: METHODS AND DIFFICULTIES

Much of the data collection in this project has had the character of 'stock-taking', in other words, qualitative and quantitative studies of the extent of media and music industry operations and their relations to music activities. The aim was to identify local and national activities in our sample countries and compare them to international developments. Such research can appear to be somewhat unstructured. On the other hand, commentators such as Blaukopf have argued convincingly for types of activities akin to the collection of artifacts (though not totally absent from a theoretical framework) when trying to penetrate a media operation that does not normally open its doors to scrutiny (Blaukopf 1974: 231–4; Mark 1981). An important part of such research consists of simply watching, questioning and trying to understand the operations of the music media production and policymaking processes.

Schlesinger has put forward another convincing argument in favour of the 'free-for-all investigation of the animal' approach, as opposed to, say, merely sending out questionnaires based on a previous choice of theoretical model, or conducting research where conclusions regarding the functioning of a media process are based mainly on analyses of output. Writing about his studies within the BBC, Schlesinger claims:

> There are good reasons for keeping the ethnographic tradition alive in this field, for it offers insights which are otherwise unavailable. The most obvious general argument is that an ethnography permits the theoretically informed observation of the social practices of cultural production. Even now, only a few studies of this kind have been undertaken – and hardly any comparative studies at all. . . . Furthermore, while there is no doubt that external analyses of cultural products, whether by using the techniques of content, textual or discourse analysis, have much to tell us, such approaches do face the crucial limitation of only being able to make inferences about the actual process of production inside cultural institutions and organizations, and thus face a lacuna in any explanations offered.
>
> (Schlesinger 1987: xxxi)

Our approach has been to collect relevant, believable, quantitative data where it was available, without devoting too much energy to comparisons which would be rendered meaningless by their lack of reliability. Often orders of magnitude were far more relevant than exact quantities in a dynamic situation where conditions could vary considerably from day to day.

Our previous studies of the phonogram industry showed that exact, comparable statistics of phonogram releases, sales and imports were almost impossible to come by in most countries. Different standards were applied; sometimes customs returns would even measure imports in kilos (Gronow 1980)! The quantitative data provided by different bodies on the music content of broadcasting media suffer the same shortcomings as data on phonogram production (Wallis and Malm 1984: 22ff.). Sweden is a partial exception; data on phonogram sales, releases (by genre) and music output on national radio are up to date and exact. In countries such as Kenya and Tanzania, no official data on music programming exist. In the other countries, data from different sources such as audience research departments and polling institutes are usually incompatible. For instance, interpretations of what is included in different musical genres such as classical music, art music, contemporary music, pop music, etc. can vary considerably between countries, institutions and individuals. Very often what is covered by different names of musical genres appearing in statistics is not even defined.

The amount of national and local music in radio/TV programmes as opposed to international or imported music was of major interest. Here again, different definitions make available data hard to handle. In Sweden, statistics from the national radio company covering the use of 'Swedish music' define this as music written by Swedish composers or music played by Swedish artists. Statistics from the same company over phonograms played on different channels define 'Swedish' as 'recorded in Sweden'; in other words, such data can even include foreign works recorded by foreign artists. In statistics from the Swedish copyright organization, however, 'Swedish music' is defined as music by composers with copyrights registered with the Swedish Copyright Society, thus excluding, for instance, all traditional music where arrangements have not been copyrighted. Cultural activists lobbying for more Swedish music in the media define it as 'music in a Swedish musical style', thus excluding all music made and played by Swedes in styles copied from abroad.

Whatever definition one opts for, there are always borderline cases and difficulties in applying categorizations in a strict and logical fashion. Again, the curious observer has to settle for rough categories and orders of magnitude when using this kind of quantitative data.

Dichotomies are often popular amongst those who have devoted their time to content analysis. Many mass communications analysts have concerned themselves with studies of information content (as opposed to entertainment content). Their understandable interest is in whether or not the media is being used to disseminate information and stimulate thought and discussion, so that citizens can carry out their democratic obligations. Entertainment is seen as a natural opposite. A notion that entertainment can provide the right style or packaging within which to purvey information is rarely compatible with this conceptual framework. Those concerned with culture in the media, particularly the fine arts, use another pair of opposites when referring to content: culture and entertainment. What isn't deemed to be culture tends to be regarded as output of lesser aesthetic value.

Our view, which focuses on music activity as a central concept, tends to cut right across these two approaches. For us, musical creativity in progress on the stage of the Stockholm Opera has just as much cultural value as reggae at a concert or in a studio in Jamaica, an afternoon ngoma show of music and dance in a suburb of Dar es Salaam, or a Welsh folk group playing in a tavern in North Wales. They are all just as valuable in their separate contexts, and just as worthy of support from the various policies and institutions which can exert influence on the conditions for their survival. Statistics that show a huge rise in entertainment output but a diminishing percentage of TV programme time being devoted to 'cultural' programmes, in other words, are of little interest in this project. Our focus is very much more on cultural elements that hold societies and subcultures together, rather than on those forms of culture which an elite deems to have transcended what is vulgar and popular. Our focus is on that which involves creative musical activity over the widest possible range; such statistics are few and far between!

The collection of data for the MISC study relied almost entirely on face-to-face interviews with people who could be expected to have a profound knowledge of the area under investigation. Interviews were geared at getting the informants to identify *significant incidents* which they had observed during the 1980s. The significant incident method is useful for highlighting strains and tensions in relations between different sectors of the music industry. Reference to significant incidents, seen from different points of view, gives valuable clues as to the relationship between different actors on the music and media scene.

The MISC project allowed us to develop a general approach to data collection which worked well. Since all the sample countries in this project were also included in the MISC project, we had a solid platform on which to stand. We were already familiar with the music media environment in the different countries. We also knew a great number of people whose reliability had been tested during MISC.

Interviews were carried out during visits to the sample countries and later supplemented by contacts via telephone or mail. Kenya and Tanzania were visited once in 1988, while Jamaica, Trinidad and Wales were visited up to four times during the period 1986–91. Data has been collected continuously in Sweden. Informants were chosen so as to cover the following main categories:

1 Direct policymakers

Government: politicians responsible for music media, bureaucrats working with culture in central and local government.
Media corporations (both phonogram/videogram and broadcasting corporations): owners, board members, directors, producers, disc jockeys, staff in marketing and market research departments.
Music press: journalists.

2 Indirect policymakers

Trade and interest organizations: board members, staff in secretariats, representatives of the membership.
Agents and their clients
Educationalists
Musical establishment: academic researchers and others.

3 Musicmakers and the audience

Individuals who have documented an interest in music media policy and its impact on local music activities through participation in debates, articles, etc.

A checklist was used to facilitate the gathering of information from several respondents about similar significant incidents, thus providing for a minimum of structuring in the interviews. This list covered the following points:

1 Are there any written or otherwise recorded policy documents or authoritative policy statements concerning music in the media? Where can these be obtained?
2 What policy determines the music content of media X, Y and Z? What is the relation between stated policy and applied policy?
3 What is the composition of the music output in the media? How much local, how much national, how much international music? What musical genres? How much consists of feature programmes, DJ programmes, video clips, etc.?
4 In what way has the musical output of the media influenced musical activities in your domain and in other domains of the music life?
5 In what way have musical activities in your domain been reflected or affected music policy in the media?

The interviews also included an updating of the general data collected during the MISC project and covered areas such as:

1 The formation of new music institutions or significant changes affecting existing music institutions.
2 The formation of new music organizations or changes in existing music organizations.
3 Significant changes in legislation affecting the music industry.
4 Changes in the structure of the music industry.
5 Changes in the structure of broadcasting, especially the establishment of satellite-cable networks, CD and music video production units.
6 Other changes or events not covered by the above.

As many relevant documents as possible were collected to supplement the interviews. The information and statistics on music content of radio programming in Kenya, Tanzania, Jamaica and Trinidad were supplemented by direct data collection. This was done through continuous sampling of the programme content of radio stations every sixth minute, in most cases during several days of broadcasting at different times. By sampling ten times an hour and classifying the programme content in each sample, fairly reliable primary data could be collected. Since the music content in all these samples was categorized according to consistent principles, the resulting data admit comparisons between different radio stations and different times of the year.

Such sampling was not needed in either Sweden or Wales. Statistics were already available in the former, and in Wales we were specifically looking at Welsh language media, i.e. where output was dominated by artists and recordings from the local music industry.

A major problem in this kind of research is that the music and media industry is always in a state of flux. Conflicts between those entrepreneurs and artists working with local/national music and those involved in the distribution of international music were often so strong (as experienced by respondents) that it became hard for a researcher asking questions to remain entirely neutral. When a person who experiences a problem meets an 'expert' from Sweden, then that person wants to know how the Swedes have tried to solve their difficulties in the same area. The answer can trigger off new activities. Even without giving any such stimuli to respondents, the mere act of encouraging informants to specify and analyse critical incidents that have affected them in the past can be sufficient to set in motion considerable changes. One often noticed this on later return visits! Thus the researcher, merely by observing phenomena and asking questions, serves to change the nature of those phenomena.

A methodological problem with such methods of data collection is that reliability becomes hard to test, since it is virtually impossible to repeat exactly the same interviews, under the same conditions. Parameters change even during the course of an interview, and such methods of data collection require an interviewer with a high degree of theoretical and practical knowledge. The fact that several respondents gave the same or similar answers, combined with the ability to make return visits and check unclear data, added positively to the reliability of the method. An important observation is that almost all respondents agreed to their answers being recorded on tape. These tapes were then transcribed and stored – a far more reliable way of recording essentially open-ended interviews than merely making sporadic notes. Even the samples of radio output used for music content logging were recorded on tape. Transcribed excerpts from our recorded data are referred to in the following sections by the letters TI (taped interview) followed by the date on which the recording was made (day/month/year).

Information describing the situation in each of our sample countries is presented in the following six chapters. Each starts with a general introduction to the media environment. International, national and local actors in both primary and secondary music media are then described in greater detail, including observations on different examples of music media policy and their effects on music activity.

Chapter 3
Case study: Jamaica

INTRODUCTION TO THE MUSIC AND MEDIA ENVIRONMENT

In 1983, the then Prime Minister of Jamaica, Edward Seaga, gave this appraisal of the significance of the music industry in his country:

> 'It is a way out for young composers who come from a ghetto background – it's a way out in terms of becoming a professional in a field that gives an income level that is not attainable in the normal occupations that would be open. . . . As in most countries, musicians come from underprivileged backgrounds. It's a path of vertical mobility that's very important in our society.'
>
> (Interview for Swedish TV, 28/01/83)

Four years later, sociologist Carl Stone made this comment on reactions in Jamaica to the influx of US entertainment culture and technology:

> 'The hatred some intellectuals feel for US culture doesn't exist at the local level. The man in the street wants a wide range of choice. There is a sense of cultural confidence amongst people at the lower end of society which doesn't exist amongst the intelligentsia – *they* feel threatened. *They* have identity problems which a man from the Trenchtown ghetto doesn't have. He feels he can deal with the foreign stuff without losing any of his identity.'
>
> (Carl Stone, TI 31/05/87)

Hidden in the two statements above are some of the more significant factors determining the complex nature of Jamaica's music and media environment.

Jamaica is a nation with a young population, poor in economic resources but rich in cultural terms. The island has long been an important source of material for the international music industry, first through the spread of Jamaican folk songs via artists such as Harry Belafonte, and more recently through the international success of reggae music, where artists such as

Bob Marley, Jimmy Cliff and many others have received worldwide acclaim.

Even if Jamaica is a Third World nation, it is hardly isolated from events and trends in the industrialized world. About two-thirds of Jamaica's population have moved overseas, mainly to the UK, Canada and the US in search of better financial conditions. Geographic proximity to the US and particularly the type of media proximity that goes with being in the footprints of US satellites, coupled with a high level of communication between Jamaicans and expatriates, leads to high access to international cultural products and media trends. Carl Stone, quoted above, describes Jamaica as 'a very internationally exposed society. There is an enormous amount of communication between Jamaicans and relatives living abroad. Foreign mail per capita is higher than for many European countries' (C. Stone, TI 31/05/87). With such a large interest in both local and international trends, it's hardly surprising that electronic industry hardware is plentiful in Jamaica.

Three Jamaica All-Media Surveys, produced by the advertising industry in 1984, 1986 and 1990, provide some growth statistics for the Jamaicans' access to media equipment. Sampled interviews with a selection of the estimated 1.5 million Jamaicans over the age of 10 produced the following statistics:

Table 3.1 Consumer electronics in Jamaica

Year	1984	1986	1990
Radio sets	976,000	931,000	1,298,000
Audio cassette machines	191,000	202,000	251,000
Television sets	387,000	394,000	500,000
VCRs	127,000	128,000	211,000
Satellite dishes	5,000	5,900	17,800

Source: Jamaica All-Media Surveys (Andersson Associates, Kingston)

Note: These figures are based on interviews with a sample of 2,000 chosen randomly over the whole of the island from the total population over 10 years of age.

The figures in Table 3.1 are hard to verify through comparison since they appear to be the only ones available. They indicate a remarkable influx of electronic hardware, despite the economic problems besetting Jamaica; virtually every third Jamaican over the age of 10 has his or her own TV set! Government officials working on a proposed satellite dish tax in 1987 estimated that there were between 6,000 and 8,000 such dishes (a sudden and spirited burst of opposition from dish-owners quickly led to such fiscal plans being shelved). Our own ocular observations indicated a move in this trend down the socio-economic scale, or as one observer put it: 'It will only

Plate 3.1 The colourful mural outside one of Jamaica's many record manufacturing plants. Bob Marley financed this one through his Tuff Gong Records Company.

be a matter of time before the dishes turn up in Jonestown' (Jonestown is a poorer, 'ghetto' district in Kingston).

Several local recording studios and manufacturing plants supply the island with vinyl records and pre-recorded cassettes. CDs, however, only started to 'catch on' in 1990 with the largest record company, Dynamic Sounds, opening its Digital Audio CD store in Kingston. DJs with huge mobile sound systems play an important role in the marketing and spread of recorded music, particularly of music deemed by the radio stations to be unsuitable for airplay, usually for reasons of lyrical content. Much more local musicmaking occurs in recording studios than in the live concert or club scene. The sound systems scene featuring large PAs in mobile discotheques has encouraged the development of DJ poets using the medium of rap, as well as 'Singjay' hybrids – DJs who sing melodies and chants to rhythmical backing tracks.

The local phonogram industry consists of a handful of locally owned larger companies which record, manufacture and distribute primarily singles and LPs, although the latter are tending to be replaced by pre-recorded cassettes (a trend which can be expected to rise as the CD gains ground). There are still no cases of subsidiaries of the Big Five multinationals in Jamaica. In our 1987 interview survey, the radio stations

Plate 3.2 No CDs! Singles are still popular sound carriers in Jamaica. The inside of Randy's Record Store in downtown Kingston – a visit here is a must for many a Western reggae pilgrim.

estimated that about 100 new Jamaican singles were received monthly from artists and companies seeking media exposure. Established artists such as Jimmy Cliff or Bunny Wailer usually have their own phonogram companies, using larger local companies for manufacture and distribution at home, but signing release deals with one or more international companies in different territories abroad.

Pre-recorded cassettes, we have noted, have gained popularity during the latter half of the 1980s – this has also been accompanied by an increase in piracy, something the local industry had previously been good at discovering and discouraging. One shopkeeper told us that pirates survived because they produced a better quality product (i.e. on higher quality tape) than local manufacturers could achieve with their mass-reproduction facilities. An owner of one of the more prominent local phonogram companies, Sonic Sound's Neville Lee, described piracy as

> 'one of the major problems in Jamaica. A few years ago it was underground. Now it has surfaced to the level that you can go into any record shop, look at the Top 20 Chart and say: "I'd like all that".'

Lee sees tourism as one factor encouraging this trend:

'There are people duplicating on a mass level, and they go into the gift shops on the north coast where there are a lot of tourists – tourists want the Top 20 reggae hits. The industry is suffering terribly.'

(N. Lee, TI 21/05/87)

THE BROADCASTING AND PRINT MEDIA

Four nationwide radio channels, all funded by commercials, as well as some regional stations, entertained and informed the Jamaicans throughout the 1980s. Three more came on air as Jamaica entered the 1990s.

The dominant service is provided by RJR which runs an AM service (Supreme Sound) and an FM channel (Fame) which came on air in 1973. RJR was originally a Rediffusion company which was sold to local interests in 1976. The employees of the station bought 24 per cent of the shares, the government 25 per cent and the rest were distributed amongst a number of mass organizations such as trade unions, co-operative movements, etc. The government divested its share at the end of 1991 in a share offer which was heavily over-subscribed by the general public.

The state-controlled JBC (Jamaica Broadcasting Corporation) emerged out of the pre-independence broadcasting organization created by the British. JBC started broadcasting its own AM radio channel back in the 1950s.

The development of unique Jamaican popular music styles can hardly be ascribed to the wisdom or otherwise of those formulating music policy in the country's first independent radio stations. On the contrary, musical impulses via foreign stations combined with local traditions seem to have been the catalyst for the development of blue beat, ska, reggae, etc. Bob Marley biographer, Timothy White, has described how Jamaican youth in the 1950s were listening to foreign radio stations, and how this began affecting their own music-making.

> turning away from the American pop foisted upon them by RJR and JBC. Weather conditions permitting, they listened to the sinewy music being played on New Orleans stations or Miami's powerful WINZ, whose playlists included records by Amos Milburn, Roscoe Gordon and Louis Jordan. They could relate to . . . Fats Domino's lamenting 'Walking Blues'. . . . Jamaican bands began covering US R&B hits, but the more adventurous took the nuts and bolts out of the sound and melded them with energetic jazz concepts . . . and emerged around 1956 with a hybrid concoction christened 'ska'. . . . Practically overnight, ska spawned a major Jamaican industry called the Sound System.

(White 1983: 18)

The 1960s saw both RJR and JBC following the success of the sound systems and hooking on to local music. As in the case of RJR, JBC added an FM channel in 1984. These two JBC channels have been run partly in conjunction with a number of regional stations which opted in and out of the signal from Kingston. During the mid-1980s, the regional outlets tended, however, to be somewhat erratic as regards operations. Radio Central, for instance, in the town of Mandeville, consisted merely of an empty office in 1987. Since then the authorities have planned and executed a certain measure of divestment, selling off radio licences to private operators, with Central becoming Radio KLAS, a western regional station in Montego Bay changing into Radio Waves, and an eastern region station in Ocho Rios emerging under private management as Radio IRIE. All of these rely heavily on music content to attract listeners.

Up to the introduction of FM radio, the two JBC and RJR channels tended to attract more or less equal shares of the audience. With the introduction of FM stereo music, the amount of international music on the airwaves increased. RJR Supreme Sound (AM) could claim the lion's share of the audience (over 52 per cent), with JBC1 (AM) noting an average share of 32 per cent and the two FM channels receiving about 7 per cent each.

One single personality, Barry Gordon, or 'Barry G', however could give JBC a virtual walk-over during his on-air hours when his popular output of local Jamaican music and political comments could be heard, generally fairly loudly, over most radios in the capital city. When Barry G moved to RJR for a year in 1988, a large part of his audience moved with him.

Jamaica has one TV channel (JBC-TV) with much programme material being taken in by a large satellite dish before being retransmitted. JBC's own production was minimal during the second half of the 1980s, partly because of financial constraints. All locally produced programmes had to be sponsored by some commercial benefactor. The government Educational Broadcasting System (EBS), in conjunction with a production and resource centre known as the CPTC (Creative Production Training Centre), financed partly by Unesco and a grant from the EC, also provided some programme material for JBC-TV. In 1986, a government decision, apparently endorsed by Unesco consultants, had led to most of the technical staff at JBC being transferred to the new CPTC.

Since then, a number of small, independent production houses producing local music videos have started to appear on the Jamaican scene. Together with the CPTC, they produce a number of video clips which are submitted to the JBC for consideration. If approved, they might appear on a weekly video show, together with international clips, or as fillers between programmes. As usual with the Jamaican music industry, the aim is dual, namely to create publicity and success in the home market (which generates international interest) as well as to provide audio-visual material for marketing abroad. A statement from record company owner Neville Lee, confirms this analysis:

'Audio-visual is a very important vehicle – not necessarily an expensive vehicle. But it's a young industry and there are still lots of people willing to do videos at very low rates. Our problem is that we cannot recoup those costs from sales in Jamaica even at the cheap price. What we do is to try to videotape in Jamaica, hoping that if the record breaks internationally, then we can use that video. We have markets like London or New York, where purchases are determined by what's going on in Jamaica.'

(N. Lee, TI 21/05/87)

As in the case of radio, plans have been mooted for the divestment of TV coupled with the sale of a licence for a further terrestrial TV channel, a matter which we shall return to later. Of course the 20,000 or more households hooked up to private dishes and, where necessary, with the right 'black box' for descrambling, can see scores of US satellite TV channels, including the music video channel, MTV. MTV output frequently gets taped and spread via video clubs and VCRs. Perry Hensell, Director of the film *The Harder They Come* (about exploitation in the Jamaican music industry), sees the satellite dishes as a middle-class phenomenon:

'Satellites and the like have made people who otherwise might have left Jamaica stay here. If you have a dish, you could be living in Des Moines or anywhere . . . that's what the middle class in Jamaica like to feel, that they are locked into the whole American network of culture.'

(Hensell, TI 23/05/87)

Marjorie Whylie of the Jamaican School of Music sees a worrying change in the media environment, brought on by the satellites:

'All round the Caribbean we are getting a steady diet of things that bear very little relationship to our culture. I think it's affecting young people so much that they strive for things which most of them within their lifetime will never realize.'

(Whylie, TI 25/05/87)

Ms Whylie's worries are echoed by another observer, Grace Livingstone, who runs a music and drama programme in a Nonconformist Church on the edge of Hannatown, one of Kingston's ghettoes. MTV's music clips form the ambitions of many young budding musicians, ambitions concerned not so much with foreign music but with the available hardware:

'Music through TV's video clips brings not a want so much to sing what Cindy Lopez is singing but a desire to get the instruments and the clothes and the baggage that comes along with it. The kids will tell me that the synthesizers and the mikes we've got here at the church are not as good as the ones they've seen on TV. There is a contradiction – they will like Barry Gordon but they will also want something more than Jamaica. MTV creates expectations which are not so much within their reach as they might think. Their world tends to be the world the video clips depict.'

(Livingstone, TI 28/05/87)

The *Daily* and *Sunday Gleaner* together with the more tabloid-style *Star* have dominated the Jamaican press throughout the 1980s, although other papers have begun to emerge of late with a popular tabloid such as the *Weekend Enquirer* finding a demand at the lower end of the socio-economic scale. There is no established music press, even if magazines with a music/show business focus come and go – the *Rockers Magazine* from the mid-1980s was one such example. The *Daily Gleaner*, however, is of importance for promoting the few live music events that take place in Jamaica, usually with the support of a business sponsor:

'Advertising is the greatest chunk of the costs for organizing a concert. Even a small ad in the *Gleaner* costs 800 dollars (US$ 150). Unless you have a very close relationship with the features editor who can give you a line to the person who does the gossip column, you need a paid advertisement. You can't hope to get an audience with only a press release. The *Gleaner* and radio/TV are the most important sources of promotion.'

(Whylie, TI 25/05/87)

MUSIC IN THE MEDIA

As in Trinidad, local music's role in the broadcasting media has increased over the past three decades. The growth of locally based popular music and its access to the phonogram media can be ascribed to factors such as urbanization and legitimization. Sociologist Carl Stone claims that:

'It has to do with a new generation emerging in the 1960s. There was massive movement into urban areas with huge concentrations of poor people. For the first time they were removed from the middle-class influence of rural teachers. They operated within their own community, their own leaders emerged, they set their own views and standards. . . . The whole notion of blackness, the impact of the Rasta movement took off in the late 1960s. Some things coming out of the USA and the civil liberties movement had an effect on the middle class, but most of it was internal. Michael Manley's PNP legitimized a lot of it – he used a whole lot of Rasta symbols at the 1972 election.'

(Stone, TI 31/05/87)

Bob Marley emerged out of this situation, and with the help of music industry entrepreneurs such as Chris Blackwell of Island records, he and other reggae artists became known over the world, but only after success at home. Many of his countrymen's minds were preoccupied with thoughts about poverty, exploitation and roots on another continent – Marley sang about such things.

As usual in the music industry, technological, economic and human factors have interacted to set the parameters for the spread of Jamaican music in various forms of mass media. Access to huge PA systems, a steady supply of singles as well as 'dubs' (usually the B-side of the single with only the backing-track) and other sources of rhythmical accompaniments have been prerequisites for the 'DJ', 'toaster', 'Rap' of 'sing-jay' scene. It's a scene that relies heavily on recorded elements becoming *de facto* public property:

> 'Your work turns up on any number of records. When I create a riff it gets played back on synthesizers and other songs. It's nothing that hurts me really, but it's worse for drummers and guitar players.'
> (Jamaica's leading sax player, Dean Fraser, TI 21/05/87)

The sound systems have traditionally provided an independent outlet for local music, particularly in recent years for dance/rap music with a high

Plate 3.3 'Your work turns up on any numbers of records' – Jamaican saxophonist Dean Fraser checking out a local record store.

jocular or obscene lyrical content of so-called 'slack talk'. The sound systems allow artists and records which would be banned on RJR/JBC to get limited exposure, whilst encouraging such lyrical trends.

Fragmentation of the radio system with the introduction of two FM-stereo channels led to the spread of more international music, i.e. music that was deemed to sound good in stereo. RJR's stereo channel actually started up in 1973 as Radio Capital, playing what the Programme Director described as 'Mantovani and endless tunes with James Last'. It went on doing so for nigh on ten years. RJR's Radio Capital wasn't a commercial success: 'it never made any money; the masses didn't go for it; it had a minority audience' (Don Toppin, RJR, TI 26/05/87). A 1984 revamp turned the FM channel into Fame radio, playing 'a better kind of reggae and pop music as it comes to us from across the world'. DJs on Fame were given a 'modified personality', which included introducing them to the public on tours, and not talking as much on the air as on the more popular AM service.

The Jamaica Broadcasting Corporation also runs an FM outlet. Originally the plan was to call it Radio Galaxy, no doubt as an alternative to RJR's Fame, but it became quite simply JBC2. A local music journalist described it as 'a bit more reggae, a bit more funky than Fame, whose emphasis is mainly on the young well-to-do market.'

Our own music-logging exercises covered three separate occasions in July 1986, May 1987 and December 1988. Whilst the total amount of Jamaican music on the airwaves varied between 32 and 40 per cent on these three occasions, JBC1 and RJR-AM (the Supreme Sound) averaged 66 and 55per cent Jamaican music respectively. The equivalent figures for the percentage of Jamaican music on the FM channels were 25 (RJR2) and 19 (RJR Fame) (see Tables 3.2–3.4).

According to the Jamaica All-Media Survey, RJR-AM and JBC had 46 per cent and 34 per cent of the total listening share in 1987. The FM channels attracted 11 per cent (RJR Fame) and 9 per cent (JBC1). A year later, in 1988, RJR's AM share had increased by over 10 per cent to around 47 per cent, with a corresponding drop in figures for JBC-AM. The reason, as we mentioned earlier, was the temporary move of radio/DJ personality Barry G to the Supreme Sound. The Jamaican music content on JBC-AM had also dropped by about 10 per cent. Barry G took his music and his audience with him to the other competing station. This illustrates the significance of radio personalities and the music associated with them in bringing different styles of music to a radio audience.

The Barry G phenomenon in Jamaica is interesting – he seems to appeal to both a large working-class audience as well as to some middle-class categories.

'There's a lot more interest in local music now. Much of the sensitivity

Table 3.2 Survey of programme content on Jamaican radio, 7 July 1986

Station	Jamaican %	Other W.I. %	USA %	Speech %	Comments
JBC1					
Total content	48	3	18	31	Most reggae
Music content	70	4	26		6–10, 14–17, 21–24
JBC2					
Total content	16	5	70	9	Middle-of-the-road,
Music content	17	6	77		easy listening
RJR1					
Total content	28	2	22	48	Interviews, public
Music content	53	4	43		affairs, reggae 12–16
RJR2					
Total content	8	0	88	7	Funk, disco
Music content	9	0	91		
All stations					
Total content	25	2	49	24	
Music content	37	4	59		

Notes: [1] Sample time 06.00–24.00.
[2] The music content of the Jamaican radio is dominated by a few kinds of music:
 (a) US funk, disco, middle-of-the-road and easy listening with the occasional gospel (in 'Jesus Saves' shows), country and jazz number (59%).
 (b) West Indian music, mainly Jamaican reggae with a sprinkle of soca and mento (41%). No Afro-Cuban or salsa music. Only music from the English-speaking Caribbean.
[3] The share of commercials is high in the early morning. Otherwise 5–10 minutes per hour. Most commercials contain US music, but many advertisers use Caribbean music to push both local and international merchandise.

that characterized the 1960s has come back again. DJs like Barry G play an important role. He comes across as someone who knows what's going on (satellites, New York and so on), so the middle-class kids accept him. The ghetto accepts him because he takes the sound systems to them.'

(Stone, TI 31/05/87)

Stone's final comment here is a reference to Barry G's perceived accessibility – he literally visits the poorer parts of urban areas with his very loud sound system; they can see and maybe even touch him. On air he also combines local music with political comments on topical issues, as Grace Livingstone from her vantage point at a Church in Hannatown observes:

GL: When Barry G goes on JBC, a ghetto-blaster will be pumping it out on William St – it's an everyday happening. You can stay upstairs and hear it. His charm is basically the music he plays, reggae in all its formations. It's put out from the grass roots, easy

Table 3.3 Survey of programme content on Jamaican radio, 27 May 1987

Station	Jamaican, incl. W.I. %	Anglo-American %	Speech %
JBC1			
Total content	22	7	71
Music content	74	26	
JBC2			
Total content	28	64	8
Music content	30	70	
RJR1			
Total content	31	16	53
Music content	66	33	
RJR2			
Total content	22	64	14
Music content	25	75	
All stations			
Total content	26	38	36
Music content	40	60	

Note: Sample time 06.00–18.00.

to identify with. He uses it to comment on all sorts of things. He has a very captive audience.
Q: What sort of issues does he take up?
GL: Right now it's apartheid – there's a lot of message music. Or if it's child abuse or teenage pregnancy, he'll play some of the DJ dub material, titles like 'pregnant, no pregnant, no mamma'.
Q: Is he an opportunist or genuinely involved?
GL: That's very subjective. I get the feel he's genuine, true, in key with the vibes. He also visits with his show the different places where he's popular. He brings his system with him to the people and doesn't stay obscure. He comes to meet you, and for the people those are the signs of genuineness. He's on key, not just playing a fast one.

(Livingstone, TI 28/05/87)

A qualitative section in the 1986 Jamaica All-Media Survey, summarizing some 2,000 interview responses, tends to support the above analysis of the Barry G phenomenon. His programme is seen as 'complete' because:

1 It was addressed to those at work and to those at home.
2 It involved music of all types but was also informational and educational.
3 The presenter was personal and involved with the listeners and his life situation.

Table 3.4 Survey of programme content on Jamaican radio, 13 December 1988

Station	Jamaican, incl. W.I. %	Anglo-American %	Speech %	Comments
JBC1				
Total content	23	15	62	
Music content	60	40		
JBC2				
Total content	27	67	6	
Music content	29	71		
RJR1				
Total content	18	20	62	Barry G had a phone-in show with Country and Western theme
Music content	48	52		
RJR2				
Total content	13	69	18	
Music content	16	84		
All stations				
Total content	20	43	37	
Music content	32	68		

Notes: [1] Sample time 06.30–18.00.
[2] Due to the season there was a fair amount of Christmas music increasing the Anglo-American content: 38% of the Christmas music was Jamaican and 62% Anglo-American. Also the C&W theme of Barry G's show increased the Anglo-American content.

4 Barry G was seen as an independent voice who spoke out regardless.

Point 4 above is interesting considering that JBC, Barry G's normal radio habitat, is government controlled and was generally perceived, according to the same survey, as being guilty of 'political bias, inefficiency and incompetence'. Barry G's attraction as a generator of commercial income for the advertising-financed station, as well as his public standing, gave him no small measure of leeway – after all, he could command an audience of around 350,000 at the 'difficult' radio time of 3pm.

A year after his 1988 move to RJR with his afternoon 2–6 show, Barry G was back at JBC ('they made him a fat offer', was one journalist's comment), but he didn't manage to take the whole of his audience to the former AM frequency. The reason would seem to be twofold: RJR has found a competing personality, Winston Williams, and new stations are on air as the result of the government's divestment of the former regional radios and their FM frequencies.

In a 1991 written report which we requested from music critic and jazz DJ Dermott Hussey, he gave this summary of the new Jamaican radio operators to whom deregulation moves had given FM access:

Plate 3.4 'On key, not just playing a fast one.' Jamaica's leading DJ, Barry G, in the JBC studio.

With regard to format and music policy, Radio Waves, which is heard in Montego Bay and not in Kingston, is similar to JBC1, i.e. Jamaican and a mix of everything else. KLAS (the old Central station in Mandeville) is international, new age and fusion and what it calls class reggae – it's not into the current dance hall stuff. IRIE says it's 95 per cent reggae in the broadest sense, and some hip hop, especially the sort that's fused with reggae. All three stations have found their audience.

A significant point is that although they were set up to provide a regional service, reflecting regional concerns that could be then heard in Kingston, they have not fulfilled that policy, particularly KLAS and IRIE. What they have done successfully is find their market niche. As a result of IRIE particularly, a lot of local music is being slotted into the FM channels at RJR and JBC – Sunday has become a big day for Jamaican oldies. In a recent survey, IRIE was placed second with 22 per cent to RJR Supreme (AM) which had 40 per cent listening share.

(Hussey, January 1991)

Dermott Hussey's summary is significant – it shows that conditions for granting radio franchises concerning, for example, regional content, don't always get transformed into reality when a larger urban market can be reached. It also indicates that a format with a very high percentage of local music can work well in a small country with a lively home music industry.

Whether this is a universal, permanent axiom or the results of a novelty effect will no doubt become apparent as we get further into the 1990s with the prospect of even more local and foreign radio finding its way into receivers on the island of Jamaica.

Most of the 1980s decade was characterized by a decrease of local programme output on Jamaica's one TV channel. The erection of a large dish in 1983 and the removal of most of its production resources and staff to the newly created CPTC three years later were important contributory factors. As in Trinidad, the now-defrocked US evangelist, Jimmy Swaggert, was an attractive source of ready cash.

The main outlet for music on JBC-TV was one weekly video show, 'Music, Music, Music' with a mix of local and international video clips. On Saturday, 30 May 1987, for instance, although JBC was on air from 8.30 am until after midnight, the only programmes with any local content apart from the news were two sports spectaculars and 'Music, Music, Music' – a far smaller percentage than, say, ten years earlier when JBC was in black-and-white on the PAL system, before easy access to NTSC satellite signals from the USA.

As Jamaica entered the 1990s, plans for a second TV station began to materialize. One effect was an internal restructuring of JBC-TV, with an increase of local production and programme content, particularly in the areas of sports and music. Religious groupings, the *Gleaner* press empire and the biggest manufacturer and distributor of music, Dynamic Sounds, were active contenders for the second TV station, CVM, which is expected to start transmissions in 1992. The franchise was finally awarded to a group including some local video production houses – this group has said its goal is to reach a 50 per cent level of local content.

The increase in private satellite dishes has obviously given more people potential access to MTV-style programming with international music videos. These can be taped on VCRs and spread via such copies. This has not necessarily led to a general increase in sales of phonograms with foreign music, according to Neville Lee, owner of Sonic Records:

> 'People who used to buy foreign records are restricted to home entertainment. They have the dishes or the videos where they get the shows from. They have less time to play music. Before he got his dish, the husband when he got home would go into his music room and play his foreign records. Now he comes home, a film is on the dish, and that's the end of it.'
>
> (Lee, TI 21/05/87)

Neville Lee noted that the ratio of local to foreign sales in 1987 was around 80:20, as oppsed to 60:40 back in 1980. Other contributory effects according to this industry spokesman were:

1 the availability of back-to-back stereo tracks of international music on Fame and JBC2, thus encouraging home-taping; and

2 the fact that 'local product has improved tremendously, both in quality and quantity. My company puts out twice as many albums with local music now.'

In both radio and TV there would seem to be different rules and procedures for defining 'airworthiness' for domestic and foreign music. RJR radio, for instance, has a record committee which meets twice a month and handles about fifty local discs. The committee consists of on-air staff and management supplemented with an external jazz musician (Marjorie Whylie) who also teaches traditional music at the Jamaican School of Music in Kingston. About 50 per cent of the discs are rejected by the committee: 'a good proportion because of its abysmal quality. We pass a lot of bad music but apply guidelines regarding libel and obscenities. A lot which we pass still doesn't get played because the station's DJs can't stand it' (Whylie, TI 25/05/87).

This description of the selection process was confirmed by RJR-AM's Programme Director, who said that records tend to be approved if 'the lyrics are catchy and not suggestive'. They then get registered in the station library and can be chosen for airplay. The same routine does *not* apply to foreign records. Here input to the station seems to rely on someone going over to Miami every month or so and filling a suitcase with latest hits. The Programme Director and the presenters then choose what to play, apparently basing their choice largely on what is featured on the US Billboard Top 100 singles and albums.

JBC-TV would also appear to apply different standards as regards clearance for local and international video clips. A local video producer with a small editing facility noted that he had access to a wonderful backdrop, Jamaica itself, and that Jamaican cameramen and producers were learning fast, even if they were still some way 'behind the Americans and the British'. But he found it hard to understand the rigorous process of checking for unsuitable content which applied to local but not to international videos. He felt you couldn't make a local video which in any way referred to problems in Jamaican society:

'If you do something nice and pleasing to watch, then they'll air it. I know they're against violence but there are real situations we would like to work with, but there we're limited. I can understand half of this – I can't understand the other half. I can understand the half that says: let's breed a society that is good and sees good things on television. But the other half I don't understand is how the international stuff which has so much violence will get through. Do they say: the international stuff is over there and will only happen over there? It's a bit complicated – but then I'm not one for politics.'

(Bailey, TI 1/06/87)

Once again we have an example of the suspicion the Establishment in small countries tends to direct against local popular mass culture, once any messages embodied in such popular media get too close to reality.

MUSIC OUTSIDE THE BROADCASTING MEDIA

Recorded or semi-recorded music, as we have noted, dominates the pop scene in Jamaica. Occasional live extravaganzas do bring out the artists and the fans. The annual Sun Splash Festival in the Montego Bay area, heavily backed by sponsors and supported officially by the Jamaica Cultural Development Commission (JCDC) is one such example. There are other one-off cases, such as a concert attended by these authors on Saturday 24 May 1987, labelled the TAXI CONNECTION. Our notes read as follows:

> We attended a marathon reggae concert featuring Sly and Robbie as the central figures and their Taxi backing group which regularly backs major Jamaican stars when they tour abroad. All the stars turned up on stage, from old-timers such as the Tamlins and Gregory Isaacs, to newcomers such as DJs like Tiger. The venue was the large drive-in cinema in New Kingston. Well over 10,000 turned up. It was meant to start at 7.30 but didn't get going until 9.30, which was a bit too much of a delay even for a Jamaican audience. The concert was sponsored by Miller Beer of the USA and the crowd showed its displeasure by chanting 'We want Red Stripe' (the local Jamaican beer). When it did get underway, the concert continued non-stop for about three and a half hours, featuring different types of reggae, without any intervals. Subject matter of the songs could be divided equally three ways; one-third 'love', one-third social comment, and one-third 'slack talk'.

The fact that organized live performances seem to be few and far between in Jamaica should not be interpreted as a lack of live, spontaneous music-making. Everywhere, particularly in the poorer areas, one finds budding musicians enjoying themselves and maybe looking for a path of upward mobility. They use what instruments they can afford or find, including makeshift sound system equipment for DJing to dubs. In the absence of instruments, they even make their own vocal accompaniment: 'We don't use instruments – we just settle 'pon a riddem.' Amateur musicmaking of this ilk rarely gets featured in the media, even if it's inspired by it; such is the relationship between music in the media and music activity at large.

In theory, any gifted songwriter can win fame by entering a song for the annual Festival Song Competition, organized by the Cultural Development Commission. Some 200 are entered each year. As with the Eurovision Song Contest in most European countries, entries have to be delivered in what might be termed a 'prefabricated form', with a lead-sheet and a cassette.

Plate 3.5 'We don't use instruments – we just settle 'pon a riddem.' Local music activity in the absence of financial resources.

This virtually requires access to at least a rudimentary studio, thereby excluding some songwriters, even if a number of studios offer their services at a very nominal cost to help young artists.

Our own logging of music output on Jamaican radio during 1986–8 showed a fairly small percentage of other West Indian music. We identified between 4 and 6 per cent of music from the English-speaking Caribbean, mainly soca, and virtually no Afro-Cuban or salsa music. Soca has become more popular as a result of the introduction of a carnival in April 1990. Byron Lee, owner of Dynamic Sounds and a regular visitor with his dance band to the Trinidad Carnival, has been one of the prime movers, backed up heavily by corporate sponsorship. The first Jamaican Carnival was a success in terms of public interest – some 400,000 turned out to watch and take part. A result of this activity has been an increasing interest in soca, and in particular a move in the focus of this interest from the middle-aged to younger groups of Jamaicans.

ACTORS, ISSUES AND POLICIES

Unesco has played an important role in the Caribbean, by carrying out various feasibility studies and thereby influencing media policy. The three regional radio stations which were closed by the Jamaican government in the early 1980s and then sold off to independent operators, were originally set up by Unesco in the 1970s as part of a policy of decentralizing and localizing media production.

Unesco's situation in the Caribbean, however, is somewhat sensitive because of the exodus of the USA from the organization, and the fact that any projects supporting local media production inevitably involve competing with the flood of US programmes coming in via satellites. The Unesco regional office in Kingston was one of the few places where we were not allowed to tape an interview – an indication of the aforementioned sensitivity. It was clear, however, that Unesco realized that any plans to regulate the flow of satellite broadcasting from outside must be coupled with a prior development of alternative local production facilities. Our notes from 1987 include this quote from a UNESCO official:

> 'What's outside is going to come in whatsoever. Use the satellite output as a vehicle for your own message. Use "Dallas", drop the commercial break and replace it with 2 minutes on the coconut crop. One must also ensure provisions for a minimum number of local programmes which are on at prime time. Our policy is to try to strengthen TV production in the East Caribbean. We are working with six TV stations, training producers in the techniques of community-oriented programming at low cost, for instance, developing 30-second, well-done community messages about things of importance such as health matters. We are not interested in programmes longer than 5 minutes or which take more than a day to produce.'

Whether the production of local music videos would be encompassed by such aims is not clear. The same Unesco official noted, however, that his organization had funded training courses for some Caribbean TV producers at the Banyan video production centre in Trinidad. He also confirmed that Jamaica's Creative Production Training Centre (CPTC) and the moving of JBC-TV's production resources to this new organization was the result of Unesco advice.

Another important international actor in the media field, of course, is the omnipresent USA, both via satellite feeds, and somewhat more indirectly via various aid programmes. When JBC-TV erected a dish and started relaying US films without paying copyright dues, US film producers lobbied their government to put pressure on Jamaica via the terms of the Caribbean Basin Initiative (an investment programme). Indications are that this leverage was successful.

With Jamaica seemingly unable to decide on the form of a modern music copyright law, international copyright collecting societies have had much influence over performance rights both for international music in Jamaica and for Jamaican music abroad. Bob Marley moved the collection rights for performance fees generated by his songs to the US organization, BMI (Broadcast Music Inc.). Previously such incomes had been collected by the

British PRS, which has had a local office in Kingston ever since Jamaica was a British colony.

A new copyright law has been on the policy books of successive Jamaican governments since the 1960s, leading to much frustration for local record company owners such as Neville Lee:

NL: Each time a new government gets into power – and this has been going on for the past twenty-five years – copyright has been an issue. Once they get into power something happens and it drags out and drags out and never materializes. We have just been told that they have looked at Trinidad's Act which protects the calypsonians and not the foreign acts. This is as much as I know. The problem is that we have nowhere to go to stop a person taking someone else's works.

Q: Why can't the government take the pirates to court?

NL: They are aware of it, but I have a suspicion that they are a trifle wary. Once we legalize things here, then *they* will be liable for copyright dues for things all over the world.

(Lee, 21/05/87)

Neville Lee's last sentence in this quote highlights the major dilemma facing successive Jamaican policymakers in the copyright field. How to protect one's own intellectual property without having to pay out too much scarce foreign exchange for cultural products coming into the country? Satellite TV signals comprise an important test case.

In 1984, Jamaica's Attorney General Tom Finson, who was working on a new copyright law, expressed the view that 'if anyone puts signals into our airspace, then it's our property – we didn't ask for them.' Three years later, another government official with the copyright brief, Deputy Permanent Secretary at the PM's Office stated a modified view, referring to the 'Mango Tree School of Communications': 'If you plant a mango tree in your garden by the fence and some of the branches hang over into my garden, then the mangoes on those are mine' (Mordecai, TI 28/05/87).

Mr Mordecai then related the tale of former Prime Minister, Edward Seaga's attempt to find fiscal revenue by taxing satellite dishes. To judge from the fuss the dish-owners made, 'you would have thought the PM was going to invade their bedrooms'. This Jamaican civil servant seemed to be happy that the satellite dish tax never got off the ground, bearing in mind dissatisfaction in the USA regarding free access to new US films via this technology. A functioning tax would have given the US Motion Pictures Association a perfect case for demanding compensation from the Jamaican government.

'It's better that copyright owners in the States are mad at the dish-owners, rather than I have to license the dish-owners and they become mad at me for not paying royalties. Let them be mad at the dish-owners – it doesn't affect me. I mean, they quarrel with me, but what am I going to do? Take the dishes away, all 6,000 of them?'

(Mordecai, TI 28/05/87)

The JBC-TV relay of US films lifted off satellites was something which even this civil servant admitted was dubious – presumably he could hardly do otherwise considering the heavy pressure apparently being put on Jamaica by the US Administration. This modified view, as compared to that expressed in 1984 by Finson (see above) was not even compatible with Mango Tree theories: 'JBC were *re-broadcasting*, rather like if you went out to the roadside and started selling mangoes from your neighbour's tree.' (Mordecai, TI 28/05/87).

With the prospect of a tax out of the way, satellite dishes increased rapidly in numbers, with an estimated total of more than 17,000 by 1990. They had become such a common phenomenon that dishes even became the subjects of popular songs. After hurricane Gilbert hit Jamaica at the end of 1988, Lovindeer had a number 1 disc with his song 'Wild Gilbert', featuring a reference to what was apparently a common problem: 'Have you seen me dish? Where me dish gone?'

Plate 3.6 'Have you seen me dish? Where me dish gone?' Satellite dishes moving down the socio-economic scale. A 'spider's web' in a poorer suburb of Kingston.

As Jamaica entered the 1990s the authorities were still wrestling with the issue of protecting intellectual property. We have previously used both print and audio/audio-visual media to chronicle the sad tale of the international exploitation of Jamaican folklore songs, and the corresponding lack of returns to the Caribbean. Our government spokesman could see no simple legal means of redressing the problem: 'There are many difficulties. What is a folk song? What is the correct arrangement, and who owns it? It's difficult to put the WIPO Tunis Model Law into practice' (Mordecai, TI 28/05/87).

Any functioning music copyright legislation for works which are protected by the terms of, say, the Berne or the Universal copyright conventions, presupposes the existence of functioning registers of works and copyright holders. This is a major problem in any country with a large amount of musical creative activity where copyright is not institutionalized.

'One of the weaknesses we are struggling with is the absence of trade unions in the artistic and cultural field. Not all musicians are in the union. There is an Association of Jamaican Record Producers but it is controlled by the four older producers – so the younger ones don't get a lot of the royalties they should receive for their records [i.e. their share of money paid by radio stations to the phonogram industry for the right to play records] . . . So one of the areas we are looking at is the way in which you build up organizations that will protect themselves. Government can only act as a kind of prop or foster parent early on. The interests of groups and individuals must be looked after by themselves. Otherwise it becomes a no-win situation. The government gets wrongly cursed by everyone and receives no thanks from anyone. . . . A massive education programme is needed. What these guys don't realize is that, yes, we will get money from Japan, the UK and so on, but then *we* will have to pay cash every time we play Stevie Wonder.'

(Mordecai, TI 28/05/87)

The process of expanding radio and TV in Jamaica by granting new transmission licences can be traced to a combination of two factors which emerged in the mid-1980s, namely a political desire to deregulate and dwindling public funds for public service broadcasting. The then Prime Minister, Edward Seaga, was clearly inspired by deregulation fervour in Reagan's USA, even if he was keen to retain a certain amount of protection for local as opposed to foreign entrepreneurs. There was also the perceived problem of:

'resources which are getting more finite by the year as the cost of public media increases. That's the dilemma we're caught up in. The only way you can afford these media is to make them commercial and let someone else pay for them. But if you hand over to that type of people, you abandon responsibilities which governments particularly in the developing world should have to a heightened extent.'

(Mordecai, TI 28/05/87)

Such a statement might seem surprising, bearing in mind that almost all broadcasting in Jamaica was already financed by advertisement revenue. Even limited public service input, in the form of programmes produced by, say, the Education Broadcasting Authority with their daily output of little more than 30 minutes of TV, was proving to be a financial strain. A government Bill, No. 5-1986, amending the Broadcast and Radio Diffusion Act, paved the way for divestment of existing radio/TV stations as well as the creation of new ones. The revised Act formally reconstituted the Broadcasting Commission. Clause 16 describes the Commission's duty to advise in relation to:

1 The terms and conditions on which licences may be granted; and
2 the allocation of time to broadcasting of programmes of Jamaican origin or performed by Jamaicans or which are particularly relevant or significant to Jamaica.

The same Act specifies loosely the Commission's role in monitoring output and its access to sanctions when broadcasting rules and agreements are contravened by licensees. A more detailed set of regulations issued by the Commission in 1988 also stresses licensee's duties, noting that programmes must maintain a 'proper balance in subject matter and a high general standard of quality' and that 'a proportion of the recorded and other matter included in the programmes shall be of Jamaican origin'. There is no indication of the percentages of local material which are envisaged.

At a second interview in December 1988 with Martin Mordecai (now Chairman of the Broadcasting Commission), he explained that the issue of Jamaican content was:

'a very contentious one. It is never a numerical prescription, but many people feel one should lay down a numerical law and say 20 per cent of your broadcast, *excluding news, music and DJ-type programmes* should be Jamaican. That would not be a problem for radio but it would be for TV.'

(Mordecai, TI 8/12/88)

To exclude music in a such a policy might seem surprising, considering the importance of the local music industry and the fact that Jamaican discs were one of the more important parts of the AM-stations' staple diet. A value judgement was hidden in these policy reflections – non-stop reggae excludes other, 'better' Jamaican music. The Broadcasting Commission's new Chairman explained:

'The arguments that stations use is that most of the music, 90 per cent, is

DJ music for youngsters. When I say "excluding music", it's because the stations say: "All our programming is Jamaican. We're playing reggae all the time." But they don't play other kinds of Jamaican music – only at Christmas, at Independence and at Easter. . . . Because of that you have to say 20 per cent Jamaican music, excluding popular discs or something like that. It's a very difficult subject to define as you can appreciate. The object is to encourage the playing of other sorts of music.'

(Mordecai, TI 8/12/88)

The 'other sorts of music' were further defined in this interview as including music by groups such as the Jamaican Folk Singers and some groups with a religious base. Possibly this search for a 'broad-range' music policy is a reflection of a middle-class concern about the lyrical content of much reggae. The religious lobby had been active producers of letters in *The Gleaner*. Under the heading, 'DJ music – a euphemism for denigrating reggae and language', one Frank Manborde expanded on thoughts previously put forward by Rev. Chisholm and Callam of the Baptist Church:

DJ music and some other songs negate the virtues of the institutions – Church, school and home. . . . DJ, more than any other type of music, cannibalizes religious songs to the gutter of its own making. . . . The silent majority detest the emancipation of reggae.

(*The Gleaner*, 23 May 1987)

This letter-writer then recommended that the public should refuse to buy records that do not enhance the quality of music, that they should speak out against garbage and trash music, and he asked for the media to be used 'to help mould public opinion'. Frank Manborde was full of praise, however, for Jamaica's more established names in the music industry (Bob Marley, Jimmy Cliff, Bunny Wailer, Gregory Isaacs, etc.).

Concern about the lyrical content of DJ music, and the ways in which it is fed to the public, did lead to one particular piece of legislation in 1988 concerning a popular form of public transport, the minibuses. These are run by private operators and ferry people around the island. The music in them had got louder and, some would say, more offensive as regards content. The government imposed a set of regulations stipulating that conductors should wear uniforms, and that music was forbidden.

Like most media regulations, there were some unexpected consequences, even if observers agree that the situation had got out of hand:

'The public was complaining a great deal about the content of some of the songs that were being played. That it was loud, full of smut and having a negative effect on the children. What the government has done now is to come in with a legislation that seems almost to have denied the playing of the radio on the buses. I'm not sure people are going to comply. How do you monitor that sort of thing? . . . People couldn't even hear the news with the new regulations. . . . they threw out the baby with the bathwater!'

(Hussey, TI 14/12/88)

Our latest information is that the law is still in force, but that many bus-drivers do use their radios to play programmes from the new, all-music regional stations. The law did have an immediate effect of getting rid of loud, very smutty songs in this form of public transport. And the radio stations, of course, have their own system of gatekeepers who monitor records that are played, making sure that those deemed NSRP (not suitable for radio play) are kept off the airwaves.

We have already noted reports from Jamaica indicating that the privatized regional radio stations rely mainly on a non-stop music/news format, with relatively little local programming. This would not seem to be compatible with the 1988 broadcasting regulations which state that: 'The regional stations as far as possible develop their programmes with a regional flavour and with regional interests being taken into account.'

Clearly the new stations have used music style, rather than geographical base, to define their profile. With signals being audible outside their own regions, the new entrepreneurs obviously found it hard to ignore the commercial lure provided by reaching a more widespread audience. IRIE, for instance, based in Ocho Rios on the north-east coast, is a favourite with minibus drivers – it functions as a virtual non-stop disco station with a high reggae/dance music content.

The disparity between policy and reality in this case illustrates once again the power of technical and economic factors in deciding how broadcasting develops. The technology in this case provides a bigger geographical reach, and the commercial possibilities embodied in this in turn decide output, even overriding the original conditions of the franchise as expressed in the Broadcasting Commission's regulations.

CURRENCY AND MEDIA FINANCING

As one might expect in a small nation with its own currency, the Bank of Jamaica does its best to regulate the flow of cash in and out of the island to protect, when necessary, the Jamaican dollar. The inflow of foreign exchange from the music industry's international activities is both formal and informal. Some of it comes back in the form of equipment – some of it never comes back but stays in US dollars. Significantly, few official statistics are available concerning music export income. Most independent entrepreneurs would probably agree with this view from film director, Perry Hensell:

'I don't think I'm going to bring my money here and subject myself to Bank of Jamaica approval. . . . I'll put it up in Panama or the Cayman Islands unless they give me a guarantee I'm free to move money around.

Maybe they can keep half. I'm not putting myself at the mercy of anyone when it comes to foreign exchange approval. We live in a world where we have to operate. I would love to work out of Jamaica if there were no problems of money coming in and out. I'm not putting myself at the mercy of left, right or centre – I'm a Huguenot.'

(Hensell, TI 23/05/87)

A film director such as Hensell does not have much in the way of heavy investments in equipment or plant in Jamaica. The local phonogram industry, on the other hand, is worrying about the possible need to finance future CD plants and the risks of their present vinyl disc factories becoming redundant.

'A lot of us are concerned that our capital investment in manufacturing will be obsolete within five years. Technology has forces that we must accept. My main concern is that when the CD comes, instead of manufacturing it, we will have to import it – a plant costs about 20 million. We will have to become importers – we will become more dependent on others.'

(Lee, TI 21/05/87)

This last statement highlights the value for local music industry companies of having independent manufacturing resources – increased mutual dependency (informal integration) on others is not a thought that is relished.

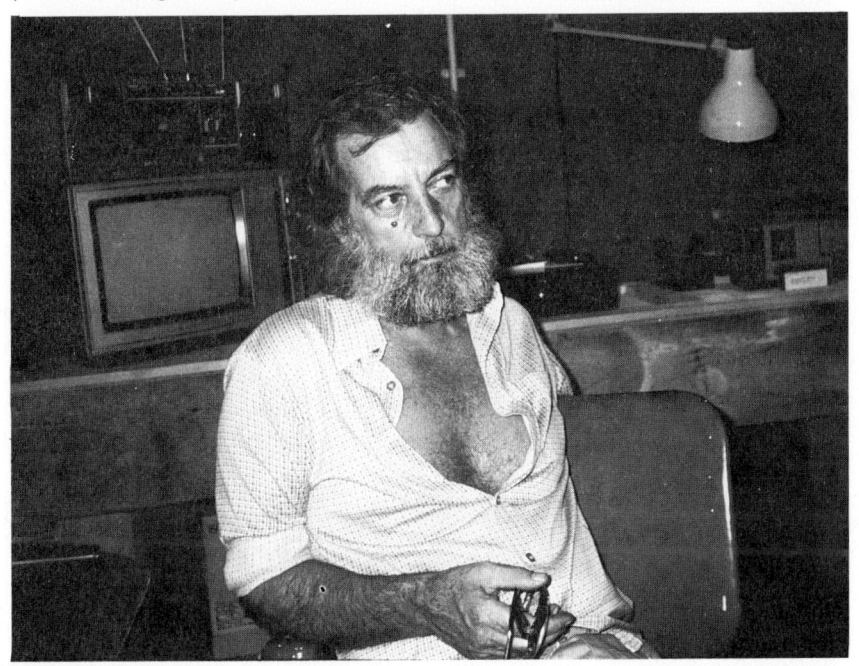

Plate 3.7 'Very little happens by policy – things happen when everything's in place.' In place here, Jamaican film director, Perry Hensell.

AT THE BOTTOM OF THE SOCIETAL PYRAMID

This heading brings us back to the start of this section, namely the notion expressed by a former Jamaican PM that the music industry is seen as providing a path of upward mobility in society, a way out of the ghetto to better things. Jamaican TV, local satellite dishes and video tapes give more and more Jamaicans access to the 'better things' as seen on US TV. Real access to the impressive orchestral and electronic instruments that can sometimes be witnessed on satellite TV is severely hampered by financial constraints. A lack of instruments is a major problem facing both formal and informal musical training:

> 'There are very few instruments in the schools. Some might find a sponsoring body in the US who would send a stock of instruments, most of them used, many in terrible condition, that would have to be reconditioned. And then there's nobody to teach – the kids are not taught the rudiments of music. Maybe there are half a dozen schools around the island with bands in place. The graduates from the School of Music have a hard time operating in such a system. They've been given the tools, and when they get there they have a head-on collision. In part the problem is that there seems to have been no policy about this at a higher level.'
>
> (Whylie, TI 25/05/87)

It is somewhat ironic that the USA serves as both source of dreams via TV shows and video clips, but source of less than perfect reject instruments when it comes to providing the tools which, in theory at least, could make those musical dreams come true. The irony becomes even stronger when one considers the immense entertainment/exploitation value which songs with an origin in the trials and tribulations of Jamaican plantation life have enjoyed in the USA.

As for the ability of government policies to sustain and develop Jamaican cultural heritage and popular culture of a high standard, well this would seem to be limited. One reason is a lack of continuity – both the people involved and their policies tend to be changed and/or discontinued after every second or third general election, as the two dominating political parties, the PNP and JLP, alternate in power. Perry Hensell would maintain that this is not necessarily a bad thing: 'I don't think you need official policies – very little happens by policy. Things happen when everything is in place – then they happen no matter what' (Hensell, TI 23/05/87).

Chapter 4
Case Study: Trinidad

A DENSE MEDIA ENVIRONMENT

Even back in the 1960s almost every household in Trinidad had at least one radio set. A decade later, televisions, record players and audio cassette machines were commonplace. By 1983, 90 per cent of all households in Trinidad had a television receiver, and around half of these were colour sets (Trinidad and Tobago Government 1987: 13). By the late 1980s, most homes with young or middle-aged occupants had audio cassette players; VCRs also became fairly common during the same decade. From around 1985 onwards, some wealthier households started erecting their own satellite dishes; such dishes, however, were still few and far between in 1991. The same can be said of compact disc players.

Trinidad has two major daily newspapers which are widely read, as well as a number of weeklies. There are no special magazines on music, but both the dailies and the weeklies devote a fair amount of space to entertainment and music.

In the early 1980s, Trinidad had two radio companies each broadcasting a programme on AM: the National Broadcasting Service (NBS), owned by the government, and Radio Trinidad, formerly owned by Rediffusion International which was part of the Lord Thomson media empire. In 1989 Radio Trinidad was taken over by the MACAL Company, a Trinidadian business conglomerate which also owns one of the country's major dailies, the *Trinidad Guardian*. During the 1980s both these companies opened up second FM channels. Thus Trinidad had four domestic radio channels, a situation which persisted until mid-1991. Both stations are financed by sales of commercials and appear to be in good financial health. Mr Alric Cross, Chairman of the NBS board declared that 'NBS is almost unique as far as government enterprises go, in that it has always made a profit albeit a small profit' (TI 11/06/87).

Government-owned Trinidad and Tobago Television (TTT) is also financed through advertising, but it has had some difficulties returning a profit. In 1986, the main channel was augmented with a second TV programme. Official government policy for Channel 2 was that it was to be devoted to educational and local programming (Laird 1987: 3). The second channel was temporarily closed after about a year after bringing TTT almost $US2m in the red. There was simply not enough revenue to be made from commercials in Trinidad to run two programmes. Since it was closed down in early 1987, the second channel has lived an 'off and on' existence, broadcasting at weekends and then mostly relaying US programming from satellite channels. There has been some debate on the effects of this practice, especially with regard to children. At times, US programming has been relayed indiscriminately with commercials and all; often the latter have promoted goods that are not even obtainable in Trinidad. All the 'free offers' that you 'mustn't miss' and US toll free telephone numbers (which do not function in Trinidad) caused no small measure of confusion, especially amongst minors.

A significant development on the Trinidad media scene during the 1980s was the emergence of independent video production houses. A prerequisite for this was the cash flowing into Trinidad during the oil price boom around 1980. Independent producers gradually took over a considerable slice of domestic programme production for TTT. By the mid-1980s, TTT only produced news, some specials and a few studio programmes with their own staff. All other local programming was commissioned from independent producers. According to TTT's Operations Manager, Lancelot Sargeant, Trinidad and Tobago Television had:

'a staff of eight in-house producers who are virtually left idle. The independent production houses are more flexible than we. Most of the equipment we use is the same as we use to transmit. There is always a clash between transmission and production. It is always easier to bring in a tape and show it to the clients and ask would you like to sponsor this . . .'

(Sargeant, TI 04/06/87)

In 1987 seven of the independent production houses formed the Teleproductions Association with the Banyan TV Production Company as its most active member. Their environment was to change radically, however, in 1991 when government deregulation led to the emergence of new radio and TV stations. A group with newspaper interests (*The Trinidad Express*) started CCN Television. An interesting and presumably unexpected result of the increase in TV stations was that commissions to independent producers from TTT, according to Christopher Laird of Banyan, actually decreased:

'It has meant less work for us now because TTT are not buying local programmes any more. They make their own. Their percentage of local programming has gone down from 30 to 20. CCN is hoping to get 20 per cent but that will not happen because there is one advertising pie to be divided now between many people. They're worried about their income so they can't afford to buy local programming. So it's going to become even more foreign programming.'

(Laird, TI 08/11/91)

We shall return to the issue of radio and TV expansion in Trinidad and Tobago later in this chapter.

Through the 1980s, vinyl records along with audio cassettes constituted the base of the music media scene in Trinidad. The first CDs with Trinidadian music appeared in 1990, but were only available in the tourist shops at the Cruise Liner jetty. Back in the 1970s, Trinidad could boast two record pressing plants and some ten recording studios. By 1983 there were no pressing facilities left and only a couple of functioning recording studios. This was partly the result of the oil price boom producing better financial conditions for the music-makers. They found they could afford to go to New York to make their recordings at the sophisticated studios available there. A network was established involving Trinidadian calypsonians (singer/songwriters) and record companies run by Trinidadian owners of record shops in Brooklyn, New York. Charlie's Records and Straker's Records are two of the more well-known examples.

Almost each and every calypsonian owns and runs his/her own record label. The 'Brooklyn connection network' has been kept going into the 1990s. A calypsonian will record either at a studio in Port of Spain or in New York and then send the tape to one of the record shops in Brooklyn. These will press a certain quantity of records, keeping as many as they need to get the money invested back with a profit through sales in the Brooklyn shop or to mail order customers. The remainder of the records will be shipped to the calypsonian in Trinidad who distributes them locally. In this way, the calypsonians avoid the need for hard currency to pay to have their records pressed in New York. An alternative administrative/financial method for getting records pressed involves custom pressing at the West Indies Records plant in Barbados. The Trinidad and Tobago government has facilitated the import of records with local music by waiving import duties on the first 3,000 copies of records with Trinidadian music brought in during any one year by a citizen of the country.

Throughout the 1980s, music piracy was rife in Trinidad. The audio cassette market, even for calypso music, was dominated by street-corner pirates. Such cassettes often provided entertainment in taxis as well as in the so-called maxitaxis (minibuses) that constitute the better part of the Trinidad public transport system. Thus they also functioned as a form of promotion of the music and artists featured/pirated. In 1986, lobbying by the Copyright Organization of Trinidad and Tobago (COTT, formed in 1985) led to the government introducing fairly severe legal sanctions for cassette piracy. These included prison sentences of up to six months for the first offence and up to two years for any subsequent offence. As a result, the more obvious forms of street-corner music piracy of calypso music have been wiped out. Cassette piracy has been limited to foreign music. Exceptions occur in the carnival season when local calypso and soca hits are likely to appear on 'top hit' sampler tapes featuring 'diverse artists'.

SOCA AND US BLACK CHARTS: MUSIC CONTENT IN THE MEDIA

Trinidad with its many ethnic groups and many musical styles has a very diversified music culture. In the 1960s the media had a tendency to avoid addressing the problems of the nation's multi-ethnic music culture, preferring instead to stay safe with a mixture of Anglo-American popular music and some Western Art music. This, of course, also reflected the conditions that had prevailed during the period of British colonialism. The colonial elite tended to consider music from Europe superior to local kinds of music.

One of the more notable developments during the past two decades has been a gradual increase in the share of Trinidadian music in the total media output. This is particularly true of the music for the carnival season: calypso, steelband, etc. But the same also applies to other kinds of music such as the Christmas parang music, forms which are known in Trinidad as East Indian music, choral music based on local folk songs, etc. Christopher Laird, owner of the Banyan TV Production Company, offered this description of developments in this area:

> 'The society as a whole has become much more mature, much more appreciative of its own. I think this is something that has been seen over the last few years. . . . There is much more consciousness among the people now of our own. I don't know about the young people, but people who now have the money, the young middle class, 25, 30, 40, are very into calypso and other local music. It is a lot of support for that. . . . There is less of treating local things as oddities and more of seeing local things as exciting, something worth putting on the air. That has certainly come up.'
>
> (Laird, TI 18/02/88)

Many forms of local music originally entered the media via live broadcasts from competitions. Parang competitions became popular around 1970. Both radio stations started to promote and broadcast such competitions (Malm 1978). Parang music also started to appear in radio commercials made for the Christmas season. Broadcasting at Christmas had previously been dominated by British carols, US 'Jingle Bells' and the type of White Christmas nostalgia which was more or less incomprehensible for the general audience in Trinidad.

The Prime Minister's Best Village Competition was one of the more significant national competitions throughout the 1970s and the 1980s. It was inaugurated by the late Prime Minister and folk hero, Eric Williams, and received much coverage from the radio stations and TTT. Different villages competed in staging programmes with folk art: music, dance, story telling, etc. The competition was organized rather like a soccer league with preliminaries, semi-finals and finals. The Best Village Competition played an important role in adapting Trinidad grass-roots folklore to the stage and the media.

Like almost everything else in Trinidad during the January–February carnival season, the media get dominated – one might even say saturated – with calypso, soca and steelband music. Radio stations broadcast several live and pre-recorded sessions from both the Panorama steelband competition as well as from the 'calypso tents'. Out of carnival season, radio music programming mainly consists of DJ shows with commercial records. Since few records with Trinidadian music are produced outside the carnival season, the variety tends to be limited.

Although the East Indian music of Trinidad and Tobago is not a regular feature of the carnival season, a form of East Indian soca music sung in Hindi and English, known as 'chutney soca', has been developed by musicians such as Sundar Popo and Drupatee. Neither is the East Indian music integrated into the regular flow of music on the radio, despite the fact that 40 per cent of the population is of Indian origin. Indian music is broadcast in special shows sponsored by the East Indian business community, usually around 7pm on weekdays.

In 1990 almost anyone could buy programme time on the radio stations at the fairly modest rate of approximtely US$150 for 30 minutes. Record shops and groups such as the National Action Cultural Committee would do this regularly in order to promote local music and make announcements about new record releases and shows.

The specific music policies that apply to the radio in the carnival season, as opposed to the remainder of the year, are clearly illustrated by our own loggings of music content. Table 4.1 shows that in 1987–8, the share of Trinidadian music outside the carnival season on the AM programmes (Radio Trinidad 1 and NBS1) was slightly more than 50 per cent, in other words quite a high figure compared to what one would expect to find in, say, a small European country. FM programmes (RT2 and NBS2) had a marked Anglo-American music format with only 10–20 per cent Trinidadian music. This gives an average share of local music on all four programmes of around 30 per cent, a share which doubles during the carnival season. Thus in January/February, AM programmes can boast almost 90 per cent Trinidadian music and on the FM band only RT2 retains

Table 4.1 Survey of programme content on Trinidadian radio, 3–4 June 1987

Station	Trinidadian incl. W. Ind. %	Anglo- American %	Speech %
Radio Trinidad 1			
Total content	26	22	52
Music content	55	45	
Radio Trinidad 2			
Total content	9	80	11
Music content	10	90	
NBS1			
Total content	21	18	61
Music content	54	46	
NBS2			
Total content	17	62	21
Music content	21	79	
All stations			
Total content	18	46	36
Music content	29	71	

Note: Time of sample on 4 June 06.00–18.00; on 3 June, 18.00–22.00.

its mainly Anglo-American format with 22 per cent Trinidadian music (local music content on NBS2 rises to 60 per cent). This dominance of Trinidadian music in the media associated with carnival fervour is further emphasized by the fact that the share of music as opposed to speech content increases from an average overall ratio of 65 per cent music/35 per cent speech out of season to 75 per cent music/25 per cent speech during the carnival period (see Table 4.2).

In actual fact, this annual periodic increase in local music content in the media starts during the Christmas season. If some special event occurs that arouses national feelings, then this too can result in the share of local music content rising. In November 1989 the Trinidad and Tobago soccer team was due to meet the USA. It was an important match; a win or even a draw for the Trinidadians would take their national team through to the World Cup finals in Italy. During the month preceding the match several new records with 'soccer soca' were released. The tunes had titles like 'The Road to Italy', 'T&T We Want ah Goal' and 'Football Dance'. These records constantly filled the music environment, either via radio plays or from cassette decks in maxitaxis. In the week before the match, the average content of Trinidadian music of all four programmes reached 50 per cent (see Table 4.3). Even Radio Trinidad 2 upped its Trinidadian content to almost 30 per cent, thus departing from the usual Anglo-American format.

Table 4.2 Survey of programme content on Trinidadian radio, 4 and 6 February 1988

Station	Trinidadian %	Anglo-American %	Speech %
Radio Trinidad 1			
Total content	58	3	39
Music content	94	6	
Radio Trinidad 2			
Total content	21	72	7
Music content	22	78	
NBS1			
Total content	47	10	43
Music content	82	18	
NBS2			
Total content	48	32	20
Music content	59	41	
All stations			
Total content	43	30	27
Music content	59	41	

Notes: [1] Sample times: 06.00–10.00 on 6 Feb.; 10.00–22.00 on 4 Feb.
[2] Carnival season. Lots of commercials for calypso tents and parties with Trinidadian music. Many live recordings from calypso tents and Panorama preliminaries.

Although we have no loggings of TV programming, anyone who visits Trinidad during the carnival season can easily observe the many broadcasts from different carnival events. Since the mid-1980s, several video clips featuring calypsonians have been produced at carnival time, most of them by TTT. These are also run as fillers out of the carnival season, as TTT Operations Manager, Lancelot Sargeant explains:

> 'We do them here. Last carnival season we did about fifty with calypsonians. But all at the carnival season. The musicians don't really publish music at rest of the year. Even if they do so, we will still do it for free. Production houses don't do that. That's too expensive for the musician. They prefer to come here.'
>
> (Sargeant, TI 04/06/87)

Of the total programme output on TV, around 30 per cent is domestic production, most of that news and game shows. Music programming out of the carnival season is dominated by US shows with a sprinkling of recordings from the Trinidad carnival. A domestic exception is the regular 'Scouting for Talent' show, run for many years by the popular TV personality Holly Betaudier. Another is the 'Masthana Bahar Show', which has

Table 4.3 Survey of programme content on Trinidadian radio, 13 November 1989

Station	Trinidadian %	Anglo-American %	Speech %
Radio Trinidad 1			
Total content	30	25	45
Music content	54	46	
Radio Trinidad 2			
Total content	30	51	19
Music content	37	63	
NBS1			
Total content	27	18	55
Music content	61	39	
NBS2			
Total content	38	25	37
Music content	59	41	
All stations			
Total content	31	30	39
Music content	51	49	

Notes: [1] Time 08.36–15.30 not recorded.
[2] A big football game against the US was coming up the next weekend and the Christmas season was beginning. Thus there were quite a lot of football soca tunes and some parang.

been very important for the East Indian music scene in Trinidad (Mohammed 1982).

CALYPSONIANS, PANMEN AND POLITICIANS: INTERACTION ON THE MUSIC AND MEDIA SCENE

From 1962, when Trinidad and Tobago gained political independence, through to 1987 the country was ruled by governments formed by the People's National Movement (PNM) party. In 1986 the PNM was voted out of power for the first time and the National Alliance for Reconstruction (NAR), a political alliance formed by a number of smaller parties and other political groupings, took over.

No clear written-down media policy had existed during the long period of PNM rule. The actual policy implemented could be described as conservative, i.e. not allowing any significant changes in the media structure. Apart from the abortive test with a second TV programme by TTT, the structure of the media scene was unchanged from the 1960s through to 1988. No new licences for radio or TV companies were granted. No official rules governing media content were formulated. Media policy was applied via *ad hoc* decisions and informal rulings in particular cases.

'No governments in the [Caribbean] area, certainly not in Trinidad, have made their own TV stations under any obligation to have a certain percentage of local programming. They make statements but they do not ever oblige the station to follow that policy. All they oblige the station to do is to make a profit.'

(Laird, Banyan TV Production Co., TI 18/02/88)

The changes we have noted above, such as the increased share of Trinidadian music on the radio, have not been the result of a government policy, but rather of the actions of different pressure groups. Some of these actions have been taken by different ethnic or religious groups. The East Indians have time and time again pointed out that they have had very little access to the media. Such protests and lobbying have gradually led to an increase in the programming of Indian music and dance (Mohammed 1982). The main pressures and protests have come, however, from the musicians.

Plate 4.1 The Trinidad Carnival providing an outlet for all manner of creative images.

Music is of paramount importance to Trinidadian society, especially at carnival time. Ever since the last century, the calypsonians have established and defended their role as spokespersons for the people by writing songs on almost every conspicuous event in Trinidad and the world at large. They have served as political commentators and creators of public opinions (Warner 1982; Malm and Wallis 1985). The authorities, as one might expect when constantly confronted by an unpredictable political force on the entertainment and cultural scene, have had an ambivalent attitude towards the calypsonians. On the one hand they have been regarded as trouble-makers, singing songs with dirty lyrics, on the other hand as representatives of a unique national music culture. Sometimes some of their songs have been banned on the radio stations. At other times, different political personalities have sought their support. The same ambivalent attitude prevails regarding the steelbands and their musicians. They have been regarded as hooligans and 'badjohns' as the Trinidadian expression goes. But the immense importance of the steelbands in community life in Trinidad has also been recognized.

> When Rudolph Charles, the leader of the Desperadoes steelband, died in 1985, his funeral was rivalled only by that of the late Prime Minister. The media mourned him as a national hero, and his body was drawn through the streets of Port of Spain in a casket fashioned from two large steel drums. Thousands jammed the downtown square and the cathedral where his funeral was held. It was attended by the country's leaders and by the people he had loved and served as a bandleader, friend, community leader, and role model for young people. His ashes were scattered by helicopter over Lavantille Hill, home base of the Desperadoes.
> (Aho 1987: 34)

Actions by the musicians to influence music policy on radio and television are legion, and have involved both individuals and organizations. Several calypsos have specifically addressed the subject of music policy in the media (Wallis and Malm 1984: 262–3). Most of the more famous calypsonians have their own record labels and thus a clear personal interest in getting airplay.

> 'Records are no important income for us. It gives publicity.'
> (Calypsonian The Mighty Chalkdust, TI 03/06/87)

> 'We make records in Trinidad not to sell, but so that people know that we have a new song, so that we get more live work, about four or five nights a week.'
> (Calypsonian David Rudder, TI 09/06/87)

Calypsonians regularly complain about payola problems, claiming that they have to pay DJs to get their records played on the radio. In 1987 calypsonian Crazy staged a one-man 'sit-down' strike in front of the NBS building in Port of Spain, accusing the station of not playing his records. Calypsonian Brother Superior (Andrew Marcano) applied for a broadcasting licence to start a new radio station with a calypso music format in June 1973. After waiting in vain for an answer from the government for thirteen years, he took the matter to court in 1986. The case was dismissed due to a judicial technicality, but the judge gave the government a severe reprimand for not having responded to the application.

Among the musicians' organizations, the steelband association Pan Trinbago has been the strongest lobbying body calling for changes in media policy on music. Pan Trinbago formulated a policy document in 1980 which they have since tried to implement. This document includes the following statement concerning the media:

> We have reported an improvement in the financial terms and conditions of recording *vis-à-vis* TTT. However, we are not yet satisfied that the highest professional standards are attained so that a product with international market potential is forthcoming. Apart from the regular Steelband Concert slot on television, steelband music is treated as a poor relation and relegated to mere fillers in the rest of the programme schedule. We believe greater initiative and creativity must be displayed by TTT in producing shows featuring steelband music and other local art forms. But perhaps these children of the media have become spoilt. Just put in a canned imported product and flip a switch. Hey Presto! Instant TV!! . . .
>
> Enough has been said about the local radio stations in the past to make further reference to them almost superfluous. The pseudo-yankee accents, the disco music and rockers continue to spew forth from these with sufficient intensity and regularity such that we may be tempted to believe that we are living somewhere in Alabama or Montego Bay. To say this is not to adopt a rabid anti-foreign stance but rather to affirm a belief that charity certainly begins at home.
>
> It is long overdue that we solicit from the various media some firm commitments for the promotion of local culture. This can take several forms, but the bottom line must read increased airtime and television programming and greater exposure through the national newspapers for local culture.
>
> (Pan Trinbago 1981: 32)

The main point of the Pan Trinbago policy document is that the government should formulate a policy on the steelbands and their music. A motivation is that the steel pan instrument and the steelband is an original invention of Trinidad and Tobago. Indeed, there are hundreds of steelbands with tens of thousands of members. The 'pan yards', i.e. rehearsing sheds, of the steelbands function as important community and neighbourhood centres. Every year around the carnival season, when the major steelband Panorama competition is held, people follow and support their neighbourhood steelband in the same manner as soccer fans support their local team.

A complaint from both calypsonians and Pan Trinbago is that the media only play their music at carnival time or when a steelband festival takes place. Media gatekeepers reply that calypsonians do not produce any new music outside the carnival season and that hardly any records with steelband music are produced at all. When steelbands are shown on TTT or heard on the radio out of carnival season, it is likely to be a recording from the Panorama competition. One problem seems to be that there are few music events outside the carnival season for the media to cover. Another is that media organizations have very small facilities for producing their own recordings and that the facilities that do exist are badly maintained.

A National Action Cultural Committee (NACC) has been formed to promote live music events throughout the year. Competition from discos, however, is rising. Even in the carnival parades, trucks with DJs and loads of loudspeakers have been replacing live steelband music. Their powerful amplifiers drown any live music competing with them. In the 1988 carnival, the most regularly played calypso by Tambu (the so-called 'roadmarch') had the refrain: 'Hey, Hey, Mr DJ play. This party is it!'

NACC spokesman, Anum Bankole, claims that it is hard to arouse any interest from the media for live performances out of carnival season. NACC has to buy airtime to get on the air. This highlights another obvious problem related to media access, namely the obligation to find sponsors for programmes. Local music is rarely a high priority for foreign companies operating in Trinidad. Furthermore the cost of making a TV show with a steelband is more than ten times as high as buying a show of US origin. With such price differences, a businessman seeking media publicity may opt to sponsor 'Dallas' instead of a steelband show. Such a decision is made even more likely by the absence of any ratings for TV or radio audiences that could have shown sponsors that money put into local productions gives a larger or specific audience. On top of this, there is always the temptation for TV and radio to sell time slots to people with money who wish to broadcast their own programmes, spreading their own ideologies. This latter category includes several US evangelical churches and preachers. In 1987 the Jimmy Swaggart organization payed TTT US$500 per day for their regular morning show. Payment came in the form of a lump sum paid a whole year in advance (this was before the aforementioned preacher was literally defrocked in connection with a sexual scandal in the USA). None the less, the dilemma of quick money versus one's own cultural interests is observed and debated:

'I fear that vested interests are more powerful than local interests such

Plate 4.2 Loudspeakers replacing live steelbands in Trinidad.

as the calypsonians. I am encouraging more groups to make more noise, to write to the press more, agitate more about a media policy. If you go to St Vincent or Grenada you get about eight American stations. The effect is absolutely disastrous on those nations. It is really unfortunate that a nation that is least able to provide any moral guidance to the world has, because of its enhanced technology, taken over that role. It's like a drunk person driving a car.'

(Brinsley Samaroo, Minister of Local Government and former Minister of Information, TI 10/06/87)

Pan Trinbago spokesman Richard Forteau states: 'We have started something we are not going to stop until we have reached our final goal. The goal is to have 65 per cent local music on the air. We are going to ensure that we get a media policy' (TI 03/06/87). There seems to be widespread agreement amongst those active within the cultural life of Trinidad that the share of local programming in the media is too small. In a call for a government media policy on this issue, Christopher Laird wrote:

No objective listener or viewer of radio and television stations in Trinidad and Tobago could conclude from the output of these stations that Trinidad and Tobago is a Caribbean island with the highest output of original music and culture in the Caribbean. Neither could such a monitor guess that Trinidad and Tobago was 6 miles from the South American mainland, within sight of a continent which fought its anti-colonial wars a century ago and continues, like ourselves, to struggle to maintain its independence while contributing significantly to the musical, literary and cultural richness of the world at large. . . . But as we say in Trinidad and Tobago, we have more vice than versa and we hear nothing from our fellow inhabitants of the area. Instead we have a non-stop North American and specifically United States culture mixed with European culture and token gestures to our own, especially at carnival time. With this state of things it's not surprising that examples of the cultures of the lands of our ancestors and other Third World and part colonial societies are also absent from our airwaves.

(Laird 1987: 6)

The view generally expressed by musicians and others in our 1987–8 interviews was that the share of local music in the media was as low as 15–20 per cent except during the carnival season. It is also interesting to note that the Copyright Society of Trinidad of Tobago retained only 25 per cent of the moneys collected to be distributed in Trinidad. We have already observed that loggings of programme content indicate the share of local music on the radio outside the carnival season averaging 30 per cent. One possible explanation for these discrepancies could be that local music content was on the rise as a result of constant debate on the matter and the actions taken by the NAR government. Another is that musicians, being only too aware of the frailty of their situation, tend to paint a somewhat bleak picture of reality when interviewed.

In 1986 the newly elected NAR government set up a task force on telecommunications. This task force reported back in August 1987 with a White Paper entitled 'The Establishment of a Telecommunications Authority for the Republic of Trinidad and Tobago'. This report did not contain any statements regarding music in the media, not even in the appendix 'Broadcast Code – General Principles' (Trinidad and Tobago Government 1987: 45–54). The task force suggested that a proposed Telecommunications Authority should take on the task of formulating and proposing a media policy for government consideration.

While the task force was at work, the Teleproductions Association teamed up with around twenty trade unions and cultural organizations and put in an application to lease the inactive second TV channel. Their plan was to run a station with programming mainly of local origin. This move, coupled with the above-mentioned high court reprimand for not having replied to Brother Superior's radio station application, produced a swift government response. Without even waiting for a Bill to go through parliament regarding the proposed Telecommunications Authority, an *ad hoc* licensing committee was set up. Applications for licences were invited for five different categories of broadcasting/narrowcasting: cable TV; regular TV with national coverage; community TV; radio with national coverage; and community radio. Subsequently, after some speedy processing of applications, a number of licences were issued. These included four for cable TV, another four for national TV, three for community television, four for national and two for community radio (Laird, TI 08/11/91). By November 1991 one new national TV and one new national radio station (Prime Radio) were on the air, both operated by CCN (Caribbean Communications Network) which, as noted previously, also incorporates the big daily newspaper, *The Trinidad Express*. Meanwhile, Radio Trinidad changed the format of their FM station (RT2) into 100 per cent local music and renamed it Radio Tempo.

The period 1989–90 saw the political alliance which held the NAR together weakening and fragmenting. Several groups left the government coalition. In July 1990 a Moslem faction attempted a coup and held government ministers hostage in the parliament building for almost two weeks. The coup did not succeed but definitely brought to a halt any 'national reconstruction' taking place, including work on a media policy. Independent producer Christopher Laird has concluded that conditions for small local video producers have become precarious, with the notion of the 'public service' concept more or less absent from government thinking and obsolete at the remaining government-owned broadcasting stations.

'You've got cross-media ownership as well as concentration. What room is left for independent people, I don't know. The government should really realize that government stations have to be run in the interests of the people. But up to now they have only made it clear to the TTT people that they have to make a profit. They have to fight in the marketplace like everyone else. And that means they have to fight for the same share. I mean they should not have to do that. There is a place for a national station with more of the public service concept. Otherwise it might die. The government has to see this and commit money to it, but as finances are now it's a slim chance.'

(Laird, TI 08/11/91)

Similar fears to those expressed here by Laird can be found in all our sample nations as we enter the 1990s.

The introduction of FM radio programmes in the early 1980s led initially to an increase of foreign music content in the media. These programmes introduced new international music styles to Trinidad, particularly music from the 'black charts' of the US such as funk and soul (and later rap and hip hop). Music from neighbouring countries (reggae and salsa) has also entered Trinidadian media via records generally produced in the US and the UK and less often directly from the Caribbean nations where such styles originated.

Video clips got their breakthrough in Trinidad during the short period in 1986–7 when the second TV programme was on the air; channel 2 relayed a lot of MTV programming. Video clips also appear to have boosted the introduction of synthesizers. The largest instrument store in Port of Spain, Sa Gomes, reported sales of no less than 2,000 Yamaha DX7 synthesizers in 1986–7. By 1987, numerous young amateur bands as well as almost all the established bands were using synthesizers. At the same time the steel pan got an equally important boost by being included in the official school music curriculum. There was competition between the synthesizers and the steel pan: 'Music from outside, MTV, is a grave problem. The children want to play more music heard from outside' (June Bacchus, music teacher, San Juan Senior Comprehensive School, TI 10/06/87).

By 1990, however, numerous youth steelbands were taking part in a national school steelband competition. Quite a few of these had women bandleaders and most had a majority of female players. This was a very new development, since the panmen (as the gender suggests) have, with very few exceptions, traditionally been men. The large number of girls performing in the school bands was said to be due to the fact that playing steel pan and sports were two alternative options in many schools. Boys tended to opt for sports and the girls for steel pan. This curious result of school curriculum scheduling is surely going to have an impact on the future of the steelband movement.

One of the most obvious effects of the influence of foreign music heard

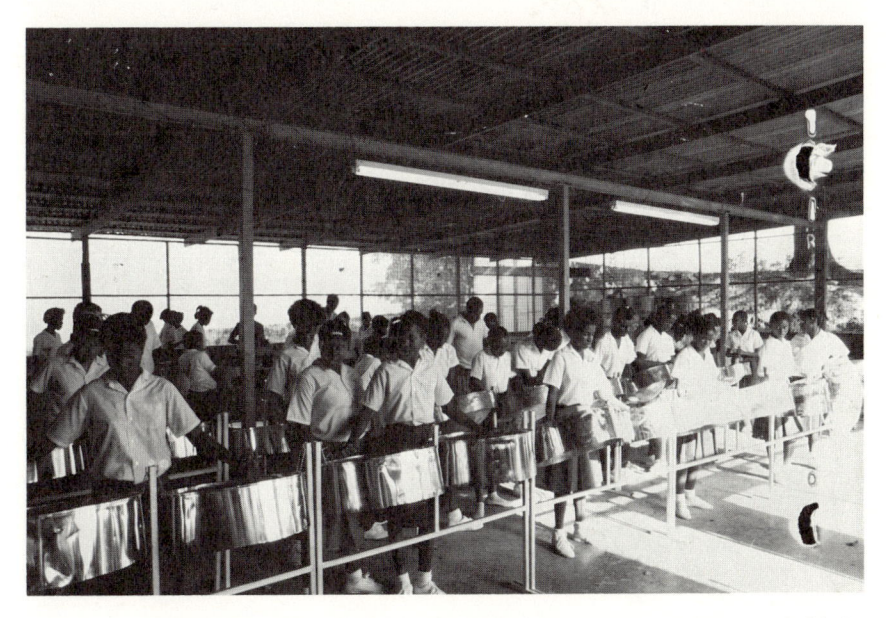

Plate 4.3 What impact for the future of the steelband movement? Lots of girls in the school band.

via the media was the creation of the soca, short for soul-calypso, around 1980. Soca became the dominant carnival music during the 1980s, replacing older often more acoustic forms of calypso. Soca music has established itself on the international music scene with several soca format radio stations in North America and increased airplay for soca on some British so-called 'incremental' stations. Even Swedish National Radio has had a regular weekly soca and reggae DJ show since 1985. Soca, renamed as 'zouk', has entered the music charts of France and Southern Europe via the French West Indian islands. In 1989, Kassav – a zouk group from Guadeloupe – was voted the most popular band in France.

The funky version of soca, incorporating elements of reggae which David Rudder and Charlie's Roots introduced in 1986, is another example of the influence of international hit music. Rudder's music was an immediate success and he won the Calypso Monarch Competition in 1986 and 1987. Like one of the inventors of soca, Lord Shorty, Rudder is very reluctant to admit any major foreign influence on his music. Instead he is keen on pointing out that his roots are in the purest calypso traditions of Trinidad. Calypso oldtimers like The Roaring Lion, however, are upset that Rudder calls his music calypso. They cannot identify his funky soca style with the calypso they know and have performed. The fact that Rudder does not wish to be identified as someone adopting foreign music

Plate 4.4 Older and younger calypsonians. The Roaring Lion upset about soca; David Rudder claims his music definitely is calypso.

styles is interesting. It suggests that success as a musician in Trinidad requires that your music appears to be Trinidadian.

> 'I always think that people in the end come back to themselves. At some point they look at themselves, at who they are. This is our saving grace. It carries me on. Because if you had said David Rudder in 1985, not many would have known me. But from 1985 there was a great cultural change here. A lot of the youths got interested in calypso. I'm so busy touring the schools. A lot of teachers are involved. It's a whole cultural upsurge.'
>
> (David Rudder, TI 09/06/87)

Rudder named his 1987 album 'Calypso Music'. Inside its double sleeve can be found pictures of calypso legends: Atilla the Hun, The Roaring Lion, The Mighty Sparrow, Lord Kitchener and others together with Rudder. The front of the sleeve carries the following proud statement:

> Trinidad and Tobago has given the world two unique gifts: the steel drum and that musical and lyrical form that is best known as the 'Trinidad Calypso', also called kaiso, wouso, carisseaux and others. And just as the pot-pourri of names reflects a culture in ascent with its ensuing conflicts and uncertainties, so it also reflects the creative zest of its people. A vibrant people moving towards its destiny; just like the hand reaching out beyond the drum towards the very source of the music . . . which itself is infinite.

Chapter 5
Case Study: Kenya

SINGLES, CASSETTES AND MULTI-ETHNIC RADIO: THE GENERAL MEDIA ENVIRONMENT

Artists are not the only category of workers whose job security has been hurt by 'productivity improvements' due to technology. But what other group has been, like them, forced to literally compete with themselves and even put themselves out of business, both figuratively in general and literally as individuals?

(Kenya Arts Co-operative Society 1988: 2)

This view of the influence of the media on the conditions of the artists reflects the worries experienced by Kenyan musicians concerning the changing media environment. Kenya has been the centre of the music and media industry in East Africa. The market-economy policies of Kenya have attracted investments from the international music industry in a number of projects. One such was 'East African Records Ltd', the now-defunct record pressing plant in the capital Nairobi. Another was a modern recording studio complex built with funds from CBS (Wallis and Malm 1984: 93–5). This influx of foreign capital has contributed to the development of the music and media scene in Kenya. As we shall see, the international companies, however, have not been very successful in controlling their interests in Kenya. Another party that has been active in developing the media in Kenya on a more local level is Unesco.

In spite of the investments in the production sector of the media industry, media penetration is very uneven. One limiting factor is the number of reception and playback devices. Radio cassette and cassette players abound, especially in the urban areas. Radio sets can be found in most households. Theoretically, radio can reach 90 per cent of the population but in some areas reception of the monopoly Voice of Kenya programmes is very bad. As in other countries, there are also cultural limits to the number of listeners. Mrs Rose Wandera, Head of School Broadcasts reports:

'Most children cannot listen to the radio because the family has only one radio set and it belongs to the father and he may have several wives and the children are not allowed to listen to the radio. So the exposure to other [i.e. than traditional] musics up country is not much.'

(Wandera, TI 20/04/88)

The Kenya Institute of Education has supplied schools with radios and radio cassette players to enable them to receive school broadcasts. Such operations are mainly financed by development aid programmes.

Most areas in the countryside and indeed many suburbs lack mains electricity, which means that TV sets and VCRs cannot be used. In middle-class urban areas, TV sets, gramophones (but in 1990 still no CD players), cassette players and even VCRs are fairly common. This is also the case on the coast where many become migrant workers in the Arab Emirates, investing part of their salaries in radio cassette players, VCRs and TV sets. As in Tanzania, video cassettes have become a substitute for television programmes in areas where TV broadcasts cannot be received.

There are three main daily papers which regularly feature articles on music. From time to time magazines dealing specifically with music have been launched, but none has lasted long. Most of these magazines were financed by the music industry; *Music Scene*, for instance, was backed up for a few years during the 1980s by CBS Kenya.

The Voice of Kenya (VoK) is the only broadcasting corporation in the country, apart from a few local experimental FM stations run as Unesco projects and a TV station run in Nairobi since 1990 by the ruling political party KANU. VoK was originally modelled on the BBC; today it has quite a different profile. VoK was a government department but was transformed into what was, at least formally, an independent corporation in 1990. The VoK is financed through commercials.

The Voice of Kenya provides four radio channels and one TV programme. Radio consists of the General Service in English, the National Service in Swahili and Vernacular Services 1 and 2 in the languages of the three main ethnic groups (tribes). English and Swahili are the official languages in Kenya. Radio programmes in five languages may seem a meagre output considering that forty-two different languages are used in Kenya. The Kenyan government, however, has quite a pluralistic approach to languages in broadcasting compared to many other governments in the area (in neighbouring Tanzania, with the exception of the External Service, only Swahili is used). Programmes for the Vernacular Services are produced by regional branches of the VoK. Educational broadcasts are produced by the Kenya Institute of Education.

VoK television can only be received in and around the main cities. It has an extensive impact all the same, since a significant proportion of the population live in the cities and the majority of viewers belong to the influential upper middle class. By 1990 cable television was established in a few wealthy neighbourhoods in Nairobi and Mombasa.

From 1976, East African Records Ltd (EAR), owned by Polygram, was the only record pressing plant in East Africa. There have been a number of attempts in East Africa by, for instance, musicians' co-operatives and the government of neighbouring Tanzania to start up new pressing plants and break the Polygram monopoly, but none has been successful. Since the mid-1980s, cassettes have gradually replaced vinyl discs to become the main medium for recorded music.

This is reflected in the production statistics from EAR. In 1981 the plant pressed 2,413,900 singles and in 1988 less than half the amount, 1,086,000. The amount of LPs remained more or less constant through the 1980s at between 130,000 and 150,000 copies per annum. The numbers of units sold of each record release is comparatively small. A thousand copies is considered a top seller. This means that production statistics from EAR reflect quite a large number of annual releases.

The growth of the cassette market (both legal and pirate) finally led Polygram to cease record production in Nairobi and to sell the record presses in 1990. At the time of the sale it was said that the new owner was about to move the presses to Zambia.

EAR also copies music cassettes (Wallis and Malm 1987: 124). This production showed an increase of almost 50 per cent from 110,000 in 1981 to 160,000 copies in 1988. EAR, however, is not the sole manufacturer of pre-recorded music cassettes. The legitimate music cassette market was estimated in 1988 to be around 2 million copies. On top of this comes the thriving business of the cassette pirates.

Polygram is both a phonogram production and manufacturing company. Over the years other transnational phonogram companies have established themselves in Kenya. AIT Records, a subsidiary of the Lonrho organization, was established in Kenya by the South African Gallo Records as early as the 1940s. At the beginning of the 1980s the company was still releasing many phonograms, but it went into receivership in 1986. EMI's operation, which was set up in 1977, went into bankruptcy due to the shifting of company assets into the pockets of the local manager (Wallis and Malm 1984: 93). In the early 1980s, CBS started a local subsidiary and was soon claiming 30 per cent of the market. In spite of this, CBS claimed it was not enjoying financial success in Kenya (Wallis and Malm 1984: 95). The CBS studio facilities were leased to a local company, Crawford Productions, and the subsidiary concentrated on distribution. By the end of the decade, CBS Kenya appeared to be completely run by local management with a minimum of interference from the mother company. Perhaps this will change when the Sony administration of CBS in New York gains momentum.

Kenya, like Jamaica, seems to be one of those smaller phonogram markets which are tricky places for subsidiaries of transnational phonogram companies. Polygram has also had a lot of problems in keeping control of its assets in Kenya. This is probably due to the very lively local phonogram company scene which includes a large number of small operators, many located in River Road in Nairobi. They are often musicians or groups of musicians. While the larger companies sell imported records and release Kenyan recordings in English and Swahili, the small ones cater mainly for different tribal groups. Both larger and smaller companies have small studios, but there is no 24- or 36-track studio. In 1988, Nairobi's most sophisticated studio was the 16–track facility leased by Crawford Productions from CBS.

A typical small record company is the one run by Kikuyu musician Joseph Kamaru in a shacky two-storey commercial building in River Road, Nairobi. This company specializes in Kikuyu music, some traditional, but most of it popular with accordion, guitar, etc. Joseph Kamaru is himself a musician/singer/songwriter in what has been called the Kikuyu Country and Western style, complete with guitar and cowboy hat! The business consists of a record shop, which is quite small but a little bigger than the 'hole-in-the-wall' kind of shop common along River Road. His premises are always filled with people chatting, laughing, and listening to records and tapes played back through old amplifiers and loudspeakers, sometimes three, four records simultaneously. Behind the counter, posters are displayed promoting the owner's records and concerts. One can also observe piles of old and new records, audio cassettes, and the odd video cassette. The company office is a small room without windows, usually guarded by a sturdy, grim-faced watchman. The recordings are made upstairs in a tiny studio with simple four-track equipment.

The single used to be the most important sound carrier for the small companies, but by the end of the 1980s the cassette had taken over. With the cassettes Kenya got its own flourishing pirate industry. Kenya does have a fairly up-to-date Copyright Act from 1983 which provides a legal framework for the prosecution of cassette pirates, but very little action seems to be taken. The following excerpt from an interview with Mr Mdsanjo, Manager of CBS Kenya, highlights the problem:

Mr M: Piracy is at a high peak at the moment. If you look in the streets you can see people dubbing and selling the pirated cassettes. We're trying to fight it.
Q: But don't you have a copyright law that forbids that?
Mr M: We do, but it's not very strong.
Q: You mean the sanctions . . .
Mr M: It's the problem of chasing down the people. Through civil law and what not, it takes a very long time to prosecute anybody.

88   Media Policy and Music Activity

Plate 5.1   Joseph Kamaru's store on River Road, Nairobi.

> *Q:*   But you do raids at times?
> *Mr M:* Yes, in fact we had one about three months ago. And they have a purpose. People are now understanding what it's all about. The people who are pirates are now feeling the pinch as they never used to do.
> *Q:*   Presumably you sell pre-recorded cassettes. Do you manufacture them yourself here?
> *Mr M:* Yes, we have our own plant. But the pirates can sell theirs at half the price of ours.
>
> (Mdsanjo, TI 21/04/88)

In Nairobi there seems, however, to be some limit to the activities of the pirates:

> 'The real problem is piracy. The stores buy the minimum number that they're allowed to buy from the distributor and they hide it under the counter and make copies. If anybody comes to check, they take out the records and say they are not selling. In Nairobi it's only in River Road you can get anything copied. In other parts of town if you bring a cassette that's not labelled they will copy it. They wouldn't care what music is on it. But if you bring a pre-recorded cassette they would not do it.'
>
> (George Kidenda, Ministry of Culture, TI 22/04/88)

COMMERCIAL RECORDS RULE: MUSIC CONTENT IN THE MEDIA

There are almost no music recording activities at the Voice of Kenya; music output in programmes throughout the 1980s was and still is completely dependent on commercially available phonograms. The VoK, however, does not purchase any records. It relies on gifts from phonogram companies and distributors. In 1988, the VoK's music library received approximately 200 new records every month. The music librarian estimated that about half consisted of singles produced in Kenya. Most LPs registered at the library were non-Kenyan records.

A major part of the Kenyan records the VoK receives are products from smaller companies working with material in the tribal languages. These can only be used on the vernacular services. Since Nairobi is the business hub of the East African music industry, several groups and musicians from neighbouring countries make the journey to Kenya to record. This means that much of the music on records sung in Swahili and English has actually been recorded by bands from Tanzania, Uganda or Zaire. The CBS Kenya distribution catalogue of August 1987 carried in its section labelled 'Local' 74 singles, 20 LPs, and 62 music cassettes. About two-thirds were recordings by foreign artists made in Kenya, including Alpha Blondy of the Ivory Coast, Burning Spear from Jamaica, and Ladysmith from South Africa. The 'International' section of the same catalogue had 24 singles, 91 LPs and 160 music cassettes, mainly with Anglo-American artists.

Although quite a few of the records labelled 'Kenyan' probably originate from other African countries, the number of Kenyan records in the VoK library seems to have increased remarkably during the 1980s. This is partly an effect of constantly increasing pressure from musicians and some officials for more Kenyan music on the radio (more on that later).

All the records that are played on VoK must come from the record library – this is seen as a way of guaranteeing that nothing deemed unsuitable is heard over the air. The DJs are not allowed to play records they get directly from the phonogram companies; the music played on VoK has to pass a vetting committee, partly for political reasons but also to avoid payola scandals. When we visited the VoK in April 1988 a record with the title 'Nelson Mandela' had just been banned because the text praised an individual, which is against the rules stipulated by the government. The staff explained that the only individual who could be praised in songs on VoK was the Kenyan President, Daniel Arap Moi.

Music content in VoK programmes was logged in April 1988. These loggings (see Table 5.1) show a music share of the total programme content of 50–60 per cent on the National and Vernacular Services and slightly more, approximately 70 per cent, on the General Service. Usually the content of spoken programming is a bit higher, since no educational

90   Media Policy and Music Activity

Table 5.1   Survey of programme content on Voice of Kenya, 21 and 25 April 1988

Programme	Kenyan tot. %	(trad.) %	(pop) %	Other African %	Anglo-American %	Speech %
National Service						
Total content	46	(0	46)	1	1	52
Music content	98	(0	98)	1	1	
General Service						
Total content	13	(0	13)	2	46	39
Music content	22	(0	22)	3	75	
Vernacular Service 1						
Total content	66	(33	33)	0	0	34
Music content	100	(50	50)	0	0	
Vernacular Service 2						
Total content	61	(6	55)	0	0	39
Music content	100	(9	91)	0	0	
All programmes						
Total content	49	(11	38)	1	9	41
Music content	84	(18	66)	1	15	

Note: Sample times on 21 April, 06.12–11.30 and 13.30–23.30; on 25 April the sample time was 11.30–13.30.

programmes were on the air due to school holidays. On the National Service almost all music played was Kenyan. Once again we must heed the proviso that some items classified as Kenyan might have featured bands from neighbouring countries singing in Swahili, thus boosting the share of Kenyan music a bit. All of this was popular music (Swahili jazz, Benga, Congolese etc.). On Vernacular Service 1, 50 per cent of the music was traditional and 50 per cent popular music from different ethnic groups, taarab music from the coast, and Indian film music. On Vernacular Service 2 only 9 per cent was traditional music and 91 per cent popular music including Indian film music. The English Language General Service had only 22 per cent Kenyan music, all of that popular music, 3 per cent other African music and 75 per cent Anglo-American popular music.

The overall average of all four programmes works out at a mix of 60 per cent music and 40 per cent speech and a share of the music content of 84 per cent Kenyan music (18 per cent traditional, 66 per cent popular), 1 per cent other African music and 15 per cent Anglo-American music. These figures point to a fairly high percentage of Kenyan music. According to comments by several of the experts we interviewed, this phenomenon was partly the result of an order issued by the Ministry of Information to the VoK in February 1988 to play more Kenyan music. There had been even more Kenyan music during the month of March. The share of Kenyan music was said to be on its way down again. One of our experts informed us in July 1989 that the shares of local music were down to a 50 per cent level on the National and General Services. In other words, we had witnessed an almost exact repeat of the somewhat unsuccessful attempt eight years earlier to increase the amount of Kenyan music on radio and TV through government edicts (cf. Wallis and Malm 1980; Wallis and Malm 1984: 257–9). These two case studies comprise almost classic examples of the difficulties involved in imposing media policies concerning national music content – we shall return to them shortly.

Most music on the National and General Service is presented in DJ-style programmes. On the Vernacular Services long recordings of uninterrupted traditional music are also featured. Music output includes special shows produced by the record companies who can buy programme slots to promote their products. These are usually transmitted on the General Service, the channel listened to by the more affluent, record-buying segments of the audience.

During school terms the Kenya Institute of Education broadcasts half a dozen 20-minute music lessons for different grades each week. They also tape both sound and video programmes from the annual Kenya Music Festival, a competition involving different schools. The programmes do not merely reflect conventional modes of teaching music.

'We have a programme called "Music and Movements". This programme is for 9-year-olds, standard 3. Apart from this programme, we want to use music as a vehicle to teach them other things. We want to use music to teach the standard-3 children, for instance, the concepts of "tall" and "high". We play some good music in the background and tell them "Try to stand as high as a tree". What we are trying to see is if that child knows the concept "stand high". In standard 1, 2 and 3 they don't use English as an instruction language. They use their mother tongue. Most children when they go home their mothers don't speak English; their fathers don't speak English. So there is no real enforcement of the English language. They know very little English. But after standard 3, English takes over as an instruction language. So they have to master enough English language to be able to learn all subjects. We have tried the method with music and it is very popular. "Spread out like a cloud" and that sort of thing.'

(Wandera, TI 20/04/88)

Radio is the most important music medium. Margaret Safari of Crawford Productions and the band Kenya Blue Stars says:

M.S.: Radio is very, very popular. Radio is a very good advertising medium for any song. You just need one airtime, one play, on the National Service and everybody knows that song. If it's a good song everybody will be humming it. So it's a very vital part of advertising. Radio reaches nearly 90 per cent of the whole population of Kenya.

Q: What about television?

M.S.: You see, not very many people own television sets, so we are talking of a very small number of people who own the TV sets and who can go to social clubs where they have TV sets. We are talking about a small number of viewers but it is still very powerful.

(TI 18/04/88)

In the early 1980s, VoK TV only broadcast the occasional music show, and then it was usually a foreign import. A change came about in 1984 with the introduction of the weekly show 'Music Variety' which featured Kenyan popular music. When video clips made their way into VoK programming in 1987, 'Music Variety' turned into a programme dominated by international video clips interpolated with a few locally produced music videos, most of them made by VoK in-house producers. Even in 1991, very few Kenyan bands had made videos sponsored by record companies.

BOLD POLICY STATEMENTS BUT LESS IMPLEMENTATION: ACTORS AND ISSUES ON THE MUSIC AND MEDIA SCENE

Nairobi used to be the main centre for the administration of colonial British East Africa. As one might expect, a strong colonial cultural heritage developed, enforced throughout Kenya by the activities of missionaries and the many European farmers who settled in the highlands during the first half of this century. The conviction, particularly amongst the urban middle-class segment of the population, that European culture is superior to African, is stronger than in many other African countries. This also holds true for music. Nairobi has a European-type Symphony Orchestra; the Kenya School of Music is modelled on European conservatories; the European tradition of polyphonic choral singing enjoys high status, etc. Many policymakers and gatekeepers in the media are firmly rooted in Euro-centric values.

On the other hand, there are several younger intellectuals who are very aware of the threat to African traditional culture posed by a colonial heritage. Many intellectuals, however, tend to be political radicals who are often in opposition to the one-party, authoritarian style of government that Kenya has experienced since independence in the mid-1960s. Thus their impact on policymaking has been limited.

Traditional and popular musicians do not, as a rule, have a middle-class background. The musicians who form the core of the Kenyan popular music scene are very aware of the low status ascribed to their music by the middle class. One of those veteran musicians, David Amunga, who is also the Chairman of the Arts Co-operative Society, says:

'Western civilization has contributed a lot to the ignorance in our society. Because if you cannot be taught the dance your mother danced, instead you're taught how Western civilization dance. And if you become a Director of VoK, you will not appreciate what is local because that particular officer was educated to look down on local values. So when he's manning the station, it takes time to convince him that the local song is as good as the Western. In fact, I have met some of them who say that if you sing in Kiswahili they would not listen to it. Sing in English!'

(Amunga, TI 22/04/88)

The tension between the African and the European perspective has been one of the main forces behind actions regarding music and media. Throughout the 1970s, the Voice of Kenya's output was clearly dominated by Western music. Little Kenyan popular music and almost no traditional music at all got on the air. Musicians and others began to voice protests. The audience also protested in their own way by tuning into Radio Tanzania and other stations that played mainly African music – this was particularly annoying for the Kenyan government since it was not on speaking terms with Tanzania at the time as a result of the Tanzanian involvement in the removal from power of Idi Amin in Uganda.

In March 1980 some politicians realized that something had to be done to curb the growing discontent and return the audience to the VoK. The Ministry of Information ordered VoK to play 75 per cent Kenyan music. The effect on VoK was traumatic. The DJs were not oriented towards Kenyan music. They said that there were not enough Kenyan records available and started to play old records from the 1950s, including tunes praising the British monarch! Music journalists, the subsidiaries of multinational record companies and other members of the affluent Western-oriented middle class started a campaign against the 75 per cent Kenyan music rule. Within two weeks the Ministry of Information revoked the directive.

The sensitive issue of music policy on the Kenyan broadcasting media was highlighted again two years later. An unsuccessful coup attempt against President Moi on 1 August 1982 started early in the morning at VoK with a change of music policy. Instead of the soothing tones of Jim Reeves, Kenya awoke to the rhythms of Swahili pop music as Kenyan Air Force personnel took over the station. This was another incident that focused attention on the music content of the VoK.

A study published in 1985 of the media habits of rural and slum-dwellers in Kenya showed a continued preference for foreign radio stations, notably Deutsche Welle broadcasting via a relay station in Zaire (46 per cent) and

Radio Tanzania (22 per cent). This study was based on data collected in 1983 and it notes that there was 'high tension in the political atmosphere. . . . there was still official condemnation of the coup, consequently a war of words raged between the VoK and Radio Tanzania' (Ugboajah 1985: 162–3). Ugboajah concludes with some advice to media policymakers in Kenya:

> Western programmes should be deemphasized on the channels of the VoK as they are bound to do more harm than good in the effort of decolonialization which is Africa's most important worry. A more ambitious socio-cultural engineering would demand the popularization of the indigenous music and songs of the Kikuyus, the Nandis, the Kambas, the Lukuyas, the Luos and the Masai in all the services of the Voice of Kenya.
>
> (Ugboajah 1985: 173)

This advice might have been taken, but it certainly did not reap the expected rewards.

The 1980s also witnessed the formation of several new music-based organizations. Most were formed to function as vehicles for putting forward the demands of different interest groups on the Kenyan popular music scene. Many of these organizations were dissolved or merely folded after a short period of activity. Others were still very much alive in 1990. Musicians have been active within the Kenya Musicians' Union and different co-operatives and copyright organizations. In the early years of the 1980s, the phonogram industry was split between the Kenyan branch of the IFPI, mainly representing the subsidiaries of international companies, and the Kenya Association of Phonogram Industries (KRPA) which attempted to organize a multitude of small, local operators. In 1983 the first phase of struggle within the popular music arena came to an end with the Kenya National Music Organizations' Treaty regulating studio fees, copyright and royalties, and other dealings of phonogram producers, musicians and composers (Wallis and Malm 1984: 143ff.).

Soon, however, new bodies were formed which were not subject to the terms of the 1983 'Treaty'. Some local phonogram producers teamed up with the IFPI group and formed the Kenya Association of Record Producers (KAPI). Musicians, together with other artists, formed a new co-operative named the Kenya Arts Co-operative Society. The new Copyright Act of 1983 triggered off a struggle between the Performing Right Society of London, which had enjoyed a monopoly dating back to colonial times, and the new Music Copyright Society of Kenya regarding the right to collect and distribute copyright dues.

Another factor constantly influencing events on the music scene is tension between different ethnic groups. Those working in the media always have to take into account the need to communicate across ethnic cultural borders. As with most 'national' concepts in Africa, the concept of 'Kenyan music' is of a multi-faceted nature. This is illustrated by the fact that the signature tune used in school broadcasts to introduce the grade 8 course on Kenyan music is the British Christmas carol 'Joy to the World'. Head of School Broadcasts, Rose Wandera, says:

> 'Initially, when we started discussing it in the subject national panel, most of the members were of the opinion that we should use an African tune. You know "that tune is very foreign" and arguments like that. Kenya is very rich in music. We have as many different types of songs as we have different tribes. Now this richness in broadcasting also becomes a problem if I choose a Luo tune as a signature tune to use, although the Luo component of the syllabus is a tiny aspect. There is a part of the syllabus that says African music as well as Western and Asian. But we can't equate Luo with Africa because Luo is only one of the many tribes. So when you choose one African melody from one group you have a problem there. Because you are not broadcasting to that tribe, you're broadcasting to the Kenyan nation, which has all the tribes as well as all the Asians as well as all the white people. It's a sort of multi-racial society. So we look for things that have some sort of communality. Something that will be general and common to everybody. Western to some extent is our music in that it does not belong to one group of people.'
>
> (Wandera, TI 20/04/88)

In 1982 the President appointed a National Music Commission with a brief to find ways of increasing the status and quality of local music culture. The Chairman was Dr Washington Omondi, an ethnomusicologist educated at the universities of Edinburgh and London, who was well aware of the importance of traditional music in society. Since music and dance are very closely connected in traditional Kenyan culture, dance was also included in the Omondi group's study. The Commission worked for a little more than a year intensively interacting with different interest groups.

The Presidential National Music Commission presented its report entitled 'Preservation and Development of Music and Dance in Kenya' in January 1984. This 200-page-plus report covers most of the significant music issues of the 1980s in Kenya. A central dual aim was to combine sometimes incompatible goals of safeguarding traditional music and dance whilst simultaneously bringing about a modernization of music activity in Kenyan life. The report has chapters on research, dissemination and development of music and dance, music education, music and dance performance, music in the media, musicians, training of music personnel, etc. It concludes with a 30–page list of main recommendations.

Some of the proposals in the report were speedily adopted and implemented. Recommendations concerning music education resulted in a music syllabus for Kenyan schools in 1985; prior to 1985, music had not been a compulsory subject. The new syllabus mirrors the struggle between European and African elements, but it definitely represents a shift of emphasis in favour of traditional Kenyan music. The introduction to the Secondary Education syllabus notes:

> This Syllabus is set upon the nature of music as a performing cultural art whose main element is expression of feelings and ideas. It explores both local and international culture. There are three main areas which are covered throughout the course at graded levels. These are: basic skills, history and analysis, and practicals. . . .
>
> By the end of the course the learner should be able to:
> (a) read and write music
> (b) perform and enjoy song, dance and instrumental music
> (c) design, make and use musical instruments and costumes
> (d) express his own ideas, feelings and experiences through the art of composing music and dance
> (e) appreciate different types of music
> (f) acquire a sense of co-operation by participating in musical activities
> (g) use acquired knowledge and skills to explore the musical environment of our country through field work
> (h) and enhance national unity and identity through exploration, appreciation and performance of indigenous music from all parts of Kenya
> (i) contribute to the world of music through the study of the subject and participation in the country's music and that of other nations
> (j) use acquired musical skills to contribute to his well-being and to the welfare of his society.
>
> (Kenya Institute of Education 1985: 1)

Even in the late 1980s, the schools were still struggling to implement this very ambitious syllabus. Approximately 15,000 music teachers versed in both Western and African music had to be trained, which is an impossible task to accomplish in a few years. There was also a clash between the traditional concepts of music and the teaching of music as a school subject. A teacher at a secondary school in Nairobi told us that his students could not be engaged in any study of music unless there was a concrete aim for the activity, like a concert or a performance at a wedding party. He had asked the students if they were interested in forming a traditional music and dance group. Sixty had announced their interest. When he called a meeting to start the group only six turned up. He found out that the reason was that he had not told the students why, where and when the group should perform.

This anecdote possibly explains why most of the music activities of the schools seem to be directed towards participation in the yearly Kenya Music Festival, a music and dance competition featuring groups from all over Kenya. The educational music broadcasts of the Kenya Institute of Education are adapted to this situation:

> 'Music programmes for children are something new. Before we only had music programmes for teachers. The music programmes we have made for the teachers have been those made under the Kenya Music Festival syllabus. A lot of the teachers cannot read staff or solfa notation. And yet they have to teach music.'
>
> (Wandera, TI 20/04/88)

The Presidential National Music Commission made forty-two recommendations regarding music in the media, thirty-nine of those concerned the VoK and three dealt with music 'through loudspeakers in public places'. The following recommendations were put forward:

- Eighty per cent of the music both on VoK and through speaker systems in public places should be of Kenyan origin.
- The VoK should strive to broadcast traditional music representing all the ethnic groups in Kenya.
- The VoK should ensure that signature tunes, background music and music advertisements are mostly Kenyan.
- The VoK should start special commercial programmes for the sole purpose of promoting new releases of records.
- School broadcasts should have their own channel.
- Music aimed at informing or educating the public should be presented in Swahili.
- The VoK should set up a special Department of Music, headed by an individual with advanced music training and administrative abilities.
- The VoK should set up a Music Advisory Council, which should institute a system of consultation and feedback from members of the public.
- The VoK should use its facilities, such as studio and others, to record the music of local musicians.
- The VoK should organize its own music groups.
- The VoK should not erase existing recordings, but keep them in the archives for posterity and make copies for safety deposit, as well as making such recordings available to the public.

(Omondi 1984: 162–4)

The Kenyan government took no immediate action to implement these proposals from the Commission. But the recommendations did put pressure, once again, on the VoK to change its music policy. More Kenyan music was introduced into radio programmes, including traditional music of different ethnic groups. Commercial programmes promoting new record releases were introduced. The Music Advisory Board was formed, but merely became a committee vetting records before they could be broadcast rather than a policy-making body. On the other hand, in 1991 the VoK still had no Music Department. Neither were VoK studios used to record Kenyan musicians. The VoK still relies mainly on commercial recordings and makes very few field recordings and video productions. The broadcasting company has no employed 'in-house' music groups and no public library of recordings.

As we mentioned earlier, in February 1988 the government again ordered the VoK to play more Kenyan music, eight years after the previous attempt. But, yet again, there was a slide back into a more Western-oriented music policy, something which the VoK staff seemed to favour. One member of the VoK music committee made this comment:

> 'The problem that I think we have here is lack of follow-up. Things like Kenyan music being played on National Service. The Ministry of Culture have recommended more Kenyan music, but the Ministry and VoK have not sat down to discuss it. We cannot go to the papers and castigate VoK. We have to discuss it with them. The recommendation of the President's Music Commission is that the foreign music should be reduced to 20 per cent. But it has not been taken up and discussed with VoK.'
>
> (TI 22/04/88)

The struggle between the Western-oriented and the African-oriented sections of Kenyan society over VoK music policy was still intense in 1991. Among the strong pressure groups lobbying for more Kenyan music we find the Kenya Arts Co-operative Society (ARTCO) with its 2,000 members. But the Chairman of ARTCO, David Amunga, also offers some self-criticism:

> 'We would like local music to be played on VoK. But before we reach that stage we have to ask ourselves how to purify our music. Because technology has changed. People have got sophisticated equipment to listen to the music. Our music does not fare well with the man we have to depend on, the one who buys a radio to listen to music. If we talk of local music featuring more on VoK, I think we're putting the cart before the horse. I think we should admit that we have failed and this is where ARTCO comes in. First we must decide on a programme to develop our music. There are studios here that are out of order, but the technician will not advise the band that it is out of order. He'll record on one track even if he has got twelve people. So I think we need a forum to discuss and plan a programme. . . . Before that, let us accept any record on the radio whether it is Kenyan, Ugandan or . . . We want good entertain-

ment. They will tune to another country's station where they would listen to better music. Take Tanzania, for example, they were actually consumers of Kenyan music. But today Kenyan listeners are switching to Radio Tanzania and Zaire for better music. So the more you play our local music today and get people hostile you are actually doing a disservice. You have to wait until the quality gets better.'

(TI 22/04/88)

The ARTCO Chairman had this to say on another issue that has constantly come up during the past decades, the Polygram monopoly on the manufacturing of records via ownership of the sole factory, which was still operating in 1988:

'We have put together this budget here in case Polygram, who are the owners of the factory, don't buy the idea of joining with the co-operative, we will challenge them and say "Your charges are too high." We are not able as a co-operative to service our members through your factory because that would mean exploiting the members more in order to earn our service charges. Our bylaws cover facilitating for our members. We intend to request the government to give us researchers. If we feel that a record factory then is necessary, it would be a complex with both cassette and disc manufacturing. Otherwise we are talking about making guitars and other instruments. ARTCO is supposed to lead the way. ARTCO means the artist deciding his own destiny. . . .

This is why I say both politically and economically this country has to take a stand. You cannot change anything of that kind without establishing a policy. CBS are simply doing cheap economics. They are not dealing with the artists practically. They just get a recorded tape from a foreign country and they find it much cheaper than dealing with me, a local musician. I will spend all the money and do all the gigs needed to reach that stage of a recording artist but it is easier for you to take a stamper from the United States and duplicate it here and pay a small percentage. So a cultural policy should really minimize their activities and they should be made partners in the development of our local music. That's our views in ARTCO.

If the government could help us to take distribution of all the records locally we don't need the money from the government. Even if we're earning one shilling on every record that passes through here it is that shilling that will build our studio, it is that one shilling that will purify our music so it becomes competitive. We don't ask the government to restrict them. But we complain because we have been disarmed and we are told to fight against foreign artists and there is no policy governing us. So we are left now to fight what I may call a cultural protracted war.'

(TI 22/04/88)

Constant criticism from local artists was probably a factor contributing to the decision of EAR-Polygram in 1990 to close the vinyl plant and sell the record presses. The Polygram company will not suffer much from this decision since it has access to other pressing plants outside Kenya. The decision amounts to a failure for the line of action advocated by Mr Amunga of ARTCO. In 1991 it was almost impossible for local musicians and small companies to get records released. This also speeded up the move towards a situation where analogue cassettes became the dominant music carrier.

THE INTERACTION OF MUSIC MEDIA POLICY AND LOCAL MUSIC ACTIVITIES

All the music organizations of Kenya have been more or less active in trying to influence the music policy of the VoK. There is a consensus that the music output of the VoK plays an important role in forming the Kenyan music culture. This consensus is also mirrored in the report of the Presidential National Music Commission. The government's interest in the VoK music output has been sporadically manifested through edicts relating to an increased output of Kenyan music. These orders have not had any real effect. Besides this, the government also maintains a close watch, for political reasons, on what is played on the VoK through the record vetting committee.

The government seems to be ambivalent about the main issue: more Kenyan music in the media. The report from the Presidential National Music Commission includes evidence suggesting that this ambivalence can be related to the use of local music to reinforce traditional values which the middle class equates with 'backwardness'; also that local music is used as a vehicle for communicating criticism against the government.

As in many other countries there is a gap between the norms applied to the teaching of music in the schools and music policy in the media. Margaret Thiongo, primary school music advisor, comments:

> *M.T.:* There is a conflict with the youngsters. What is very popular with them is popular music and disco music. But according to what we have laid down, the most important area in music in schools is the reading and writing of music. Once they are able to interpret that piece of music from whatever source, then they will be able to appreciate the good music we are offering at school level. . . .
>
> *Q:* Do you think it is important to introduce any of this outside musical environment into the music appreciation or music teaching?
>
> *M.T.:* With this syllabus it might be difficult because we have so much to cover and it's very broad. We don't have much time. We

prefer to tackle the syllabus as much as possible. When they get to secondary school they have periods for appreciation where they do jazz, classical . . . and they have to learn to appreciate music from other cultures. That has to be limited at primary level because the teachers also have to be very conversant with it and they also have to appreciate it first you see. So some of the teachers may not be familiar with music from other areas but only from just here.

(TI 18/04/88)

The ways in which the school curriculum will influence Kenyan music culture in the future remain to be evaluated. Music in the media has obviously affected traditional attitudes in a number of areas. There is a preference for modern Western instruments such as electric guitars and synthesizers. Most Kenyan popular music bands use these instruments. Even small local bands in outlying villages try at least to make simple box guitars and jazz-style drum sets from available objects and materials such as tin cans. The Makuyu Stars of Kimorore village, Makuyu, in Central Province are an example of this phenomenon. This band of teenage music enthusiasts rehearses in a round thatched mud hut with their home-made instruments. In order to meet and rehearse they have to have a formal organization (so as not to contravene Kenyan laws of assembly restricting conditions under which private persons may congregate). This problem has been solved by paying a membership fee of 50 shillings a year, to the local self-help association. Since the musicians are unemployed, this is quite a considerable sum. But if they don't pay up, on the other hand, the police could detain them since rehearsals could be deemed to be illegal meetings.

The Makuyu Stars play pop music with texts in Kikuyu. They have learnt this style by listening to the radio. On weekend evenings they play in the local pub. The band made a recording, 'Heri Uende', which Polygram in Nairobi released as a single in 1987 (Polydor POP 623–211 1386). This disc has been available in some record shops and has also been heard over the radio. A small local band thus became linked up with the media. Since the members of the band are illiterate and Nairobi is far away they have little means of protecting their rights. They told us they had never received any fee or royalties for their recording.

A musician in Saba Saba close to Makuyo also made a recording in Nairobi which was released as a single. He said that the arrangement was that he should get one Kenyan shilling per record, but he never received any money. He proudly showed us his Music Copyright Society of Kenya membership certificate, but maintained that it hadn't helped him at all.

The story of these village musicians' dealings with the media and the music industry has been told many times before. A classic Kenyan case is that of the tune 'Malaika', a world hit that has turned evergreen. The

Plate 5.2 The Makuyu Stars' rehearsal hut from the outside.

person who is widely recognized as the composer of the tune, Fadhili William, has received almost no copyright money for his work. He lives in the slums of Nairobi while other names appear as composers on the record labels (Wallis and Malm 1984: 182ff.).

Even established Kenyan musicians complain about difficulties experienced in their dealings with the media. The Mushrooms are a six-man band, five of whom are brothers, who have worked for many years in the tourist hotels of Mombasa. In 1988 they were fully equipped with high-powered amplifiers, electric and electronic instruments. They have had several hits, the most famous being 'Jambo Bwana'. The spokesman for the band, Teddy Kalanda, had this to say about the income from records and air plays:

> *T.K.:* It's pocket money. The market is very small here, especially for a group like ours. We don't depend on our tribe because our tribe, the Gidyama, is a very very small tribe. You know people like Kamaru and Luos, they have big tribes and they can survive only playing for their tribes. For us, we sort of play for everybody. We sing in Swahili and English. We rely more on the live gigs than recording. We're only doing recordings because we feel that we have to contribute something by doing our own thing and hoping

Plate 5.3 Inside the hut of the Makuyu Stars – homemade drums and a simple box guitar.

Plate 5.4 A lone operator: the Kahabati one-man band from Saba Saba, also available on disc.

    that some day we will make it on the international scene and sell more records than we are doing now. At the moment we are just doing it as a hobby or whatever it is. It isn't much we get out of it. The only record that did sell very well and is still selling is our first recording that we did in 1980. It is called 'Jambo Bwana'. This one is selling up till now. We've got silver, gold and platinum disc for this song. It's been done by Boney M in Germany and other German artists.

Q: Do you get any copyright money?
T.K.: We're still fighting for that [Laughs].

(TI 21/04/88)

    In traditional society, the world of music is segregated into gender and age groups. When played on the radio, music from different contexts are mixed in the same time slot. This contributes to a change in the status of traditional music. A local traditional music that is favoured by media producers, like some of the Luo and Luhija music, is picked up by other ethnic groups or subgroups within a tribe which have not performed that music before.

    The media have also contributed to the change of the status of women in music. In popular media music, women have started performing alongside men. Singers Margaret Safari and Sheila Tett of the Kenya Blue Stars recall:

> 'At first when we started singing there was a lot of objection from the society. Normally the African society look at the singing or the world of show business as a male kind of restricted area. And then we started to go into music there was a lot of objection. But then we showed them that even women could be in show business. It is nothing wrong with it. It is just an occupation like any other occupation. They have started now to accept it. Since we broke into the market there has been several other lady groups singing. They saw that we started and we have kept to it and we have protected ourself and we want to break through.'
> (TI 18/04/88)

Among the Islamic population in the towns along the coast, video cassette recorders are fairly common. A case study reports that women and children in Lamu town are big consumers of Indian entertainment films. They gather during leisure hours in private houses to watch new films (Fuglesang 1990: 34ff.). It is the music and dance scenes and the 'romance' theme that make Indian films so popular. Here the film heroes and heroines sing out the pains and pleasures of love. The heroines become idols; their radical behaviour, dress fashion and lifestyle admired and emulated. They represent new role models for the women in this sex-segregated community, women who, until recently, have led secluded lives at home and submitted to 'arranged' marriages by parents. Romantic 'love' marriages with a partner of one's own choice becomes the new ideal. The increased access to media such as Indian film has had a profound influence on social relations as well as local music and text traditions, i.e. in the taarab music.

What is seen on TV and heard on the radio awakens dreams among young people of upward mobility in society through 'making it' in the music business. They see how other Africans like Miriam Makeba, Mori Kante, Salif Keita, etc., have become international stars. Since the information available on those stars is very fragmented, the village musician cannot put the phenomenon into a wider context. The dream gets stronger. At the same time the gap is constantly becoming wider between the international star and, say, the Nairobi night club musician with a salary of less than US$100 a month. The latter probably doesn't even own his own instrument. We have even seen musicians who have come to Nairobi to seek their music industry fortune performing in a cage because the club owner, who also owns the amplifiers, microphones and guitars, doesn't want anyone stealing or damaging his equipment.

The fight through the 1980s over the music policy of the VoK mirrors the importance large groups of the population ascribe to the music output in

Plate 5.5 'A musician's life is a . . .' Playing in the cage on the club owner's instructions.

Plate 5.5 While a few customers drink and dance outside.

the media. The affluent middle class wants the international superstars and says Kenyan music is not good enough. Teddy Kalanda of The Mushrooms has this comment:

> 'When we got our independence some years back and they stopped the importation of clothes, there was a big outcry from the people. But they gave a chance to the local textile mills. And with time people didn't complain that much because by that time there was a lot of improvement in the products that came from KIKUMI and ARIWATEX. And now we can do without any imported stuff so it could be the same with music. People will complain for some time. But as time goes by musicians will improve and sooner or later we are definitely going to have a very healthy Kenyan music scene. I mean it's just a matter of giving it a chance.'
>
> (Kalanda, TI 21/04/88)

Chapter 6
Case Study: Tanzania

ECONOMIC CONSTRAINTS SHAPING THE GENERAL MEDIA ENVIRONMENT

As with so many other aspects of modern life, the media environment in Tanzania is heavily influenced by the fact that this nation is one of the poorest in the world. Economic constraints, especially the lack of hard currency, have been decisive factors in forming the general media environment. Even in the early 1970s, foreign currency considerations lay behind a decision not to introduce television to mainland Tanzania. The island of Zanzibar did start a small television station in the 1970s, but it was barely functioning a decade later. The data in this section refer primarily to conditions on the mainland.

The oil price boom in the 1970s and the Tanzanian involvement in the Kagera War in Uganda in 1979 created a desperate economic situation. Severe import restrictions were imposed with a list of items that could be imported being drawn up by the government. That list did not include musical instruments, media hardware (i.e. cassette players, radio sets, etc.) or software (records, cassette tapes, etc.). This meant that no foreign currency was supplied by the Bank of Tanzania for payments of such imports. The only way to acquire, say, a radio cassette recorder was through relatives abroad or via purchasing it with Tanzanian currency from a tourist or foreign development project employee who could use local money. During the early 1980s, some media hardware such as TV sets and VCRs were even included in a list of items that could not be brought into the country at all.

Little quantitative data exist regarding the availability of consumer-electronic hardware; we can only offer a rough qualitative overview based on information gleaned from diverse informants and personal 'on-site' observations.

Radio sets have been produced in Tanzania by a subsidiary of the Philips company. The majority of the population have access to a radio, even if every household does not have its own set. During the 1960s and 1970s

Plate 6.1 Despite import restrictions and a lack of hard currency, there are plenty of cassettes for sale in Dar es Salaam.

there were quite a few gramophones, but these gradually disappeared as spare parts ran out, and have not as a rule been replaced by new ones.

In spite of nominally tough import restrictions, cassette players and audio cassettes became fairly plentiful throughout the 1980s at least in the urban areas. Smart businessmen find ways and means of bringing media hardware into the country when there is a demand.

Although there are no TV transmissions there has been a rapid growth of the number of TV sets since the mid-1980s. These are used with VCRs to show video tapes in village shops, drinking places, upper- and middle-class homes. Kivikuru notes a distinct difference between 1978 and 1987: 'the urban middle class prefers video to movies in the 1980s' (Kivikuru 1990: 375).

There is one government-run radio corporation, Radio Tanzania. Radio Tanzania broadcasts mainly on AM although there is one FM transmitter in Dar es Salaam and a couple of shortwave transmitters which are used for programmes beamed to Southern Africa; for many years these provided a means for the ANC to be heard at home, despite the banning of the organization by the South African authorities.

In theory, Radio Tanzania can be heard all over Tanzania, but reception is very poor in some areas. Throughout most of the 1980s, three programme services were maintained: the National Service and the Commercial Service in Swahili and the External Service in English, as well as some local languages of Southern Africa. The National Service broadcasts throughout the day, the Commercial Service opens up at 4pm and the External Service broadcasts one hour in the morning and returns at 6.30pm. All three services close down around 11pm. Only the Commercial Service has commercial advertising spots. In November 1989, the National and Commercial Services were combined into one advertising-financed channel, 'temporarily, it was said, because of broken transmission machinery' (Kivikuru 1990: 377). A year later, however, the authorities had repaired the broken equipment and the channels were separated once again.

There is one English language daily newspaper (the *Daily News*) and four or five dailies printed in Swahili. These carry advertisements for musical events and the odd article on music and dance. There is no specialist music press.

Although Tanzania has been extremely successful in stamping out illiteracy, most of the culture is still an oral one. Cassette recorders have gradually started to play a role as mediators of the oral culture. The country, however, has no facilities for mass production of recorded cassettes. There are also very few recording studios. Not even the studios at Radio Tanzania and the Tanzania Film Company (with a formal monopoly on film, video and phonogram production/distribution) are particularly well equipped or maintained. The film company tried to start a gramophone disc pressing plant in the early 1980s despite advice that it would be better to go for a cassette copying plant. Equipment was bought and a building was erected, but the project was never completed.

By the mid-1980s there was no market left for vinyl records in Tanzania. At the end of the decade, virtually all pre-recorded cassettes were supplied by pirates; these would connect a few cassette recorders together and copy tapes of Radio Tanzania broadcasts or music acquired from abroad. Pirate tapes are sold in local stores or are played at the discos which have opened more recently in urban areas.

HIGH TANZANIAN MUSIC CONTENT IN THE MEDIA

Tanzania has more than 100 ethnic groups, most of them with a language and a music style of their own. Since independence from British rule in 1961, one of the major goals of the government has been to promote unity within the country. The media have been used to this end. In contrast to neighbouring Kenya, all broadcasts as well as other official activities are conducted in either Swahili or English, the two official languages, and not in any of the many local languages. Although traditional music from

Plate 6.2 An impressive notice points the way to a record pressing plant which was never completed.

different ethnic groups is broadcast from time to time on Radio Tanzania, the main emphasis is on music that is deemed to be common to the whole nation. This includes the neo-traditional music created by the National Ngoma Troupe or at the College of Arts in Bagamoyo. Another example of the music that is regularly heard on Radio Tanzania is 'Swahili jazz', a popular form that has developed from a mixture of Afro-American, mainly Caribbean, and African music and is played by bands with singers, Western brass instruments, electric guitars and percussion.

The music officially promoted both live and in the media has usually featured texts or dancing that convey a concrete message. This is not something new since the traditional *ngoma* (a word meaning music, dance, drama and drum) has always been and still is used to teach traditional knowledge in areas such as farming or hunting methods, baby care and so on. In the 1970s and 1980s, the official line was that Swahili jazz bands, choirs or modern ngoma groups were supposed to use their art to inform people of the advantages of learning to read or write, or of boiling water before drinking it. Bands could be involved in specific campaigns, such as how to build modern houses, how to avoid getting AIDS, etc. This message music has also dominated the music programming of Radio Tanzania.

Prior to 1973, Radio Tanzania's music profile was dominated by foreign

Plate 6.3 A typical line-up of a Swahili jazz band – the now-defunct Safari Sound Band entertaining at a restaurant just outside Dar es Salaam.

imports, mostly Anglo-American popular recordings. In that year it was decided that the music played on the Swahili language service should be 100 per cent Tanzanian (cf. Wallis and Malm 1984: 260ff.). Since very few records with Tanzanian music were available, the radio had to start its own recording activities. This was also in compliance with the ideology of 'self-reliance' that had been a cornerstone of the teachings of the then Tanzanian President, Julius Nyerere, and the ruling CCM party. Every week for almost two decades, a number of traditional and popular music groups have been recorded by engineers from Radio Tanzania (assisted somewhat by equipment and know-how supplied as foreign aid grants from countries such as Sweden and Denmark). Over the years Radio Tanzania has amassed a huge tape library with recordings of Tanzanian music and Tanzanian musicians. The station uses these tapes in much the same way as other stations use their libraries of commercial recordings.

During the 1980s, the 100 per cent Tanzanian rule was relaxed somewhat. Some music from neighbouring countries and Anglo-American phonograms could occasionally be heard on the Swahili languages programmes of Radio Tanzania. Tanzanian music, however, still dominates output. This is shown by the loggings of music content of the radio programmes in Table 6.1. On the other hand, none of Radio Tanzania's programmes can be said to have a marked music format. There is a high level of educational and information programmes. Loggings show that the Swahili-language programmes were 60 to 70 per cent speech and that the mainly English-language External Service had a speech/music ratio of around 45:55.

Around 85 per cent of the music played on the National and the Commercial Services was Tanzanian. Around 10 per cent of the music was of Anglo-American origin and less than 10 per cent came from other African countries. The Anglo-American content was slightly higher in the Commercial Service. The External Service shows a different profile with only around 21 per cent of the music being Tanzanian, while 36 per cent came from other African countries and 43 per cent was Anglo-American. The share of traditional Tanzanian music of the music programming was 18 per cent in the National Service and 7 per cent in the Commercial and External Services. The bulk of the Tanzanian music output was Swahili jazz-band music with a few items of the coastal *taarab* style. Taarab is a traditional form of Swahili music of Arabic origin which has become mixed with Indian film music in its modern form. It is very popular in coastal areas and in Zanzibar, where it is regularly featured on Radio Zanzibar.

As one might expect, there is very little musical content in what is shown in the cinemas and on the VCRs besides background music and, in the case of some Indian films – much music and dance. Tanzanian music hardly features at all in an audio-visual context because of the absence of a functioning Tanzanian film or video production industry.

114 Media Policy and Music Activity

Table 6.1 Survey of programme content on Tanzanian Radio, 11–13 April 1988

Programme	Tanzanian tot. %	(trad. %	pop) %	Other African %	Anglo-American %	Speech %
Radio Tanzania National Service						
Total content	35	(7	28)	4	3	58
Music content	85	(18	67)	9	6	
Radio Tanzania Commercial Service						
Total content	20	(2	17)	0	3	77
Music content	88	(7	81)	0	12	
Radio Tanzania External Service						
Total content	12	(4	8)	21	24	43
Music content	21	(7	14)	36	43	
All programmes						
Total content	27	(5	22)	6	7	60
Music content	69	(13	56)	15	16	

Note: Times of samples: 06.24–11.00 on 12 April; 12.18–17.00 on 13 April; 17.00–23.00 on 11 April.

BUILDING THE NATION: ACTORS AND ISSUES ON THE MUSIC AND MEDIA SCENE

From 1961 onwards, Tanzania was governed by the Tanganyika African National Union on the mainland, and the Afro-Shirazi Party on Zanzibar; these two then merged in 1977 to form the present ruling Chama Cha Mapinduzi or CCM. The CCM's political ideology can be described as the variant of African socialism conceived by, amongst others, Tanzania's first President, Julius Nyerere.

As Tanzania left its British Protectorate status and embarked on independence, 90 per cent of the population were illiterate. The number of persons with an academic training was minimal. The CCM's stated priorities have been clear and basic: to teach all citizens to speak, read and write the same language, Swahili (a goal nearly accomplished), and to improve basic living conditions. Co-operative efforts have been seen as the means for reaching the latter goal. The overriding goal of 'building the nation' has also been the point of departure for official policies applied to music and media.

Official music and media policy has been formulated by the ruling party, i.e. the intellectual elite of the country. Such policymaking has inevitably been restricted by severe economic constraints. Different government institutions have been established to implement policies, thus creating an institutional structure which has been altered from time to time. During the 1980s, the main institutions were the Office of the Director of Culture, responsible for the College of Arts and a network of cultural officers all over the country, the National Arts Council, Radio Tanzania and the Tanzania Film Company (TFC). TFC, as we have noted, was entrusted with a monopoly covering the manufacturing and importing of phonograms, videograms and film. There are also a few musicians' organizations such as CHAMUDATA (the Musicians' Union), but these have tended to maintain a low profile in the policymaking process. One reason for this could be the practice whereby musical groups and bands are often sponsored or 'owned' by more influential organizations in society such as trade unions or co-operatives.

As mentioned above, music has been seen as a means of conveying messages in a society based on oral tradition. To a certain extent this has been achieved directly through the party political system. Singing and dancing have always comprised an integral part of political activity, particularly in the case of the CCM Youth League. This has involved both touring groups and exposure on the radio. The basic view of music as a conveyor of messages is reflected by this statement:

'The Minister [of Culture] would know that music and the other arts could contribute to the national development both on the political and the economic level. Because it's through the music of the nation that people understand the message of the nation: political, economic. When the Census is coming up in June it is the musicians that will pass the message to the people. We had a meeting here about the Census and we shall use the musicians, the ngoma groups, to sing about Census, why Census. So the message will be passed by those humble artists. In other words what I'm trying to say is the government knows that these people must be promoted. The problem is funds, foreign exchange.'
(P. Chani, Chairman of the National Arts Council, TI 13/04/88)

The traditional music of the different ethnic groups is still very much alive. These forms of music have been one point of departure in the creation of new national forms of music. In the early 1970s, the best young performers from different parts of the country were brought to Dar es Salaam to form the National Ngoma Troupe. This troupe was used at home to represent Tanzania when important foreign guests arrived and on tours abroad. The National Ngoma Troupe developed a 'modernized' ngoma adapted to stage performance, combining stylistic elements from different parts of the country. This modernized ngoma style became the model for younger performers all over the country. It also formed the nucleus of the teaching syllabus at the College of Arts.

Over the past decade, competitions have provided a means of observing activity and developments in the field of traditional music:

'Ours has been an oral community. Much of the history has been handed down by word of mouth. For that matter we use the competitions and festivals as ways and means of research. We actually have to research into the arts, into the crafts and thereby re-create them. And so we are also aiming at preserving the findings we may come up with for purposes of future analysis and effective utilization. We think we involve many more artists by inviting them to participate in the competitions and the festivals that take place in this country. The objective is actually to go back to the owners of this country's culture in the rural areas and find out information about specific aspects of their crafts and bring them on to the stage. In the final analysis we shall bring them to the book or the tape recorder. We do not wish to urge people not to modernize as such. What we are trying to point out is: We have to modernize that which belongs to the society, and thereafter incorporate whatever foreign material we deem to be relevant and that we deem to be not too destructive to our own ways and means of livelihood in this community.'

(Elikunda Matteru, Assistant Director of Culture, TI 16/04/88)

For many intellectuals, however, modernised ngoma cannot represent development. To them the symbol of development is the Swahili jazz band with its Western instruments like trumpets, saxophones, electric guitars and synthesizers. Many of the employees at Radio Tanzania and the Tanzania Film Company prefer jazz band music to the ngoma. This is also mirrored in the dominance of Swahili jazz in the music output of the radio. In the late 1980s, an increasing share of Radio Tanzania's programming was provided as ready-made sponsored programmes. These sponsors, mainly young businessmen, also prefer modern East African and Western popular music to more traditional kinds of music.

A constant problem for the jazz bands is getting hold of instruments. With the exception of a few simple guitars at a factory in Moshi in northern Tanzania, Western instruments are not manufactured in Tanzania. This means that all instruments have to be imported and paid for with hard currency. No musicians can do this on their own. This partly explains the system referred to earlier whereby trade unions, government parastatals and some private club owners buy instruments and then employ the musicians. Since the musicians do not own their instruments, they become very dependent on the management of the body that controls them.

Since only a trickle of new instruments found their way into Tanzania during the 1980s, young musicians who do not wish to go into traditional ngoma encounter considerable problems. But in spite of the difficulties, young aspiring musicians tend to be very confident. Justine Kalikawe is the leader of Black Systems Youth, a group of young musicians trying to play their own kind of reggae music with home-made instruments. We interviewed him at their open-air 'rehearsal venue', a school sports ground in Dar es Salaam:

> 'The main difficulty here is instruments. You can see our instruments here. They are poor. . . . We need somebody to sponsor us. The kind of music we play is to spread. This is reggae music and most people of Africa they like the pop music world so it would be easy for us to get to the top very soon. We have to establish a group like this one. There is no band in this town that would take us up. This is the only way we could play music [i.e. outdoors in the sports ground].'
>
> (Kalikawe, TI 13/04/88)

The recognized power of music and dance to convey messages also encourages the authorities to attempt to control music. Together with the musicians' dependency on government sponsorship and very few media channels, such things limit the freedom of the individual musician. This, however, tends to be the case in most African countries; the musicians are aware of the fact that their difficulties are not a uniquely Tanzanian problem. Michael Okema, jazz band musician and Lecturer in Political Science at the Dar es Salaam University, sums up the views of the musicians:

> 'There is no concerted effort to aid popular music in this country. And this is not because people have sat down and decided not to aid music, but a question of priorities. You need to buy this, you need to buy that. Along all this line where does the popular music come in as far as equipment is concerned? They don't give it the weight you and I would have liked. The end product is that musicians are used a lot with a minimum of input into the industry. Minimum of input, maximum of output. Although musicians are more tolerated here than in other areas. Well, let's say in Zaire, the President is so involved with the musicians and buys instruments for them, but also crimes by musicians are very heavily punished. If a musician sings something he shouldn't sing in Zaire it's a very serious offence because of the sensitivity of music. But in Tanzania there is more leeway. The only thing they could ever do is to ban your song from being played on radio. For example, one very interesting case happened last year. They refused to record a certain band on radio because they said their song was not interesting. The band complained and the song was published in the newspaper and they said this is what has been refused. Is this something unclean?
> There was another one in 1983. This song was banned. . . . First it was recorded and it came out and it was very popular. It is "Bomwa tota yenga kechua". It means "Destroy, we will rebuild tomorrow". That

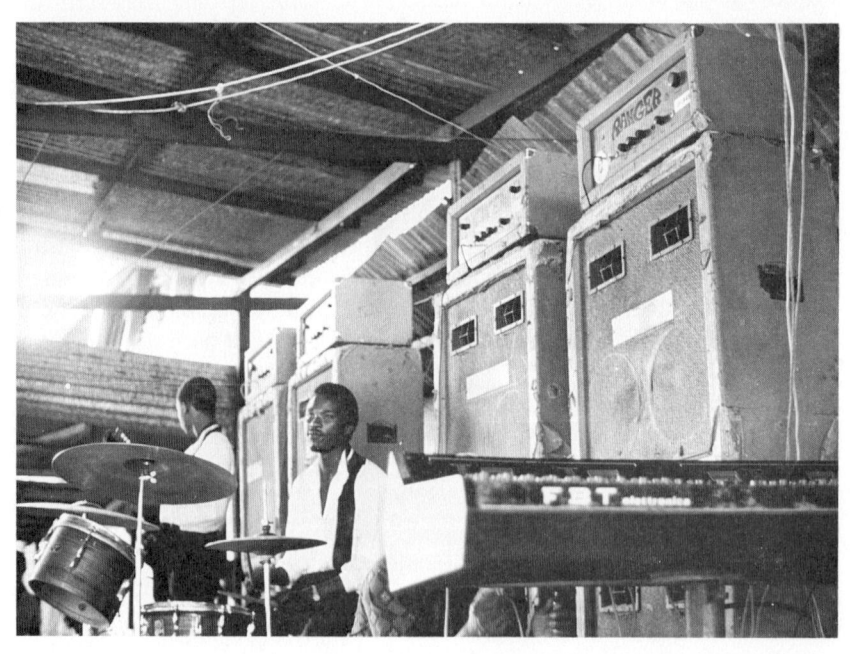

Plate 6.4 The Tanzanites playing at Dar es Salaam's biggest hotel have fairly modern synthesizers. Many other jazz bands have to make do with amplifiers that are almost antique.

Plate 6.5 The Black Systems Youth at their open-air rehearsal venue, a sports ground in Dar es Salaam.

could be interpreted in many ways. It shocked the politicians. They thought that this was a song preaching revolution, but what the musicians was saying was "If you have money let's spend it. We'll make money tomorrow." The youth wing of the party intervened so the song was banned from the radio. But the band was not banned or punished in any other way. In Tanzania the punishments are rather small. But later on the song was re-allowed and it plays again on radio.'

(Okema, TI 12/04/88)

Most Swahili jazz musicians consider their status to be low in Tanzanian society:

'The average Tanzanian they don't much appreciate culture. They just look down on that. They probably think you don't do something that could benefit the rest of the people or anything. But anyway we try hard to make them understand that we are also part and parcel of the society.'

(George Kapinga of the group Tanzanites, TI 16/04/88)

The Government Director of Culture, Godwin Kaduma, clearly recognizes the importance of creative artists. His attitude could point to improvements for the musicians in the 1990s:

'I think our main concern is laying a policy that is going to make it absolutely necessary for decision-makers to recognize the importance of culture in general and the importance of the various aspects of culture. I think that we have been looking at culture in a rather upside-down pyramid view. The artist will always be there whether there is a government or not, whether there is a party or not. To an extent the society in general will be contributing to what the artist does, is going to be inspiring the artist, but to another extent the artist is always going to remain the spokesman of the society. To an extent therefore we should leave the artist and give him enough room and ability to decide what he should do, how he should develop. We should try and give him all the possible facilities to develop and grow. But somehow we have been tending to look at culture and arts as something that can be dictated by government and authority. In doing so we have actually dwarfed artistic development. So any policy that is going to be layed down must accept and respect that the artist is there and will always be there.'

(Kaduma, TI 16/04/88)

THE INTERACTION OF MEDIA MUSIC POLICY AND LOCAL MUSIC ACTIVITIES

As Tanzania enters the 1990s, the music media environment consists mainly of broadcasts from Radio Tanzania and a limited number of audio cassettes. There is no terrestrial and virtually no satellite TV, no music video clips. Tanzania has no sophisticated recording studios, no means of pressing discs or mass-copying cassettes. The TFC studio in Dar es Salaam was built in the late 1970s with funds and know-how from Denmark; a lack of spare parts and expertise rendered it virtually unusable as the 1980s progressed. For a short period around 1980, the TFC engaged in a co-operation agreement with CBS Records. CBS released a number of singles from master tapes recorded in Tanzania (e.g. 'Kaka Adam' by the trade-union sponsored Juwata Jazz Band on S-CBS(K)005). TFC cancelled the agreement because of suspicions that CBS were selling Tanzanian music in South Africa.

A fair generalization is that developments in the Tanzanian music media scene during the 1980s have been minimal compared to what has happened in most other countries. MTV is not available in urban areas; there is no sign of a deregulation of radio allowing new commercial entrepreneurs to enter the market. Still the media, and sometimes the lack of media, have had a marked impact on the Tanzanian music scene.

The promotion of the modernized ngoma in radio broadcasts has certainly had the intended effect of spreading a national music style. It seems that radio broadcasts have been very significant for the interaction between the traditional ngoma and the new styles of ngoma in the towns. S. F. Kamba of the Music Department at the Dar es Salaam University describes this interaction:

> 'They've got a programme four or five times a week: "The Music of our Country". It broadcasts the music of the ngoma groups in the villages or those in town. This has influenced the formation of groups. . . .
>
> The things that are broadcast here that have originated in the urban area, it changes things when it gets back to the villages again. For example if somebody just takes a song from the village it is sung in indigenous language. It comes here. It is given new words in Swahili with maybe a political message. Then it is broadcast and gets back to the village. Then the villagers sing the old song with the new words.'
>
> (Kamba, TI 12/04/88)

From 1985 onwards, there has been a rapid growth of what could be called commercial ngoma groups in the towns. They put on a variety show with music, dance and drama to a paying audience in a fenced-in yard or drinking place. Their performances are influenced by radio broadcasts and what can be seen in cinemas and on video. The lack of TV as a medium has surely contributed to the rapidly growing popularity of these ngoma performances. They constitute a kind of 'folk medium'.

> 'Families go to the places where dancing is taking place. Saturdays and even during the weekdays you see whole families moving out of their

Plate 6.6 Ngoma shows are enjoying more and more popularity in a Tanzania without television

homes with their children, some mothers will be nursing their children right there watching. . . . The performances are putting families together. You can say that going to traditional dances is much cheaper than going to the cinema. But one tries to watch the children in the streets afterwards who pick up cans and pieces of metal pipes, and sometimes get hold of drums starting to do their own performances, giving themselves names of the famous dancers and actors, taking pride in what they've seen and what they're doing. I think the artists are managing to bring a new, or revive an awareness of pride and deeper participation in cultural life to quite a lot of people.'

(Kaduma, TI 16/04/88)

The all-Tanzanian music policy of Radio Tanzania has given a promotion boost to Tanzanian bands creating a buoyant music scene. This policy was so successful that Radio Tanzania had became a very popular station even in neighbouring countries by the early 1970s. This has certainly contributed to the strong position that Tanzanian jazz bands have enjoyed on the music scene in neighbouring Kenya. It also contributed to the various attempts of the Kenyan government to try to make the Voice of Kenya play more local music, attempts which did not work probably because the VoK, unlike Radio Tanzania, did not have its own recorded library of domestic music.

The popularity of Tanzanian jazz music has also made it possible for Tanzanian bands to get records recorded and released in Kenya, in the absence of a local phonogram industry in Tanzania. The story of records with Tanzanian bands released in Kenya involves many rip-offs, master tapes getting stolen from Radio Tanzania, etc. Even so, such activities have meant that Tanzanian Swahili jazz has received at least a limited international exposure.

In Tanzania itself the lack of even a rudimentary phonogram industry has left the phonogram market to the pirates. These pirates sell cassettes with international and Tanzanian music to private customers but also to the growing number of small discotheques. The discotheque operators seem to prefer international hit list music. One reason for this could be the poor sound quality of local recordings with Tanzanian music. There has been some concern in the political establishment about the music of the discotheques – but there has been no attempt at censorship.

> 'This is another problem. We don't have a phonogram industry here or even cassettes so there is a lot of things to solve. We must have our songs on cassettes or discs. When you say "stop playing foreign music in the discos" you must be able to offer them your own music also.'
>
> (M. F. Farahani, Secretary of the Musicians' Union, TI 12/04/88)

Even if the Tanzanian government establishes a functioning phonogram production facility there is little hope that this would contribute significantly to the financial state of the Tanzanian music scene. It would be very hard to curb the activities of the pirates and there is no system for collecting copyright dues. In spite of the lively music scene in Tanzania during the 1970s and 1980s, many Tanzanian musicians and media people express a pessimistic view of the future. But some also express their hope for a solution in the form of fairer international music policies:

> 'There are certain trends, and these trends are determined by the international environment. You try to think of the world as a market, everybody sensing what he can sense. Is it the best – that is, the one that is going to sell? I think the developed world has the sophistication to market their goods. We are going to have more from them. . . . This is what is going to happen. There is nobody who is going to decide against it really. Not a long time ago the politicians would have tried to keep the African culture pure, to keep it healthy. It has always failed. Because with a bit of more technological sophistication certain parts of the world will be favoured.
>
> When it comes to African culture it is going to be promoted but Africans are not going to gain from it. Why? For example, I make a record and I send this to Sweden. Somebody is going to make discs or

cassettes from it. He's a businessman. He's going to sell it back to Tanzania. He'll make the money which he keeps in Sweden. I may gain personally because the contract will maybe give me a car or a house. But this has nothing to do with the general society. You have to do it to so many people before it begins to have an impact on the society. So African culture will be promoted, and you know this better than I do, because in Europe now there is this craze for African music. This will make a lot of money. To that extent African culture will be promoted but it will not be promoted in a way that would boost music here. What will boost music here is again countries like Sweden, Denmark which make up a deliberate policy to help through SIDA or DANIDA [Sweden and Denmark's international aid agencies]. It is not going to come directly from music itself but is going to come from some charitable attitude. It is not going to be done at the level of the market. It's going to be done at the level of deliberate policy.'

(Michael Okema, TI 12/04/88)

Chapter 7
Case Study: Cymru – Wales

THE MEDIA ENVIRONMENT FOR A MINORITY CULTURE

Approximately one-fifth of the 3 million inhabitants of the Principality of Wales speak or have a working knowledge of the Celtic language. Wales, or Cymru, provides a fascinating example of the interaction between modern media and a minority culture. The success of enthusiasts of Welsh culture, language and political nationalism, has not been limited solely to campaigns for bilingual road signs (one of the first cultural statements a visitor to Wales observes). A local phonogram industry has survived almost three decades of commercial and cultural ups and downs. FM Radio (Radio Cymru) since 1979, and the S4C TV channel (1982) are also firmly established local media; both can be seen in terms of British government response to pressure, not so much from militant nationalists, but rather from an intellectual elite demanding media access in the interests of the survival of their own culture. A common denominator in these media is the use of the Welsh language. Music with Welsh lyrics plays an important role in such a media environment (Wallis and Malm 1983: 77–105; 1984: 139–43), not least because of the sheer volume of competition from national UK media emanating from London and other external sources.

With the exception of signals coming in from abroad, the parameters for all broadcasting in Wales are set by the British government via the Home Office in London. Specific radio services for Wales as a whole are organized by the BBC from its headquarters in Cardiff. BBC regional studios in Swansea and Bangor and three commercial companies provide more localized services.

Welsh national broadcasters frequently express dissatisfaction over allocated transmitting resources and frequencies. Welsh-language services, exclusively on FM, are more or less inaudible in some mountainous areas where over 80 per cent of the population are Welsh-speakers. In typical Welsh fashion, broadcasters tend somewhat despondently to dismiss their difficulties as ironic facts of life related to technical limitations of the resources that have been made available to them (an attitude which should not, however, be misconstrued as a sign of an inferiority complex).

> 'You can recognize a Radio Cymru listener by the number of dents on his car. He spends so much time changing frequencies and getting a stiff neck . . . there are pockets where you can't hear us at all; FM waves refuse to go up and down mountains.'
> (Lyn Jones, Programme Director, Radio Cymru, TI 21/09/89)

Reception of Radio Wales, an English-language service for Wales on AM Medium Waves has also not received the same priority as that of the four national British BBC radio channels:

> 'There have been central political decisions about the allocation of English-language frequencies in Wales. London has always made quite sure that network signals have been better received and more properly received in Wales before allowing us to go our own way. So the Radio 4 signal [the British speech channel] on Long Waves is guaranteed to reach a far greater audience that our own signal on Medium Waves.'
> (Dewi Smith, Senior Producer, Radio Wales, TI 21/09/89)

Reception problems have encouraged radio listeners to seek other alternatives. Along the coast strong signals coming over the water from Ireland have found Welsh listeners. In 1989, commercial interests in Ireland, with backing from Radio Luxembourg, opened up Radio Atlantic 252 (252 kHz, Long Waves). Atlanta uses a Long Wave frequency allocated to the Republic of Ireland to beam non-stop pop with a 'never more than 90 seconds away from music' chart format into western Wales and north-west England. After a massive advertising campaign, and despite its mono Long Wave signal, Atlantic 252 has won a considerable following amongst younger listeners in its target area, particularly in north-west Wales where youth unemployment is high and there is no competition from any local commercial radio station.

The division of the former BBC Welsh Home Service into a Medium Wave service (Radio Wales) and an FM all-Welsh channel (Radio Cymru) took place in 1979. Previously some Welsh programmes had been included in the former Welsh Home service output. But a growing amount of pressure from lobbying groups enjoying support from the intellectual elite forced a change. Activists in the Welsh Nationalist political party (Plaid Cymru) and the Welsh Language Society (Cymdeithas Yr Iaith Gymraeg) demanded more Welsh-language content in the broadcasting media (Williams 1977; 1982: 145–202). The campaign included some militant actions such as prominent cultural personalities climbing up BBC transmitter masts.

The extraordinary media developments that took place in Wales during the 1970s and early 1980s encompassed not only radio but also the local phonogram industry – notably the growth of the SAIN company (Wallis and Malm 1984: 88–9), and, by and by, the emergence of S4C TV.

> 'The coming of SAIN came at the same time as Radio Cymru. The protests of the Sixties led to new establishments. . . . It was a wave of awareness, whether it was nationalism with a small "n", or even with a capital "N", or whether it was an awareness that we had our own culture and identity. Everything seemed more or less to gel at the same time. You can't separate one thing from another. The existence of Radio Cymru was what caused the existence of S4C TV. Without Radio Cymru, I don't think the concept would have ever come up . . . of course there were several Agit Prop pressure groups involved in road-sign campaigns and transmitter attacks. Radio Cymru was partly a result of their pressure; S4C definitely was.'
>
> (Lyn Jones, Radio Cymru, TI 21/09/89)

A hunger strike by a prominent intellectual, Gwynfor Evans, was one of the more spectacular actions heralding the introduction of a Welsh-language TV channel. The administrative procedure was similar to that in radio. Both BBC-TV Wales and the commercial company holding the franchise for Wales, HTV, had been bound to include a certain number of hours of Welsh-language material in their schedules. With the birth of S4C in November 1982, they became suppliers of news and other programmes to a Welsh variant of Britain's Channel 4, i.e. a TV channel with a small central administration commissioning most of its programmes from outside producers and companies. The transfer of the BBC TV's Welsh-language output to S4C was the first instance of programmes from British licence-financed, non-commercial television appearing in the UK on a commercial channel.

The advantage of these developments for the Welsh-speaking community was that both radio and TV programmes could be transmitted at 'prime time', instead of being banished to off-peak spots on the former bilingual channels. A disadvantage might be a risk for 'ghettoization' by removing Welsh-language output from channels which not only the primarily English-speaking majority but even many with a working knowledge of Welsh would tend to watch. S4C have actually tried to minimize the latter risk by adding English subtitles to some Welsh series and music video programmes (and getting an English-speaking audience in the process).

RADIO AND MUSIC POLICY

The English-language service, BBC Radio Wales, is only broadcast on Medium Waves. This naturally amounts to a technical limitation to the styles of music which can be featured. Art music projects within BBC Welsh radio normally involve co-operation with the British national network, Radio 3, which enjoys FM coverage of Wales. These would generally feature the BBC Welsh Symphony Orchestra which is jointly financed by the BBC and the UK-funded Welsh Arts Council.

Radio Wales broadcasts daily approximately twelve hours per day. In the early morning and late at night, BBC Radio 2 (middle-of-the-road format) is used as a sustaining service. In the daytime, however, BBC Radio 2 is Radio Wales's toughest competitor:

> 'In terms of English-language broadcasting, listeners react to what they can hear on adjacent frequencies. We broadcast within one eighth of an inch on the dial from Radio 2. So if there's anything they don't like which we are doing, if it's too narrow, or offensive, then they've got the safety of Radio 2, and they're gone.'
>
> (Dewi Smith, Radio Wales, TI 21/09/89)

Radio Wales's estimated average audience of between 500,000 and three-quarters of a million get a 50/50 music/speech mix. The music policy, as the above quote illustrates, is 'non-offensive' in essence.

> 'It's a policy that aims not to alienate too many listeners. We would hesitate from the crash, bang, wollop of BBC Radio 1 [the BBC national pop/rock channel]. Ideally the music should be recognizable, tuneful and memorable.'
>
> (Smith, TI 21/09/89)

Although our spokesman is what an Englishman would describe as 'typically Welsh' (very proud of his country, traditions and culture), this Senior Producer at Radio Wales is well aware of the risks of including Welsh music in his own channel. The two cultures are so divided:

> 'The music industry is so divided. There's much more activity on the Welsh-language side than on the English side, simply because English-language professional musicians would gravitate towards London, perhaps Birmingham, Manchester [i.e. larger cities across the border in England]. Apart from the other industrially influenced interests of choral singing and brass bands, there's little Anglo-Welsh folk music. Radio Wales doesn't have an interest in linking up with the local recording industry because most of it's in Welsh.
>
> I'd be very careful about how much music with Welsh lyrics I'd introduce into our radio programmes. The majority of our listeners are English-speakers. I would like to generate their respect for Welsh music, but I wouldn't like to alienate them. There's no rule of thumb regarding the limit, but if we use Welsh lyrics I make sure the presenters translate so that the listeners understand the sympathies expressed in the music . . . I don't think there's a lot we can do in terms of [music] policy. We can only create a profile by acknowledging where we live. If

it's a matter of a symphony orchestra concert, I'd look through a list of Welsh conductors before I'd turn to a Belgian or French, as long as I'm *not* compromising standards. . . . as elitist as we might feel inclined to be, we must not allow ouselves to indulge our own tastes too much.'

(Smith, TI 21/09/89)

Radio Wales does get involved in the 'industrially influenced' areas of music activity which are so closely associated with Wales, namely male voice choirs and brass bands. Two competitions for these genres were established in the late 1970s. This was in response to a desire to reflect grass-roots activities that would involve the widest audience. Brass bands and choirs, being community activities involving families and workmates, were seen as a way of 'getting through to the audience'. The competitions are still running even if their character has changed. The BBC Wales Choral Competition is no longer entirely Welsh; participating choirs come from all over the United Kingdom. Brass bands have inevitably been affected by the changing industrial structure of Wales, since they have always been closely aligned to traditional industrial activities such as coal mines or steel works.

'The camaraderie of the coal mine would be reflected in the cultural activity – but industries have gone and the work environment is not the same. It seems that the white-collar workers don't want to blow their instruments in the evening. It's a very strange phenomenon . . . the number of brass bands is going down. But there are still more brass bands in Wales than Rugby Football clubs.'

(Smith, TI 21/09/89)

Betwen fifty and sixty Welsh choirs enter the BBC Wales annual Male Voice Choir Competition; equally as many enter from the rest of the United Kingdom. Around twenty-five Welsh bands enter the brass competition. Several of the recordings made during the adjudication sessions are relayed over the whole of the British Isles on BBC Radio 2, thus according some national status to these traditionally Welsh activities, but also attracting more entrants from outside Wales.

In one respect Radio Cymru is similar to BBC Radio Wales. With its comprehensive brief to offer something for every Welsh-speaker, it becomes important, in the words of Programme Editor Lyn Jones, 'to antagonize as few listeners as possible'. In other respects, Radio Cymru is the exact opposite side of the coin from BBC Radio Wales. Mixing English chart music in a Welsh language programme would create animosity, 'a very hostile reaction', and the Welsh music industry is its main source of music; mutual dependence or informal integration tend towards a maximum. 'If you look at the industry and radio, you see that the one has suckled the other in a way' (Lyn Jones, Editor, Radio Cymru, TI 21/11/89).

Radio Cymru's potential audience amounts to around 600,000 Welsh-speakers plus a fast-growing group of Welsh-learners (estimated at around 80,000–100,000 in 1989). The audience is not evenly spread over Wales. The highest concentration of Welsh-speakers can be found in the most sparsely populated areas of the north. This presents a dilemma; Radio Cymru has to function both as a national service, bridging the gap between the different dialects spoken in the north and the south, whilst also functioning as a local service for certain communities. Listeners also demand a full service from Radio Cymru, for example in the form of world news and correspondents' reports from different parts of the globe in Welsh.

Daytime programming consists of a mix of news, magazine programmes and phone-ins. Music accounts for around 35 per cent of output but tends to decrease as phone-in programmes increase in popularity (the more who phone in, the less time is devoted to music as a filler). The Welsh-only rule is not as sacrosanct as the above statements might suggest. Anglo-American music is frequently heard on Radio Cymru, both in general daytime output and in specialist programmes. The Welshness of Radio Cymru's Country and Western slot is provided by the mode and language of presentation.

Music selection presents problems because of the station's wide demographic and generic brief. From 1980–4, pop, rock and folk music was catered for mainly via a daily late-night magazine programme for a youth audience. During this period, Radio Cymru went off the air during the afternoons. Because of low audience figures (so low as not to appear in audience surveys, i.e. under 1 per cent) the evening programmes were scrapped and the money was used to fill the empty afternoon slot.

> 'The financial argument was overpowering. We needed an audience to give our important news magazine the support it needed between 5 and 6pm. It had become like a pelican in the desert. So we went for the afternoon sequence from 3.30 to 5, and decided it would be music-based. . . . We found five presenters and tried to build programmes around them. It didn't always work. Sometimes they could go from a harp solo to heavy rock music within two minutes – which meant that you lost both audiences very quickly. We lived with this for two years and then it ended.'
>
> (Lyn Jones, TI 21/09/89)

The removal of the evening youth programmes in 1984 met with the disapproval of one of the pressure groups mentioned earlier, the Welsh Language Society. Lyn Jones, who took over the control of Radio Cymru in 1989, recalls that the first protests took place in 1986. Stickers calling for the return of late-night youth programmes were plastered over the BBC stand at the big annual Welsh cultural manifestation, the Eisteddfod.

'To add to the confusion, the Home Office in London created a young people's unit for radio in Northern Ireland. The Welsh kids felt that if Northern Ireland could have it, why shouldn't they. They didn't accept that circumstances were totally different there. Last autumn [1988] they started breaking into BBC studios, sit-down protests and so forth on a Saturday morning in Swansea. At that point I'd already made my position clear. I wanted youth programmes back at night.

I think one must accept that the protests had an effect to the extent that it became an embarrassment to certain sectors of management, as you would in any organization to have your house broken into and people objecting to what you were doing. The Broadcasting Council [a British-government appointed body] had to meet the protesters. Out of that I got an agreement that we would start brand new late-night programmes aimed at a youth group from 13 up to 24-ish.'

(Lyn Jones, TI 21/09/89)

The money came through a devious combination of savings in other areas, partly through internal routines and partly through dividends from farming out certain BBC Television productions to independent contractors (the BBC had been required by the Thatcher government to shift up to 25 per cent in-house production to outside suppliers by 1993). A TV-unit at BBC Wales was about to be privatized and, according to Radio Cymru, 'management persuaded that new independent company to carry as part of their brief, two radio programmes as well. . . . It was a political, er whatever . . . call it a package deal' (Lyn Jones, TI 21/09/89).

One of the problems encountered when reinstating the evening shows was a lack of competent presenters. Radio Cymru's Head of Youth Programmes, Geraint Davies, explained:

'If music content is to be credible at all, it has to match the personality of the person who is hosting the show. There's no point in coming up with a grand concept and putting a cardboard cut-out in front of it – it won't work.

In the Sixties there were many more Welsh-language discos. There weren't any bands and the Welsh pop scene evolved from discos. As groups have grown, the need for DJs has dropped. Those that have left have mainly found their way into the media anyway. At the moment we're training new people.'

(G. Davies, TI 21/09/89)

The new series was introduced in October 1989. The nightly broadcasts follow a Welsh-language lesson and last from 10.15pm to 11.30pm. By October, 1991, audience figures were 'measurable', i.e. in the region of 2 per cent, regarded as a considerable success in a small minority world.

Co-operation between different sectors of the small Welsh-language music industry, as one might expect, is intimate almost to the point of incest, an aspect Radio Cymru staff are only too aware of:

'Any record release of any minimal standard, be it a disc, cassette, whatever, is likely to get airplay; because it's there, it's new, it's something else to play. We have the reverse problem to a BBC Radio 1 type of set-up where they are getting flooded with stuff every day and are having to make artistic, policy and editorial decisions all the time.'
(G. Davies, TI 21/09/89)

The net result is that the major company of twenty years' standing, SAIN, get airplay on virtually everything they produce. Radio plays mean extra income for SAIN since Britain is a signatory to the Rome Convention. This is one of two ways in which Radio Cymru has an initiating role. Radio Cymru also commissions and records music; the tapes are then sold for a nominal fee to the artists or groups concerned, who can then release their own discs. Production amounts to around fifteen such sessions a year (where three or four numbers would be recorded).

Plate 7.1 'Trying to reflect the audience': a Radio Cymru outside broadcast unit preparing for a Saturday morning live transmission from the Town Square in Caernarfon, North Wales.

'Radio must reflect the audience. We also want to initiate, for example by helping young groups who haven't recorded. Sometimes we promote young groups, not so much for the record, but more for the promoters arranging gigs who might say: that's not a bad group. We always announce their contact numbers, addresses – by doing that you start pushing that group around different areas. We accept that that's part and parcel of our creative element. But there is a dilemma. There are two coins – both of which have flip sides. There's the tightrope element – the line between reflecting and initiating. If we initiate too much, it becomes almost a state industry. It can become incestuous.

The other worry in the back of my head is that we could end up, given the amount of material available . . . by playing the stuff too often. If there's too little music available, then there's no need for people to go and buy the record. They're hearing it and hearing it until they're fed up, which means the reverse. No-one knows where the limit goes.'

(G. Davies, TI 21/09/89)

Most musicians and record companies would probably agree with such sentiments regarding the pitfalls that go with increased informal integration between broadcasters and other sectors of the music industry/music scene. SAIN Records founder and manager, Dafydd Iwan, agrees that access to the media in a small market can sometimes be too easy.

'There are school bands, who within a few months of starting find themselves on the radio – and there's nothing left to do! Apathy and disillusion can set in. This is a constant theme with us. It's important to keep people's feet on the ground as regards the commercial viability of Welsh records.'

(Iwan, TI 26/09/89)

Many musicians and record company producers would like to see what they term a 'more enlightened' attitude at the English channel, BBC Radio Wales, one that is less 'London-orientated'. Radio Cymru's initiating role is widely appreciated though viewed with occasional suspicion by groups in the 'post-punk' genre which have emerged from the mid-1980s onwards.

Rhys Mwyn, founder of the Welsh rock group Anhrefn and owner of a small record company with the same name, sees Radio Cymru as an example of media under the control of an establishment not always in touch with new ideas (a common expression of criticism in relationships between newer and older segments of a music culture).

Mwyn: The media like to have one thing in common. They like to say: look we know what's going on. They have great problems when music starts that's outside their control. When we started as a young band they thought we were playing deliberately out of tune, not being musicians as an art form. Radio Cymru wouldn't play us – now they do.

Q: Is that because you've learnt to tune your guitars?

Mwyn: No, because they've changed their attitudes. When bands make records and get an audience and become popular, then eventually the media have no choice but to accept them. It took time for Radio Cymru to realize that teenagers don't want to listen to bands who look like their parents. It's a conspiracy – the media want to control. Welsh culture has always been dominated by religion, schools and middle-class people.'

(TI, 23/09/89)

Such sentiments reflect not only a generation conflict, with the group Anhrefn's musical content and style finding its *raison d'être* partly in a position of opposition to the establishment. Rhys Mwyn's views also mirror a new attitude amongst younger Welsh musicians, one where the focal point is neither Cardiff and the Welsh media centre, nor London and British rule, but a wider concept of minorities in Europe (his group has contacts and exchanges with similar constellations in the Basque country): 'It's not nationalism, it's culturalism and internationalism. Welsh nationalism doesn't seem relevant.' But this same musician also expresses considerable pride about the fact that national UK radio via the Radio 1 BBC pop guru, John Peel, played his recordings before Radio Cymru: 'The change has come with people like John Peel playing records on national UK radio which Radio Cymru banned saying they weren't suitable for daytime airplay' (Mwyn, TI 23/09/89).

An old hand at Welsh nationalism like SAIN's Dafydd Iwan would probably regard any sign of media exposure emerging from London as an attempt at repressive tolerance. Iwan is more cool in his analysis:

'There is a gradual change in the English psyche – they are beginning to be aware of other cultures and languages, 1992 Europe and all that. It could filter through and perhaps be to our advantage.'

(Iwan, TI 26/09/89)

The early 1980s saw one of the more unusual experiments in British local commercial radio coming and going in the Welsh capital, Cardiff. A number of local community interests combined to form the Cardiff Community Trust and applied for the first commercial radio franchise in the city. Unlike most other commercial franchises in Britain, the Cardiff licence was not won by a consortium of local business interests and national media personalities. A stencil from the Trust distributed in August of 1980 declared that:

When Cardiff Broadcasting won the franchise, it startled those of us who had initiated the project because for once, we felt, our voices had been heard and we had challenged the status quo by defeating the obvious favourites. A different 'voice' had been heard in two different aspects. Firstly, we were not representative of solely commercial interests and were not drawn from the well-marked lines of the 'establishment' in terms of media, business and political backgrounds – the traditional recruiting ground for hand-picked ILR [local commercial radio] Consortia. Secondly, public debate and discussion had formed the basis of our application and a democratic element had been written into the structure which enabled potential listeners to Cardiff ILR to elect half the Board of the Broadcasting Company and the Council of Management of Cardiff Trust which would own 50 per cent of the shares of the company.

(Hutt 1980)

The experiment was regarded as a unique case of deregulation allowing community interests access to the media. The emphasis was to be not so much on music, but on speech and news content. Indeed, little can be discerned from the Cardiff Trust's application regarding music policy. The Trust's charter ratified in 1979 called for a 'non-profit distributing legal form'. This attempt, however, to combine a plurality of community interests with the business realities of local commercial radio failed.

In 1986, the company was amalgamated with a nearby commercial station (taken over is probably the correct term) and became Red Dragon Radio. The Community Trust lost its veto on programmes and policy. An epitaph for the experiment from the new Managing Director quoted in the local paper read:

The community venture was not commercial and it was a recipe for disaster from day one. We will not hesitate to be as commercial as necessary. We have, however, invited two directors from the Trust to be on the Board. I see their role as advisory without the veto they used to have. . . . I am pleased that they have accepted their role.

(*Western Mail*, 14 Oct. 1986)

In the same article, the station's new Programme Director promised that 'the music policy will be very much more chart-orientated than at present'. Shortly afterwards, Red Dragon began transmitting two different programmes by splitting its AM and FM frequencies; Red Dragon FM plays mainly chart music and the AM outlet 'Touch AM' provides an unoriginal standard fare of Golden Oldies. In contrast to the former CBC set-up, Red Dragon carries virtually no Welsh-language/music output.

Marcher Sound in Wrexham (in the north-east, near to the English border) has a similar set up to Red Dragon. The third commercial station, Swansea Sound, is situated about 60 miles west of Cardiff and covers a large area of south-west Wales.

Rules requiring a certain minimum Welsh-language content were included in the promises all three commercial stations originally made when bidding for their franchises. With the replacement of the IBA regulatory body with a new Radio Authority in 1989, such rules were relaxed. With the exception of Radio Swansea, amounts of Welsh music are small and such programme slots usually get banished to what the cynics would term the 'graveyard slots', between 6.30 and 8.30pm when the majority of listeners either turn to television or do something entirely different. BBC staff tend to dismiss the ILR stations' Welsh music activity as 'a token gesture': 'Management [at these stations] have written off that time. Presenters might get paid £5 to come in if they get paid at all. It's a private ego-booster, the next step up from hospital radio' (Jones, Radio Cymru, TI 21/09/89).

That Welsh presenters at the local commercial stations get paid a pittance for a token gesture is also the opinion of the phonogram company Fflach in Cardigan. Cardigan is some 80 miles from Swansea but within Radio Swansea's signal area. Welsh music, however, even at off-peak times on a local station does allow interested listeners to discover more new sounds, and results in phonogram sales, according to Fflach. In late 1991, Swansea Sound was still broadcasting solely in Welsh (i.e. on both AM and FM frequencies) about two hours between 6.30 and 9pm from Sunday through to Friday. On the other hand, all those who worked with these programmes were 'contract' employees and not on the staff of the station. The management were also toying with the idea of cancelling Welsh news bulletins within these segments.

In the early 1980s, local commercial stations were also required to invest 3 per cent of their advertising revenue in live music recordings. In Wales, this usually resulted in far more choirs getting taped than pop or rock groups, simply because of cost-efficiency considerations. These rules waned as the 1980s proceeded and the power of the British Musicians' Union to impose needle-time restrictions on the use of commercial recordings decreased. Once again, the deregulatory policies of the then Conservative government, embodied in the creation of a new Radio Authority, served to decrease further the significance of such content regulations.

TELEVISION IN WALES: THE S4C EXPERIMENT

> 'If we, in ten years' time have got a little model for all minority cultures throughout the world, I'll be thrilled to bits. That should be the goal!'
> (Euryn Ogwen Williams, S4C's first Programme Director, interviewed in July 1981, a year before the new Welsh-language channel went on air)

Most TV viewers in Wales have access to five terrestrial channels, i.e. one more than in the rest of the UK. BBC1 offers general fare whilst BBC2 is slightly more specialist. HTV runs the main independent (ITV) commercial channel. Channel 4 UK can be received in many parts of southern and western Wales. S4C (Sianel Pedwar Cymru) is the Welsh alternative which emerged in 1982 in response to a combination of political considerations in London and a flood of demands and protests in the Principality.

Britain is one of the least-cabled territories in the world (Roe and Wallis 1989: 35–41). An MTV-Europe Programme Director has said that this is because 'the British don't like people digging up their streets' (B. Diamond, TI 14/09/88). There is little cable in Wales, though individual dishes pointing at the Astra satellite are appearing on walls and roofs, allowing reception of the various British Sky Broadcasting channels. They are particularly prevalent in the working-class areas of south Wales.

All the main independent TV franchises in Britain were auctioned off in the autumn of 1991 in line with the Conservative government's broadcasting policy. Even the then incumbents (including HTV in Wales) had to bid for their own franchises. HTV's winning bid inevitably affected its operations, forcing the company to cut down its own facilities base and commission more programming from outside contractors with lower cost structures.

The BBC's funding through the licence fee system is likely to remain until at least 1996. BBC Wales are also bound to deliver 10 hours of Welsh-language programmes/week to S4C, mainly news and sports programmes, financed through BBC licence funding. S4C commission some 6 hours per week from HTV and another 14 on average are provided by scores of smaller independent production companies which have sprung up in the wake of the new channel.

The £50m S4C costs per annum are currently funded by a subsidy from all other commercial TV companies in the UK. This is pegged at 3.4 per cent of net UK advertising revenue and thus follows to a certain extent the fortunes of the British economy. S4C does carry advertising but income is handled by HTV and goes into the total pot (i.e. before the redistribution of the 3.4 per cent grant). The British government has decided that this will change from 1993. S4C will sell its own advertising – currently earning a mere £2m–4m or 4–8 per cent of annual budget – and its deficit will be covered by a grant from the state. This, of course, could mean in reality less independence or even more opportunities for a London government to exert influence over the Welsh channel, should it so wish.

S4C's main target audience for its Welsh programmes is roughly the same as that of Radio Cymru (600,000 plus 100,000 Welsh learners). S4C also wants to reach English speakers with Welsh-language output and does this by adding subtitles to Welsh series, mixing world-music videos in programmes with Welsh-language popular music, etc. 'A million viewers by the year 2000' has been one brave, commonly stated, goal for the channel. Outside the Welsh prime-time segment, S4C also transmits 70 hours of English TV weekly, all rescheduled from the UK Channel 4.

Views about S4C's significance vary depending on whom one interviews. Some see it as a political gesture from London intended to defuse militant elements in Wales:

> 'S4C channels young middle-class people into jobs so that they can stay in Wales and do things they find interesting and stimulating. If S4C wasn't there, a heck of a lot of jobs would disappear, leaving a lot of disaffected young people who can't find creative jobs. It's a very subtle argument but the government aren't stupid. They realize that S4C keeps many potential young Welsh militants in good jobs, keeping them quiet. Thus, politically, it would be a disaster for any British government to get rid of S4C.'
>
> (Independent Producer, Cardiff, TI 22/09/89)

Another S4C employee put this view even more succinctly with an Irish allusion: 'S4C is cheaper than a Chieftain tank'.

S4C certainly has created employment in parts of Wales where jobs have been few and far between. Huw Jones, former founder of SAIN Records with Dafydd Iwan, is co-owner of the video facility/production company Teledu'r Tir Glas in Caernarfon, North Wales. He estimates that: 'S4C has created around 400 jobs in North Wales. Another 400 have been also created indirectly in ancillary services such as catering and transport' (Jones, TI 20/11/91).

Providing opportunities in the media could also deprive other professions of much-needed human resources: for example, teaching. Euryn Ogwen Williams, Programme Director at S4C for the first eight years is aware of the risks of the media attracting resources which might be needed elsewhere:

> 'You do get a problem when other essential bits of the scene are left denuded. The money paid in TV makes it more attractive than teaching. So you lose particularly primary school teachers who are the very people who are going to make sure that the children of immigrants coming to Wales speak Welsh. The size of the Welsh community is on the margin of being viable – not just commercially, but also in terms of talent. There's a point, and this is where the Gaels in Scotland have a problem, a point where you cannot produce talent of a sufficiently high quality to please enough of the audience, because there are so many things to do in a culture like this. If you are going for a professional culture as well, you need to nurture the talent over a long period of time. And we probably need to target at least a 50 per cent increase in the number of people who will appreciate Welsh-language programming.'
>
> (Williams, TI 27/09/89)

The maximum audiences recorded so far for S4C are in the region of 200,000 viewers (sports and certain series). Popular music programmes attract smaller audiences of between 40,000 and 60,000. The future is viewed with cautious optimism. The fact that the channel could start from scratch without having a historic organizational legacy is seen as a competitive advantage by the station's first Programme Director:

> 'We've been very lucky. We're about the only people who have been lucky to have a Thatcherite government when we've been growing up – it hurts me to say that – in the sense that it gave us a very clear and easy brief to follow. We had to create a structure that would be the structure of broadcasting in the 1990s. If you start up in the 1980s that's not difficult. If you started back in the 1960s that would have been impossible since you've taken on staff on a permanent basis, when structures and high employment was the measure of success. That measure has changed to efficiency and cost effectiveness – that has helped us. Of our 50 million pounds, less than 10 per cent is spent on running the show, and that includes training as well.'
>
> (Williams, TI 27/09/89)

Critics have complained that S4C is the most expensive channel in the world. This postulate is based on the premise that S4C only tries to reach Welsh-speakers, something S4C would refute. Assuming that the whole of Wales is there as a potential audience, then the average per capita figure becomes lower than the equivalent for commercial television as a whole in the UK. In 1989, the SKY satellite television service beamed at Britain was making a net annual loss equal to twice S4C's annual budget (Wallis and Baran 1990: 112).

Another valid point is that virtually everything on S4C is home-made, since the channel cannot import English-language programmes. Output thus amounts to around 1,000 hours per annum, which includes ten feature films. The management proudly claim that 'we enrich the European cultural scene by being there'.

MUSIC POLICY ON S4C

> 'It's very *ad hoc*. I don't think they have a particular policy. They have to cover a huge range of audiences and variety of tastes.'
>
> (Video producer in Cardiff, TI 22/09/89)

'S4C may have a policy – it's not clear what it is. It's too conservative anyway, which makes them less attractive to young people. Production tends to be very static with the audience neatly sitting in rows. Instead of becoming more adventurous, they've become more static.

In the early days of S4C you could get a series of folk music artists filmed in a pub with drinking, smoking and talking going on. Adventurous camera work was edited to a programme afterwards. That was early on.'

(Iwan, SAIN, TI 26/09/89)

S4C have the same problems as Radio Cymru when formulating music policy. They believe they have to put on a programme which will appeal to every part of the audience. It is assumed that older people want hymn singing and a soap opera on Sunday afternoons. Others might still want the soap but also underground music or a risqué comedy.

Interviewed in 1989, Euryn Ogwen Williams concluded that S4C had generally made a mess of its music policy (which he maintained had never really got past the stage of being a loose strategy). The euphoria of the early 1980s with the achievements of national Welsh radio and TV led those working in the TV media to assume everything would be both static and simple:

'We began at the back end of quite a successful period of indigenous musicmaking, at the end of the 1970s when people had a reason for making music, a lot of it because they were lacking the TV channel they needed.

Because it was there, we actually botched it up. We didn't see the fact that our existence would change the nature of the music that was there. . . . I missed reading the signs – there was a breaking-up of the consensus. Particularly young people were moving into different areas. All of a sudden the market wasn't there. We carried on for too long trading on the idea that you could just stick a group in the studio and they bashed out and everyone would buy their records. We missed what what was happening at the grass roots – you were getting a break-up of the consensus that had kept the scene going, a scene which partly existed because TV *wasn't* there. We even went through a period in 1983–4 when we were putting out groups that were created to go on television. They had no real basis in society. We were filling up the hours with overnight groups who couldn't do a gig or fill a hall any more. What we did – and it was a very deliberate policy – we stopped putting out any young people's popular pop programmes for a whole year, to create aggravation. A lot of people wrote in. It worked.'

(Williams, TI 27/09/89)

The development described here coincided with the decision of Radio Cymru to drop its evening youth music programmes, but the two were probably not co-ordinated. The Welsh Language Society directed its attention towards both the radio and the TV channels, agitating for more Welsh pop music programmes.

Some four years later, music programmes for a youth audience were put back on again (as at Radio Cymru). This time the policy was to reflect what bands were doing, where they were doing it, rather than by bringing them into studios. An independent production company in Cardiff, Criw Byw, was commissioned to produce weekly music video programmes, 'Fideo 9'. The horizon was also widened as part of a policy to 'define ourselves as outside a British or American culture but still be viable'. This involved taking advantage of the current interest in world music and mixing Welsh videos with some international material ('trying to reflect what's going on not only here but in Europe, Russia or anywhere' as Commissioning Editor Mari Owen put it).

The production company, Criw Byw seemed to agree with this assessment:

'There are about a hundred bands in Wales singing in Welsh. Of these, about thirty to forty play regularly. That's far more than ten years ago. Then you only had a few big bands. Now it tends to be smaller venues with more groups playing. It's harder to fill a stadium with a thousand but there's more activity. When we've done live things on "Fideo 9", we've tried to arrange smaller venues instead of large concerts with five cameras, which is a bit artificial. Instead we go to smaller events with a very simple three-camera set-up. The natural audience are there and we don't promote it as a sort of media-television gig.'

(Gethin Scourfield, Criw Byw, TI 22/09/89)

Criw Byw have also been close to the move to extend horizons beyond Cardiff or London. Welsh groups have been filmed in the Basque country in Spain, in Prague, etc.

'The side-stepping of the Anglo-American Top 10 market allows groups from Wales to be popular in Germany or Spain. It might be exotic in a sense, but people are coming more open to the thought of listening to singing in languages other than English. They don't understand the words but they can listen and feel the emotion of the song.'

(Scourfield, TI 27/09/89)

This development in its turn has had an initiating effect on S4C, encouraging the channel to try to sell commissioned material of Welsh groups performing outside Wales to the BBC for viewing all over the UK on BBC2. These attempts have succeeded and have had the same type of status-boosting effect as the exposure mentioned above that John Peel has given to certain Welsh bands by featuring them on both BBC national radio and the BBC World Service. These are significant examples of how status on a national level can be strengthened through a bilateral exchange and international publicity. Both exposure on British national radio or TV networks and appreciation in other European contexts (other nationalities/ cultures) has the effect of strengthening Welsh cultural identity, even if the angry young post-punkers hate the Welsh 'Establishment' that has done so much to create that same identity.

Welsh pop/rock programmes account, of course, for a fairly small percentage of total output on S4C. Middle-of-the-road shows featuring tenors such as the singing farmer, Trebor Edwards, are also featured. The older age group of Welsh speakers are important in size; they get their much-appreciated hymns on each Sunday. These are accompanied by subtitles in Welsh so the whole thing becomes a grand sing-along.

S4C adheres to the principle of massive block coverage (rather like CNN at world summits) of certain major cultural events. The most spectacular is the annual Welsh Eisteddfod, held during the first week of August alternately in North and South Wales.

> 'We broadcasters question that – the people don't. It's a service – it's wallpaper for 90 per cent of the time and then 10 per cent will be really exciting. But you wouldn't get the 10 per cent if you weren't doing the 90.'
>
> (Williams, TI 27/09/89)

Other such events which are based mainly on musical activity are the Youth Eisteddfod, held in June, and events such as the traditional Penillion Festival, featuring a style of folk music where a singer is accompanied by a harpist, held on a Saturday each November. S4C goes live for hours and hours on such occasions; there is no evidence to suggest that this is not appreciated by the audience at large. Culturally, one can argue that such a mode of media attention is vital, since it involves a commitment to a basically amateur culture which does not always translate terribly well to the demands of a slick, high-tempo mode of television.

The demand for home-grown programme concepts has been an important stimulus for producers to present new ideas, especially where they are related to Welsh cultural traditions. The combination of the licence-financed BBC providing a fixed number of hours of programming to a subsidized S4C with advertisements, has resulted in some interesting experiments and changes of attitudes at BBC Television in Cardiff. Most noticeable is a new approach to folk music at the predominantly classical BBC Music Department. A documentary was made in 1988 of a South American tour by the Welsh folk group Ar Log; versions were made in both English and Welsh and were shown both on S4C and for the whole of Britain. Another folk project was a variant of the popular BBC2 'Antiques Road Show', where a TV team visit different towns or villages and invite people to bring out possessions and have them identified, dated and valued. The Welsh variant involved going round villages getting people to expose aspects of folk music, folk lore or folk life in general. As folk music enthusiast and Bangor University Lecturer, Lyn Thomas, noted:

Plate 7.2 Meeting your target group – the SAIN stall at the annual Eisteddfod.

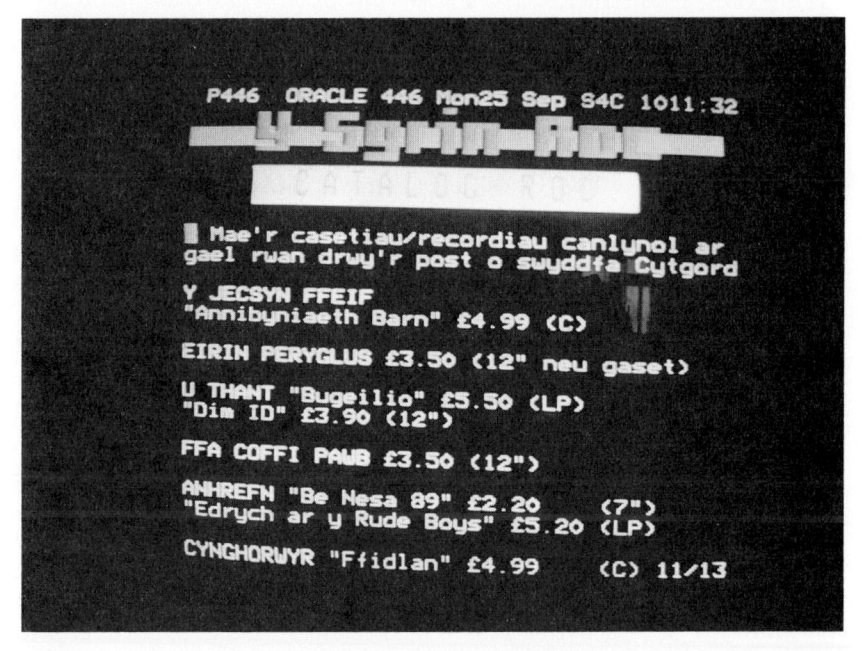

Plate 7.3 Latest communication technology spreading local music industry information. A Teletext page with record prices from Cytgord.

'People bring out traditional instruments, for instance a triple harp that had literally been kept in an attic for centuries. It hadn't been restored and was actually in a house that had belonged to a revival minister who would usually have told people to burn their harps.'
(Thomas, TI 25/09/89)

Thomas was the first lecturer to be appointed to teach aspects of Welsh music at a university level. He considers that S4C has a considerable capacity for bringing regional traditions to the eyes and ears of the whole of Wales, without such media popularization necessarily having the detrimental effect many purists might fear:

'Concerts can be arranged which bring a local community together but which can produce material which can be of worth for the whole of Wales – things which would not have been produced for television previously. For instance, Christmas carolling in north-east Wales, a form which is very regional. Such traditions are so deeply rooted that they would stay regional and not be affected by TV deciding new norms.

It gives an opportunity for Welsh people to appreciate if not adopt – otherwise things like this would be reserved for the Folk Museum and a few enthusiasts. People are becoming more aware of aspects of Welsh life in general and of music in particular.'
(Thomas, TI 25/09/89)

Even some of the latest communications technology is used to spread music information via S4C. The Teletext system includes a number of Welsh-language pages in Wales; information is commissioned from different suppliers. In the late 1980s, a section was added with rock and pop music news, aiming at a youth audience. The information was co-ordinated and updated by Cytgord. Cytgord is based in the small, slate-mining town of Bethesda in North Wales and functions as a combined rock news agency/magazine publisher ('Sothach' or Rubbish) and record distributor.

Cytgord maintain that teletext is more common in Wales than in the rest of the UK because lower incomes/high unemployment lead to more viewers renting than buying TV sets (teletext being offered as an added attraction). From their little office in the winding main street of Bethesda, these young enthusiasts could update their own pages daily using a PC and dedicated telephone lines. The pages included data about Welsh clubs, pending gigs, rock news and details of their mail order record and cassette distribution service. The service always lived a fragile existence, competing with S4C programme-making funds. In 1990, Cytgord lost the contract to a competitor in Aberystwyth (West Wales) but managed to survive through a combination of research contracts for a number of BBC programmes and subscriptions for their monthly colour magazine, *Sothach*.

THE PHONOGRAM INDUSTRY IN WALES

We have previously chronicled the emergence of a Welsh recording industry up to the early 1980s (Wallis and Malm 1983: 77–105). Our research noted how two multinationals, EMI and Decca, came and left the area of Welsh music. Decca had a marked presence in the Welsh music scene in the late 1970s with a catalogue encompassing some thirty standard-priced LPs and about as many budget priced reissues. This company had also sold about 300,000 copies of a compilation album 'The World of Wales', most of them outside Wales to expatriates in Australia, Canada and the USA. When Decca was merged with Polygram in 1980, the Welsh operation was closed. The Welsh catalogue manager, Raymond Ware explained: 'Some companies the size of this one (Polygram) feel that if a record isn't selling 1,500 copies a year, then it costs too much to keep it on the shelves in the factory' (Ware, Decca, TI 30/07/81).

With Decca's disappearance, the dominant position was left to SAIN Recordiau, a company started in the early 1970s by two young nationalists who sang songs in Welsh in the Bob Dylan idiom, Dafydd Iwan and Huw Jones.

SAIN has continued to grow in relative strength, even if record sales have been low in terms of units. In 1989, SAIN celebrated its twentieth anniversary. By British standards, the leading Welsh phonogram company was still a rebel, insisting on filing its annual reports with the company register in Cardiff *solely* in the Welsh language. In Wales, new generations of musicians, and new small record companies had emerged; for many of them, SAIN was the Establishment – Dafydd Iwan was a middle-aged hippie. The boss at SAIN pleads only partially guilty:

> 'A presenter on Radio Cymru interviewed me the other day and kept on calling me the Establishment, which is rather ironic. We produce records that are banned by the BBC. We refuse to file company reports in English. We hold back money for tax because of their nuclear policies. I mean, we're certainly a very rebel company. We constantly produce political songs. Suddenly you are labelled "the Establishment". What the presenter meant, of course, was our music, that we tend to avoid groups that are limited in their support. We plead guilty to that. But we *have* recorded young groups all the time.
>
> Also we face competition from small studios with one-man operations – bands are actually *paying* for that. There's strong competition from studios with musicians/engineers working throughout the night. They have something we had lost – we had become a 9 to 5 operation with people working on overtime with families at home. We can't handle groups who are booked to arrive at the studio at 10 but who arrive at 3.'
>
> (Iwan, TI 26/09/89)

The Welsh phonogram industry is subject to the same pressures as comparative industries elsewhere; sales are decreasing as access to recorded music in the media increases. An article in the Welsh arts magazine *Golwg* entitled 'A crack in the record', focused on the apparent lack of Welsh record-buyers.

> Nearly twenty years after establishing SAIN, the record company is facing a very changing situation. Some of the leading artists are selling fewer copies. The rock world is in disarray and records for young people don't reach a large enough audience . . . at the same time, some of the main groups such as U-Thant and Datblygu have turned to the Cartel company [an independent distributor which went bankrupt in 1991] claiming that support is not available in Wales. . . . The average sales for SAIN's rock records is by now a few hundred. The only ones to sell in substantial quantities are the more traditional ones, or the television stars – the very performers defamed by the new pundits. But the bad news for a company like SAIN is that sales on the whole are going down. One of those to suffer most dramatically is Trebor Edwards [a tenor singer who is also a farmer] His first record . . . reached 32,500 copies by mid-1988. His latest record has had difficulties reaching 5,000.
> (*Golwg* 1988)

The article concludes that television has not helped many of the traditional phonogram artists, and that the state-funded Arts Council should start putting money into phonogram subsidies for recordings of popular music (something which has not occurred as yet).

Dafydd Iwan of SAIN agrees that his home market is diminishing and offers the same explanation as colleagues in many other countries (e.g. Neville Lee in our Jamaican chapter), namely the increased media output of both recorded music and competing audio-visual products:

> 'The areas of people and communities who ten to fifteen years ago spoke Welsh most of the time are far more bilingual. That plus depopulation plus unemployment has affected it. Plus the fact that the Welsh people are affected by a multitude of media. When we started, if people wanted to hear Welsh music in the afternoon, the only way they could do it was by playing a record. Now they can switch on radio, video or look at TV. Choice has meant that we sell less. Rather than helping us, S4C has worked the other way. Trebor Edwards is a case. He has been the popular, lyrical tenor, singing well-known sentimental songs. He sold over 30,000 of his best LP; it's still selling. He's had three or four series on TV. During that time his sales have steadily dropped. The Trebor Edwards they see on TV was not the Trebor Edwards they saw on stage, and certainly not the one they heard on record. We could

smooth out a few rough edges via production – on TV they couldn't do that.'

(Iwan, TI 26/09/89)

Dafydd Iwan has come to the same conclusion arrived at by national record company executives in many other countries (e.g. Sonet in Sweden) that the only way open is to expand into other media as TV changes the rules of the ball game. SAIN thus makes children's videos, buys cartoon videos from other European countries and dubs them into Welsh for S4C. The SAIN strategy for dealing with younger musicians' suspicion of its establishmentarian role was to start a specific, separate label for new rock groups, CRAI (meaning raw, rough or unpolished). A group with the curious name Y Jecsyn Ffeif or J5, and pronounced 'Jackson Five' in English, playing a Welsh-language form of reggae was one of the first CRAI releases in 1989 ('Annibyniaeth Barn', CRAI C004A). They were released solely on cassette, reflecting the belief that the pre-recorded cassette will replace the vinyl LP/single as the most convenient sound carrier for such artists. SAIN has also started to use CDs for releases of choral and classical recordings as well as for some more well-known popular artists.

Decreasing sales have encouraged a relatively large phonogram company such as SAIN to hunt for more secondary income. SAIN insists on publishing, where possible, all the works that artists record. Via Phonogram Performance Ltd (the PPL) SAIN receives money from record plays on Radio Cymru. Publishing rights allows SAIN to retain a slice of mechanical copyright dues as well as receive one-third of PRS receipts (performing rights fees) when SAIN phonograms are broadcast in Wales or the rest of the UK. Dafydd Iwan describes such income as 'a small amount per play but very important, more so than record sales in the rock category'. This would indicate that secondary income has superseded primary from phonogram sales as the main source of remuneration for certain genres of recorded music in Wales, assuming that the phonogram company in question can register all recorded works and thereby monitor to some extent payments. This probably does not apply to many of the smaller 'enthusiasts' amongst the Welsh phonogram producers, who often don't even bother to provide a unique registration number for each new release.

SAIN's position is helped by the fact that the company, by virtue of its dominant position in Wales, has a seat on the Board of the British PPL, thereby gaining some insight into the workings of what is otherwise a very secretive organization in the service of the 'official' British phonogram industry. On the other hand, money that the PPL collects from public performances on juke boxes, at discos and shops cannot be collated with any reports on what is actually performed. Such dues are distributed according to the distribution of phonogram performances on BBC national

Radios 1 and 2, which doesn't help SAIN since their discs rarely filter through to these national channels.

Recording studios and phonogram companies can be found all over Wales. There are at least three 16- or 24-track analogue recording studios in sparsely populated north Wales:

1. the SAIN studios in Penygroes, 7 miles south of Caernarfon, established in the mid-1980s, partly with the help of subsidies from regional development funds (i.e. government subsidies);
2. a studio at Bangor University, used in conjunction with music courses but also accessible to people outside the university;
3. Studio Les in Bethesda (the home of the Cytgord agency), housed in the basement of a regular three-storey building on the main street and accessible from a rear entrance through a back yard.

In west Wales, the most active phonogram producer is Fflach in Cardigan. Fflach have two full-time studio employees with 24-track facilities. Their aim is to produce around twenty productions per annum, thus becoming the second most productive phonogram company in Wales after SAIN, 'in between the establishment SAIN and the angry young men of

Plate 7.4 The somewhat confused entrance through a backyard to the Studio Les 16-track facility in the little slate-mining town of Bethesda, Wales.

Anhrefn'. Fflach's main source of income is the recording of choirs who order phonograms and sell to friends, relatives and fans. The profit is used to record groups and artists which Fflach finds interesting. The group 'Jess' is one such group which has been particularly successful as far as Fflach are concerned:

— Jess were still selling over 500 copies a month half a year after an LP/cassette had been released.
— Jess had been featured on national BBC radio (Radio 1) in the breakfast show.

Fflach, too, represent the outward-looking attitude of younger Welsh pop musicians: 'The market to go for with Welsh music is the European market. We would tend to forget about the English market because it's a bit of a closed shop. We must promote Welsh music on the European scene' (Kevin Davies, Fflach, TI 27/09/89).

An interesting aspect of Fflach's operations was the company's differentiated choice of carrier for different purposes. Most bands were sold on pre-recorded cassettes (CDs in the late 1980s were still reserved for choirs and the tourist souvenir market). Because of local radio's unwillingness to play cassettes, Fflach produced a limited number of vinyl discs of different releases as well as 'samplers', merely as a service and publicity gesture to radio stations in the hope of getting more airplay.

As regards the rest of the Welsh phonogram industry, the agency Cytgord estimate that approximately a dozen companies are active in Wales (i.e. producing and releasing at least five phonograms per annum) and that a further handful based in England work with similar material. Examples of the latter are: Workers Playtime and Side Effects in London, and Probe Plus in Liverpool.

There are no manufacturing resources in Wales. Apart from the Nimbus company dealing with high-quality classical recordings on CD, the Welsh phonogram industry has to make its discs and cassettes in England. EMI produce CDs for SAIN. A variety of companies mainly in the north of England provide cassette-copying services.

Since Decca was bought up by Polygram and closed its Welsh catalogue, the major phonogram companies have shown only sporadic interest in Welsh music phenomena. The occasional compilation album with titles such as 'Poems and Pints' (EMI EMC 3138) or 'The World of Max Boyce' (a singer/comedian on EMI OU 2033) have been sold around the world to expatriates or to tourists in Wales. When stars perceived to have international potential turn up, then interest can awaken amongst A&R bosses in London. Such was the case with the Welsh boy soprano, Aled Jones, who was 'discovered' by SAIN and who recorded material for three LP albums.

'He became so big that he had an agent and solicitor in London. Then Virgin came here to stake their claim. They even sent a contract in Welsh and said they would help us market him around the world. Then they found that our contract with him wasn't as watertight as they had thought and said: "we're taking him over as an artist". It was a bit unpleasant all round. We didn't fight it in court.'

(Iwan, TI 26/09/89)

Dafydd Iwan admits, however, that a small company cannot compete with the majors when it comes to publicity; that artistic acknowledgement in London can still have a critical positive effect back in Wales; and that major international phonogram companies have a lot of muscle when they want a particular artistic phenomenon.

'We learnt a lot of lessons the hard way. One was that for a year and a half, we tried to sell his albums and only sold a few hundred. Once we got the big publicity and the media wheels turning, our LPs sold thousands. Even Welsh people only bought him after they had heard from London that he was the best Welsh boy soprano ever.

We learnt that we can't conquer the world without the help of the big people – but they have no qualms at all about walking over small companies.'

(Iwan, TI 26/09/89)

SAIN still have material for the third Aled Jones album (which Virgin never released in its entirety), are on good terms with the artist (who, of course, is no longer a soprano) and intend to release more 'this is what Aled Jones sounded like' material when his Virgin contract runs out.

An interesting example of the Big coming back to the Small is provided by the internationally successful rock group, The Alarm, which has Welsh-speaking members. In 1989 they produced a limited edition of an LP with Welsh versions of their English lyrics. In 1991, a second Welsh album with some exclusive material was recorded by The Alarm and SAIN were asked to distribute it on their CRAI label ('TAN' on CRAI CD 014). Most of our respondents agreed that this event gave Welsh music a boost: 'It will make some people realize for the first time that there is a thing called the Welsh language.'

OFFICIAL POLICIES RELEVANT TO MEDIA AND MUSIC ACTIVITY

The Welsh Arts Council has given some support in the past to phonogram production of Welsh music, mainly symphonic works of relatively established contemporary composers such as Alun Hoddinott, William Matthias, Grace Williams and Gareth Walters (Bohana 1977: 23–8). By

1982, some twenty-six of such sponsored recordings had been released, usually in co-operation with Decca or EMI. Since then, little has happened because funds have not increased at the same rate as wages in the various institutions the Arts Council supports. All available funds have been needed to maintain operations such as the Welsh National Opera, which are labour-intensive commitments. Calls for the Arts Council to support phonogram production in other fields of music are unlikely to meet with a positive response in the immediate future.

With the tendency of successful professional musicians in the classical field to 'gravitate towards London', it is of interest to consider to what extent the Arts Council actually supports Welsh activities and people via subsidies to such expensive, labour-intensive art forms.

> 'There are very few professional artists in any field of music-making who are happy to remain in Wales working in the English language. Take the National Welsh Opera, for instance. Practically all the front-line talent is imported, the majority of the chorus, the professional musicians that we sustain in the orchestra here, the Welsh Opera Orchestra, a lot of it is imported, from all parts, not just of the UK but of Europe now. . . . I think we should have a policy of favouring or encouraging somehow our own people. . . . Perhaps the BBC should favour Welsh talent rather than the open-arms policy that it has.'
>
> (Smith, BBC Radio Wales, TI 21/09/89)

A prerequisite for the survival of the Welsh media we have described in this chapter is the survival and growth of the Welsh language. Education, media and employment policies are all relevant in this context.

Education

The 1990 Core Curriculum, introduced by the British government, specifies certain standard subjects which have to be taught to a certain level. Welsh is included for schools in Wales. Although schools can opt out of certain subjects, only a few in border areas have requested to be exempt from Welsh tuition. A problem, which we have already touched on, is the difficulty of finding qualified Welsh-language teachers, especially when many have been attracted to the media.

As regards music eduction, the traditional policy related closely to European art music has been expanded to include Welsh music forms at least at an advanced level:

> 'In 1985, approaches were made by the Penillion Singing Society to the Welsh Education Authority noting that folk music was on the Advanced Level syllabus in Scotland and Ireland. For instance, one could be asked to compose a jig in traditional style as part of A-level exams. Wales, up

to six years ago (1983) had absolutely no Welsh music on the syllabus, no Welsh music history, no composition in any Welsh style, no composing a harp tune or even a folksong, nothing at all. It was totally un-Welsh. The first steps were taken in 1983–4. Welsh art music was included among the set works students had to be familiar with. In the next step, aspects of Welsh classical music history were added. . . . Now we have writing in traditional (Penillion) style. Penillion, after all is pure counterpoint just like Bach or Palestrina. Now the student gets a harp melody and has to write a vocal melody. Many classical composers in Wales went up in arms when this was introduced [1987], but it has remained on the syllabus. This is a very important development – it gives local traditional music the same academic status as Bach or Purcell.'

(Thomas, Bangor University, TI 25/09/89)

Media policies *vis-à-vis* the Welsh language

The 100 per cent Welsh rule is not sacrosanct, as we have noted, in either Radio Cymru or S4C. S4C allows a certain measure of English to be broadcast in some programmes from South Wales where the concentration of Welsh-speakers is low. Policy would not seem to be clear in this respect.

Employment policies

Many jobs have disappeared in areas where the Welsh language dominated, particularly in rural mid-Wales and the mountainous areas of the north. Regional development boards have endeavoured to fund new business activities in these areas. The SAIN studio in Penygroes was built partly with the support of such a grant. This, in combination with a decentralization of media production to such areas, encourages an increase in the use of the Welsh language in everyday business life.

FURTHER OBSERVATIONS ON MUSIC ACTIVITY

Attitudes towards Welsh folk music are changing. Traditional Welsh instruments are returning in revivalist forms. The crwth is used as a present-day violin, the pibgorn as a recorder. Folk music lecturer, Lyn Thomas, at Bangor University maintains that: 'The number of primary and secondary school pupils learning instruments in Wales is phenomenal. Unfortunately, as regards folk instruments, we have no equivalent of southern Ireland where the Aeolian pipes are studied in secondary school: no sadly not' (Thomas, TI 25/09/89).

Whether the majority of these pupils cease playing instruments after school, as seems to be the case in Sweden, is more than our data can answer.

It does seem clear that those working in the folk or ballad music vein tend to seek regional affinity with the rest of the Celtic minorities (in Brittany, Eire, Gaelic Scotland and even what's left of a Celtic culture in Cornwall and the Isle of Man). The annual Celtic Song Festival features artists singing in their variants of Celtic (even the extinct Cornish language) and functions rather like a miniature Eurovision Song Contest with far less of the commercial trappings.

The Welsh rock groups, estimated at between 100 and 150, might appreciate the publicity boost involved in exposure on John Peel's national Radio 1 programme in London, or The Alarm's decision to release albums in Welsh. But this has not led them to move *en masse* to the English capital, despite its role as a music industry hub, or to start singing in English, although there have been exceptions (Jess caused much debate when they produced an English version of one of their albums). A greater Europe where national boundaries and minorities are receiving much attention has also given them a focus. Here, their interests coincide perfectly with those of S4C as regards spreading Welsh culture to other nations without going through London.

Something interesting must have happened in the mid-1980s. S4C realized they had got it all wrong. A totally new generation of rock musicians emerged who were considerably dissatisfied with the 'Establishment' (including the old rebels at SAIN records). Radio Cymru took its youth music programmes off the air. Maybe this was all part and parcel of the backlash that followed the euphoria of getting those Welsh-language radio and TV channels after a long hard fight. Maybe the music activity just couldn't survive a media explosion that had lost touch with grass-roots feelings.

Huw Jones, founder of SAIN and producer of entertainment programmes for S4C, summed up his impressions of the mid-1980s with these words in a personal communication from late 1988:

'I would tentatively suggest that there is a reduction in the perceived importance of pop and rock for the population in general in Wales. . . . Whereas ten to twenty years ago, pop music was in the forefront of cultural life in Wales, particularly for young people, and particularly also in the ability of some songs to make a very strong impact on the collective consciousness, the general impression I get now is that, apart from the new "enthusiasts" who tend to be very active in their own fields, that for the population at large, including the younger element, Welsh rock features as a background against which other social activities take place, rather than forming a strong focal point to their cultural consciousness. . . . comparatively few individual songs have engraved themselves on people's minds during the past few years.

Plate 7.5 The Welsh love to sing – anywhere. An impromptu gathering of folk musicians at the Eisteddfod.

This may partly be a matter of style, in that many of the new groups seem almost to go out of their way to be amelodic and "alternative" in their appeal. High sales would probably mean a loss of street credibility. . . . However, perhaps an outsider could come to more accurate conclusions than those who are or have been involved in the business within Wales.'

(Huw Jones, 11/10/88)

Chapter 8
Case Study: Sweden

SMALL BUT WEALTHY: THE GENERAL MEDIA ENVIRONMENT

Sweden is a rich yet sparsely populated, industrialized nation in Northern Europe which enjoys a close cultural and linguistic affinity with its Nordic neighbours, particularly Norway and Denmark. Of the 8.5 million Swedes, about 10 per cent are first- or second-generation immigrants, mostly from the other Nordic countries and from Southern Europe.

Sweden's wealth grew rapidly throughout the 1950s and 1960s. Formal neutrality during the Second World War had not excluded the selling of iron ore to both the Allies and Germany. The policy had also left the nation's industry intact. Urbanization, a relatively recent phenomenon in Sweden compared to many other Western European countries, increased rapidly in the postwar years. It was accompanied by a marked population shift from the north to areas around the three main cities, Stockholm, Gothenburg and Malmö.

Personal incomes also grew quickly in the postwar decades, as did spending on leisure activities. By the mid-1970s, statistics showed the Swedes spending more per capita on phonograms (US$18/annum) than any other nation including the USA where the equivalent figure was US$13 (Kulturrådet 1979: 41).

The contours of Sweden's electronic media environment have long been moulded by two types of opposing forces. Government policy, formulated by the Social Democrats who have dominated politics since the 1930s, has been to delay firmly the introduction of commercially funded broadcasting. The licence-funded, public service Swedish Broadcasting Corporation, Sveriges Radio, enjoyed protected-species status for decades. Entrepreneurs have understandably seen rich Sweden as a potential financial El Dorado for commercial radio and TV, and have exerted corresponding pressures. National policies could do little to stop the advance of satellite channels funded by financiers with very deep pockets.

Sweden was the first country in Europe to be exposed to commercial radio pirates broadcasting from international waters and beaming transmissions at a specific territory (Radio Nord and Radio Syd – one of their boats later became Radio Caroline off the UK). In 1962, the government outlawed them by making it a criminal offence to buy advertising time on such stations. At the same time, the non-commercial Swedish Broadcasting Corporation, Sveriges Radio, was ordered to start up a replacement, light-music channel. Exactly the same legal procedure was to be employed some six years later by Britain to solve the maritime pirate problem, with the BBC being told to create an alternative service which was to become BBC Radio 1.

A similar problem cropped up once more when satellites began broadcasting pan-European TV services in the early 1980s and local Swedish companies (including the state-owned Swedish Telecom) started offering cabled relays, including Rupert Murdoch's SKY-television with commercials.

Once again the ruling Social Democrats followed an apparent belief that commercial programming is incompatible with public service ideals. Legislation was introduced that banned the carrying of satellite programmes containing advertising directed 'specifically at a Swedish audience'. No attempt was made to outlaw individual dishes which were starting to appear in the gardens and on the rooftops of houses in the wealthier suburbs. There was no attempt to change the output of Swedish television's two national channels, for understandable reasons. Any movement of programme policy in the direction of the new satellite channel's output would have entailed more US material, and less local productions. This would hardly have been compatible with a public service ethos.

The Swedish Cable Law was so loose that it offered any number of loopholes. By taking a Swedish filmed commercial and inserting a word of Norwegian (almost the same language), it could be claimed that an advert on satellite TV was not aimed 'specifically' at Sweden. And, after all, which politician of any political complexion could conceive a situation where Sweden's car manufacturer, Volvo, could not aim TV adverts at its large, important domestic market, whilst Mercedes could from abroad?

By 1990, although there had been no changes of legislation, most cable systems in Sweden provided up to a dozen or more international channels, including non-stop news (CNN) and non-stop music videos (MTV). They were also offering what were three *de facto* new national TV channels. TV3 was broadcasting out of London via Luxembourg's Astra medium-power satellite. Two others, Nordic Channel and TV4, were broadcasting from Swedish soil, with commercials, but avoiding trouble with the law by making their signal take a round-about trip of 70,000km up and down from a satellite. TV4 even managed to use the Tele-X satellite, a high-power DBS which had been financed by the Swedish taxpayers as part of a huge $500m industrial subsidy aimed at Sweden's electronic industry. Tele-X was originally intended to be a pan-Nordic project, to be used for making the Nordic countries' national TV channels available all over the region. Denmark, Norway and Finland pulled out of the project and left Sweden to foot the bill. The price TV4 paid to lease a transponder was classed as classified business information and thereby withheld from the Swedish taxpayers.

TV4 started transmitting from studios in Stockholm via Tele-X in September 1990, the day before the ruling Social Democrats decided at their annual conference to allow commercial TV in principle over a third terrestrial network. They could hardly have arrived at any other decision since cable penetration was already up to around 35 per cent of all households (SCB 1991: 50). By July 1991, TV3 were claiming that TV household penetration had risen to 53 per cent, equivalent to almost four of Sweden's 8.5 million inhabitants (TV3 1991: 3). Although Sweden in 1991 was the only country in Europe apart from Albania not to formally allow commercial broadcasting, the Swedes probably had more access via satellite signals to TV advertising than even the British. Once again we have a striking example of how financial and technological constraints decide the media agenda in the absence of functioning, realistic legislation. The 'semi-legal' Swedish satellite TV channels, TV3 and TV4, were made legal by a new government in November 1991. The business solution chosen involved a strange combination of the two; both channels continued but TV4 got access to a third Swedish terrestrial transmitter network. The owner of TV3 also got the largest stake in the company owning TV4. Deregulation of the *non-commercial* Sveriges Radio's TV monopoly had more or less created a new *commercial* monopoly.

In parallel with the 1980s satellite explosion, there was a corresponding growth of video in Sweden. Almost 4 million VCRs had been sold in Sweden by 1986, and by 1988 it was estimated that 41 per cent of Swedes in the 9–79 age group had their own video machines (Strid and Weibull 1988: 118). In 1988, VCR sales were showing signs of a saturation but still amounted to almost 300,000 per annum (Kulturrådet 1989: 78). Figures for 1991 show a further increase in penetration with 58 per cent of the total population (ages 7–99) having access to VCRs, equivalent to 45 per cent of all households (Nordström 1991: 5).

The video rental business had also exploded, with turnover increasing from an estimated $10m in 1980 to almost $300m by 1988 (Strid and Weibull 1988: 119). Little of this software, however, could be categorized as 'music videos'. Categories such as 'action', 'thrillers' and 'Westerns' dominated the rental stores (68 per cent in 1987) with 'music videos' accounting for only 7 per cent.

On the audio side, the numbers of gramophones and cassette players also continued to increase (see Table 8.1).

Radio, too, was part of the Swedish media explosion throughout the 1980s, with output increasing from around 20,000 hours to well over

Table 8.1 Audio hardware in Sweden as % ownership amongst 9–79 age group

Type of apparatus	1985	1987	1991
Gramophones	79	81	84
Cassette players (cars)	54	62	69
Cassette players/recorders	39	52	62
Freestyles	29	42	55
CD players	1	4	29

Source: PUB (audience research unit, Sveriges Radio)

300,000 hours per annum. Firstly, the monopoly Sveriges Radio was instructed by parliament to expand its local radio activities. Twenty-four new non-commercial, licence-financed stations were started – all of them had separate frequencies/transmitters by 1990 and accounted for over 70,000 hours of programming per annum.

Community or 'Neighbourhood Radio' was also introduced around 1980. The intended operators were bona fide non-profit organizations such as churches, trade unions or other associations representing common interests of particular groups. Once again, a somewhat diffuse legislation which had carefully avoided the issue of programme content (responding to a strong 'freedom of speech' lobby) left the door more than ajar for entrepreneurs wishing to introduce commercial radio. By 1991, little more than a decade after its introduction, Swedish Neighbourhood Radio had been more or less taken over by large operators providing hours of non-stop pop music, with many of them regularly calling in the public debate for the introduction of 'free radio'. From a faltering start back in 1979, Swedish Neighbourhood Radio entered the 1990s accounting for more than a quarter of a million hours of radio output per annum. Even though listeners on average were single figure percentages, this output dwarfed that of the established national radio channels (20,000 hours per annum) and even the relatively new local radio stations (70,000 hours per annum).

As we formulate this summary, Sweden's current non-socialist government is wondering how to satisfy pressures from different influential groups by introducing commercial radio in an orderly fashion, i.e. with some minimum rules to govern the distribution of licences and frequencies, ethical standards, etc. The social democrats, voted out of office in 1991, are at the forefront of a move to 'jump the queue', by starting their own network of pirate commercial stations. One problem the present political regulators face is that most available FM frequencies in the main cities are already occupied by Neighbourhood Radio stations and the comprehensive existing network of Sveriges Radio transmitters. Another is the 'Catch 22' dilemma of how to keep Neighbourhood Radio non-commercial, i.e. for genuine non-profit-making associations who do not wish to be associated with advertising, if new commercial stations licences are distributed according to a franchise system. Unless the strict rules forbidding commercial content in Neighbourhood Radio are enforced rigorously (which has not been the case so far), then those not awarded commercial franchises or who do not wish to pay for them, will probably gravitate back into Neighbourhood Radio. The effect will once again be to exclude those for whom media access was originally intended.

Satellite radio typified by SKY radio (offering what its publicity people call: 'non-stop CDs' or 'music with a low irritation factor') is also on its way into the Swedish cable systems. The policymakers face the same problems they helped to create with television by sitting on the sideline too long.

An interesting Swedish characteristic, which can function as both a boon and a curse for any observer, is the ready access to detailed statistics, whether they be of the number of blades of grass in an average lawn or the number of daily minutes an average Swede in a particular age group devotes to listening to pre-recorded audio cassettes. Some are compiled by media researchers at universities, often in collaboration with the Audience Research Department of Swedish Radio, known by the delightful acronym PUB. Others come from studies emerging from the National Council for Cultural Affairs ('Kulturrådet'), or from the State Bureau of Statistics (SCB).

Since 1986, detailed figures covering the activities of the phonogram industry have been published by the Swedish branch of the IFPI – they even cover companies and groups of companies not affiliated to the IFPI. More data follow in the next sections as we turn to the issues of what music the media play and what the music industry produces.

SVERIGES RADIO: THE SWEDISH BROADCASTING CORPORATION

Despite the fragmentation of radio services and the availability of extra TV channels thanks to satellite distribution offering a loophole in the law curtailing commercial broadcasting, Sweden entered the 1990s with its old 'monopoly', Sveriges Radio, more or less intact. The corporation consisted of a parent company and four subsidiaries (television, national radio, local radio and education radio/TV). Television provided two national channels with Channel 1 nominally based on production resources in the capital, Stockholm, and Channel 2 comprising a mixture of output from different regional studios. In fact, both channels compete with each other, offering almost the same output profile, the differences being the results of scheduling ('Dallas' on one, 'Falcon Crest' on the other; the 'News' on Channel 1 at 9pm, the 'News' on Channel 2 at 7.30).

National radio is run mainly from Stockholm, with some input from regional district studios. Local radio's twenty-four stations are co-ordinated via a central management organization, also based in Stockholm, and educational radio/TV provides programmes for all the other companies as well as material on cassettes and books which are sold to institutions and private individuals. Parliament decided that the national and local radio companies would be amalgamated in 1992; the stated aim of this move was to produce a stronger public service radio organization capable of meeting competition from new commercial operators.

Sweden has three national radio channels, each with separate FM frequencies. Programme 1 or P1 is mainly a speech channel with only about 8 per cent music content, attracting on average a daily audience of 16 per cent. P2 contains a mixture of immigrant and educational programmes during the daytime and becomes an art music channel in the evenings and through the night (called 'Music Radio'). Almost 90 per cent of its output is so-called 'serious' music and its average reach is 2 per cent.

P3 is the most popular overall channel, created, as we noted, in the early 1960s as a replacement for the pirates. The birth of such a channel was an important policy decision; it marked a shift away from an educational view of radio to one where entertainment and relaxation were acceptable goals and rewards for broadcasters and listeners. Listener statistics for 1989 showed an average daily reach for P3 of 59 per cent of the Swedish population; earlier in the decade this figure had been in the region of 70 per cent but dropped steadily as local radio stations received their own separate frequencies and transmitters. Almost 70 per cent of P3's output consists of popular music, almost 93 per cent of which is recorded music off phonograms. P3's use of live music, i.e. simulcast concerts or recordings produced with the organization's own resources, was reduced drastically during the 1980s in order to save money. With almost a 60 per cent daily reach, this increased reliance on commercially recorded material has augmented even further the significance of this national radio channel for the phonogram industry.

Even the classical channel P2 has increased its dependency on commercial recordings. In connection with a decision to keep this channel running throughout the night, more phonograms were played, which meant in essence an increase in the amount of imported music disseminated via Swedish Radio (Strid and Weibull 1988: 178). Swedish Radio's own statistics for a week in November 1989 confirm this observation; the daytime percentage of serious music featuring Swedish composers and performers amounted to 40 per cent, much of which would have been recorded by the company. The equivalent night-time figure for the Swedish content of P2 was only 15 per cent.

Statistics concerning the music played on P3, based on annual detailed weekly samples, give some insight regarding the role and extent of the Swedish content.

The first peak in the table below came in 1986 and coincided with the granting of a new franchise to the Swedish Broadcasting Corporation. As we noted in our preface, the terms of this agreement stipulated, amongst other things, that the Board of Directors of Sveriges Radio should 'take

Table 8.2 Percentage of Swedish music on P3

Sample month/year	Oct. 84	Oct. 85	Oct. 86	Oct. 87	Oct. 88	Nov. 89
Music by Swedish Composers[1]	28.2	28.6	34.4	33.4	31.5	36.0
Swedish performers/ foreign composers[2]	5.1	6.1	4.5	4.5	3.8	3.0
TOTAL	33.3	34.7	38.9	37.9	35.3	39.0

Source: Riksradions Programstatistik, Swedish Radio
Notes: [1] Swedish composers with or without Swedish performers
[2] Swedish performers playing works by foreign composers

action in connection with the distribution of funds should, for instance, the Swedish element in the corporation's music output tend to decrease' (Swedish Government 1985, section 3.5). Despite three years of a clear downward trend which Swedish Radio's own statisticians highlighted in their written comments, no such 'action' seemed to be forthcoming. Swedish composers were outraged and went so far as to organize a general strike during one of the most national of Swedish holidays, Midsummer, in 1989. The boycott was organized by the Swedish Association of Popular Music Composers (SKAP) whose members forbade the national radio channels to play any Swedish music available on phonograms during this holiday (the terms of the agreement between the Swedish Composers' Collecting Society, STIM, and Sveriges Radio allow for a composer to withdraw his/her work should the composer so request). The result of this very unique action would seem to have been a turnabout in the trend: Table 8.2 shows an increase in the number of Swedish compositions played on P3 of almost 5 percentage points up from 31 per cent, an increase of 16 per cent.

With P3 functioning as an important trendsetter, and providing large sums of copyright dues, this constituted an important contribution to the well-being of local composers. Informal integration, in other words, could be expected to provide a multiplier effect!

SECOND-TIER RADIO: SWEDISH LOCAL RADIO

Although Sweden's twenty-four second-tier radio stations were known as 'local' stations, the term 'regional' would be more correct – essentially they cover counties and there is considerable overlap between their transmission areas. As in the case of national radio, music from commercially available phonograms has been the most important tool used to fill increased programme time. Total music content (around 33 per cent on average) is less than in the two national music channels (P2 and P3 average between 60 and 70 per cent music content). All twenty-four local stations are fairly autonomous in their operation, but the centralized management structure of the company that formally owns them and co-ordinates their funding has formulated goals regarding music output and the use of commercial recordings. The aim, specified clearly in the local radio company's funding request to the government, involves a '50 per cent content of local music' and an increased emphasis on 'stations recording their own music'. Even if the latter increased from 500 to 2,000 hours a year during the 1980s, equivalent to an impressive '4,000 LPs a year' (Lokalradio 1990, section 4.3.3.), the actual percentage of live music decreased as stations got their own separate transmitters and tended to use more and more phonograms to fill out time. Stations have even started to join together and provide common regional music feeds, pooling resources to make their scarce budgets go further – offering, in effect, a service at some times of the day which differs little from that of the national music channel P3 (see Table 8.3).

Table 8.3 Music output of Swedish local radio stations, comparing music off phonograms/live recordings and total output

Year	1977/8 hrs	1977/8 %	1983/4 hrs	1983/4 %	1989 hrs	1989 %	1990 hrs	1990 %
Live music (own recordings)	503	2.4	1,142	4.2	2,023	3.6	2,000	2.7
Music off phonograms	1,494	7.3	5,737	21.0	20,019	36.0	23,800	33.0
Total hrs of transmission	20,521		27,303		55,600		72,000	

Source: SCB 1991 and Lokalradio funding application 1990

Swedish local radio, unlike its national 'Big Brother' has had centrally formulated goals regarding Swedish music content on its stations. For this reason it was exempted from 'industrial action' during the 1988 composers' strike referred to above. The central management of the local radio organization has presented figures supporting its claim that members are living up to the local music goals. Its data suggest that the Swedish content on different local stations varies from 45 to 70 per cent.

About 25 per cent of the Swedish population listen on average to a local radio station each day – the actual figure can vary, however, from town to town depending on the type of alternatives provided by the latest competitor to traditional, public service radio within the corporation umbrella, namely '*Närradio*' or Neighbourhood Radio.

The output of the Swedish local radio stations can be expected to change radically in the 1990s, not least because of a government decision to amalgamate the two national and local radio companies. The new joint-management team announced early in 1992 that a plan was being drawn up to prepare public service radio for competition from commercial stations in the 1990s. This would entail the old local radio stations forming a *de facto* fourth national network where music for listeners 'over the age of 37½' would define the format. The former P3 programme would aim for a younger audience and compete directly with new commercial radio stations. Maybe this can be seen as an inevitable consequence of public service broadcasters feeling more and more competition from Neighbourhood Radio, which was producing a staggering 400,000 hours of radio per annum by the end of the 1980s.

THIRD-TIER RADIO IN SWEDEN: COMMUNITY RADIO OR AN ALTERNATIVE TO COMMERCIAL RADIO?

The biggest increase of radio, in terms of programme production and transmission, is that provided by Swedish '*Närradio*' – 'Neighbourhood' or 'Community' radio. Introduced as an experiment in 1978, this step towards the decentralization of broadcasting comprised in effect the first formal attack on the traditional monopoly of the Swedish Broadcasting Corporation (Sveriges Radio). As such, it was a controversial move by a non-socialist coalition during a short six-year period in charge of running Sweden from 1976–82 (a government with a similar complexion was voted in again in September 1991).

The 'Neighbourhood' airwaves were opened up on 1 June 1978, at first for a three-year trial period. The briefly worded Act of Parliament makes little mention of content, but merely states that any body involved in 'voluntary, political, trade union or religious activities' could apply to the newly created Neighbourhood Radio Board for time on a local transmitter (Swedish Government 1978). Finance via advertising was forbidden.

Three years later, in 1981, the experiment was reviewed and made permanent (Swedish Government 1981). The many comments from a wide range of organizations which are summarized in the Bill's postscript concentrate mainly on the need for wide tolerance as regards safeguards for freedom of expression, as well as legal issues such as the right of reply. Some of the early programme suppliers do make references to the role of commercially available music in the output, and the emergence during the trial period of groups whose main interest appeared to be disco-radio for the sake of attracting listeners, not primarily for informing members of an organization about forthcoming activities or issues of mutual interest

(Swedish Government 1981: 50). 'Radio for the sake of radio' was a category specifically excluded in the original regulations. The law-makers, however, ignored such concerns. The Bill included no conditions which would limit the available range of programme material, nor did it specify a relationship between style and content of programmes and the intended purpose of Neighbourhood Radio. The door was thus left open for a wide range of interpretations and activities.

The term 'Neighbourhood Radio' actually is somewhat misleading. It does not refer to tiny transmitters covering a block of flats or a village. Swedish Neighbourhood Radio transmitters cover in principle a radius of about 5 kilometres. In practice, however, with the use of various boosting techniques, signals can be heard up to 20 kilometres from the transmitters. In some rural, sparsely populated municipalities, the Neighbourhood Radio Board which controls this form of broadcasting has allowed increases in transmitting power to cover even larger areas. In city areas such as Stockholm and Gothenburg, the law allows the same programme producer to transmit the same material over several transmitters simultaneously, as long as they are situated within the same municipality (i.e. within the city limits). The result, in effect, is that the Swedish local radio described above, which covers whole counties, has become even more regional in character, being replaced on a local level by Neighbourhood Radio.

The 1981 Act making Neighbourhood Radio permanent also confirmed that it would continue to be non-commercial. Any non-profit-making association could apply for time on a Neighbourhood Radio Station, ostensibly to spread information about its activities (the politicians described the new medium as 'the stencil of the airwaves'). Since 1981 the volume of programme production has increased to a staggering 250,000 hours per annum, produced by 2,500 groups and disseminated via 150 FM transmitters. Once again, recorded music has been a major prerequisite for this growth, a growth which has contributed to a fifteen-fold expansion of radio production in Sweden during the 1980s.

Neighbourhood Radio is also beginning to make its presence felt in the annual Swedish media statistics, even if the relevance is hard to interpret since not all Swedes can actually hear Neighbourhood Radio. The annual 'media barometer' from October 1988 (produced by Gothenburg University and Sveriges Radio's audience research department) showed that on average, over the whole country, 9 per cent of Swedish 15–24 year-olds listened regularly to Neighbourhood Radio (compared to a figure of 4 per cent for the combined values of listening to the two national channels, P1 and P2 in the same age group). In the major cities where several small transmitters overlap, sometimes transmitting the same music-based programmes, the figure is much higher, especially where trendy pop stations have entered the radio spectrum through the Neighbourhood Radio door.

In Gothenburg, for instance, one Neighbourhood Radio station with a pop/rock format has more listeners in the 15–24 age group than Swedish national and local radio put together (Hedman and Strid 1990).

A point of music policy to be emphasized here is the role of recorded popular music in creating very similar programme profiles for operators with nominally different ideological backgrounds; their common prime aim being to attract listeners. One can thus hear Michael Jackson both on programmes sponsored by the trade unions/Social Democrats supposedly supporting the labour movement, as well as on those run by the Employers' Federation selling a 'Free Enterprise and Capitalism is good for you' message. The only discernible differences are in short propaganda messages inserted between records. This trend is most noticeable in the larger towns and cities, where non-stop disco stations functioning within the Neighbourhood Radio umbrella can be regarded as 'pre-commercial'. The staff of the Swedish Employers' Federation's Gothenburg station, Radio City, make no secret of the fact that they are only occupying a Neighbourhood Radio frequency as a stop-gap measure until the government agrees to allow commercial radio. Others openly flout the law and sell advertising slots.

This development has presented the public service non-commercial local stations with a competitive dilemma. Their policy of 50 per cent Swedish music, retaining traditions and the role of the Swedish language in popular culture, has to survive alongside an increasing number of Top 40, high-tempo stations which attract listeners with a flood of competitions, give-aways, lotto and the like.

MUSIC ON PUBLIC-SERVICE TV IN SWEDEN

Exact figures of music use on Sweden's two national, non-commercial channels are hard to come by. Pure music productions, mainly in the serious vein, account for a mere 3.9 per cent of output or 3.6 hours a week (SCB 1991). Music also plays an important role in light entertainment programmes and feature films, as signatures and as a general background. A study carried out by Swedish television in connection with the composers' strike mentioned in the previous section looked at four weeks' output on both channels (November 1988). It found that 21.9 hours of music a week (excluding music in feature films), or 44 per cent on average, featured Swedish composers and/or performers, with the highest rate for Swedish music (86 per cent) being found in Swedish series. The second highest concentration of Swedish music (62 per cent) was recorded in entertainment programmes and shows. The channel that ran the most foreign imports, TV1, recorded a correspondingly lower figure for Swedish music usage.

Swedish national TV discovered the video clip as a source of cheap programme material around 1984. Swedish subsidiaries of the transnational phonogram companies were keen for the new marketing tool to provide publicity for their international artists. Satellite channels such as SKY and Music Box were still available only to a relatively small number of subscribers in Sweden; video clips were made available to the national, terrestrial channels at a very cheap rate.

Swedish TV also introduced its own Video Top 10 programme, 'Baggen' (The Bag). Videos were screened in advance and chosen by youth panels around the country. In principle, Swedish artists could compete. In practice this was impossible since there were so few Swedish videos – the costs were deemed prohibitive in such a small market. In a ten-week period during the autumn of 1984 (Wallis and Malm 1987: 148ff.), only one Swedish video appeared on 'Baggen'. Four of the Big Five phonogram companies accounted for 72 per cent of the videos on the programme. The impact on sales of phonograms was immense. The final Top 20 singles sales chart, published by the Swedish phonogram industry on 21 December 1984, featured nineteen singles which had been shown as video clips on 'Baggen'. The twentieth was the Band Aid single for Ethiopia which had also been run as a video clip on other Swedish TV programmes. No Swedish singles made this chart on that occasion. This observation would certainly seem to support the following quote from a 1985 industrial analysis of the significance of the video clip for international promotion:

> The prime aim of the promo video is firmly defined: to sell records . . . for the glamour rock greats, to whom image is all, the video clip gives the fans what they want, tempts the TV producers, and, of course, sells more records. . . . Companies can comfort themselves by looking at the international success of British acts purely through the screening of promo clips on cable and TV stations . . . it certainly does alter the balance of the charts.
>
> (*Music Week*, 1985)

Swedish phonogram companies working with local music complained bitterly about the 'altered balance of the charts' brought about by 'Baggen'. At this time, TV3 and TV4 had not appeared, and cable competition to the national channels was still marginal. Producers at Swedish TV, in their safe protected haven, dismissed all such criticism, claiming that local entrepreneurs just wanted to earn more money. The fact was that costs for making a video, which could only be recouped in the relatively small Swedish-language market, were prohibitively high. Even the National Council for Cultural Affairs started considering whether subsidies should be provided for making local videos. More and more observers began asking why Swedish TV, with all its technical resources and a brief to support local culture of all types, was not making its own videos featuring domestic artists and composers.

In 1987 there was a clear change of policy *vis-à-vis* local music videos at

Swedish TV. The company started paying local phonogram companies SEK10,000 or US$1,600 (about 15 per cent of the average cost of production) for each viewing of a local video. A new video Top 10 was introduced, 'Listan' (The List), which *only* featured Swedish videos. This project involved a closer degree of informal integration with the phonogram industry than ever before. Production was put out on contract to one of the few remaining national Swedish media companies, Sonet, which also ran its own phonogram operation at that time.

'Listan' was screened at prime time on Sunday evenings (around 19.00), as had been the case with 'Baggen'. The effect on the 'balance of the charts' was immediate and remarkable. Speaking at the 1990 International Music and Media Conference in Amsterdam, Dag Häggkvist of Sonet referred to the problems of surviving as an independent phonogram company when most others had been:

> swallowed up by WEA, EIM or Polygram. . . . he cited a TV hit show devoted only to local records made by Sonet for Swedish Television (but not restricted to Sonet releases), as a result of which sales of all local repertoire have rocketed.
>
> (*Europe* 1990)

The publicity value was summed up thus by two popular singing sisters, Lili and Sussie: 'Suddenly people know who we are' (*Sweden Now* 1989: 40).

For many, the thought of a commercial phonogram company producing a chart show for non-commercial national TV was somewhat hard to stomach. Had this happened in the 1970s, the Swedish music movement would have been up in arms. But it certainly had the effect of boosting sales of Swedish pop phonograms. An interesting observation is that this impact could be achieved by a 30-minute burst of local videos on prime-time national TV, despite the round-the-clock international output of MTV entering more and more homes via cable.

MUSIC OF THE SPHERES: SATELLITE CHANNELS AND THEIR MUSIC POLICY

Satellite operators began to enter Europe with Rupert Murdoch's SKY Channel in 1983, looking for a giant, lucrative pan-European market for advertising and entertainment. Satellite footprints gave media magnates the opportunity to run cross-frontier transmissions without having to be too concerned with national legislation in separate countries. Up to the arrival of CNN, the emphasis was clearly on entertainment and sport. At a January 1985 seminar organized by the Manchester-based European Institute for the Media, a SKY senior executive included the question 'More choice or less?' in his address. His answer was 'More choice is inevitable' (Cox 1985: 14). The aim was broad entertainment. The target group had been identified in the lower half of the socio-economic scale:

'In Europe, the people who pay the most (for media) – both in absolute terms and as a percentage of their resources – are the lower income earners. . . . While television obviously has an educational role . . . it should for both moral and economic reasons seek to meet the desires and requirements of its principal audience at those times when they are most able to watch . . . we at Sky have a profound trust in the public's ability to select the entertainment it desires.

(Cox 1985: 22)

Such statements reflect a clear ideological standpoint; recognized authorities, the Good and the Wise, etc. should not try to regulate what is made available through radio/TV. That should be left entirely to Mr Cox and his colleagues, leaving the ratings to decide whether or not they should survive in the job. Was satellite TV offering a wide choice to the viewer in 1985? There was certainly a heavy dependence on music videos. In connection with an in-depth study of the introduction of cable to the southern Swedish university town of Lund, Roe analysed the content of seven satellite channels, including one French (TV5) and one Soviet (Ghorisont) and found no less than 84,065 minutes of popular music programming in a 9-week period. This corresponds to 42 per cent of total output (Roe 1985: 29). SKY and Europe's first non-stop music video channel, Music Box, contributed heavily to this statistic.

Well aware that Sweden had been more or less untouched by commercial television, but somewhat uncertain as to how to woo the Swedes, SKY announced in 1986 that it was launching a project called 'Switch on to Sweden'. The idea was presented by a SKY manager, Australian David Ciclitira, at a seminar organized by the Swedish Composers' Copyright Society, STIM, in March of 1986.

'SKY channel runs about 40 per cent of its programming as video clips. We are very committed to playing European music. The problem for us is that first, there aren't many videos to play: 80–90 per cent of the videos sent in for selection come from the UK or the USA. . . . and second, people who want to make videos presumably want to get them played on TV. It seems to be more a matter of luck if a group from Switzerland or Norway do end up on a European station. SKY is slightly different because we actually start out trying to play your videos.'

(Ciclitira, TI 18/03/86)

Ciclitira then announced that SKY intended to focus all its programming on Sweden for a two-week period during the coming summer:

'From 26 May, we will start playing everything from Sweden out of

London. Then from 1 June, we'll be playing a week of recorded shows from Sweden. . . . We hope to make fifteen to twenty videos with Swedish groups. We would like to carry on, returning every two months making videos for the Swedish record industry. Videos we are involved in are guaranteed airplay on SKY in most cases. We feel this is something very important for us. What I would like to stress is that this will be an annual event. . . . Like all good things it will grow. This will be a starting point. Next year it will be bigger. . . . The ratings we are getting in Scandinavia are quite sensational – we want to do as much as possible for the Swedish record industry.'

(Ciclitera, TI 18/03/86)

The SKY representative went on to explain how music played on SKY gets seen all around the world thanks to a network of contacts being established with Hong Kong, Monte Carlo, Canada, etc. (via SKY's family relation to Rupert Murdoch). SKY, he explained, was going to introduce a special Scandinavian chart show. Swedish musicians, composers and their organizations were understandably thrilled by this sudden surge of interest in their local music scene.

SKY aims were not totally philanthropic in this project – the satellite channel persuaded the STIM to pay a cash support grant of £10,000 towards the cost of recording Swedish video clips on location in Stockholm. STIM also agreed to administer part of the project, which cost another £10,000 (all in all around US$35,000). The composers' organization recouped some of this investment by selling off the videos which were actually made to independent phonogram companies who would not normally have been able to afford such investments.

As often happens, 'the best laid plans o' mice an' men gang aft a-gley'. One week in June 1986 SKY did focus on Sweden. Forty-three video clips made by Swedish phonogram companies were sent in for consideration (seventeen of these had Swedish lyrics or were instrumental). SKY recorded on location another twelve videos. Sixty-eight viewings were noted during the Swedish week from a total of 48 videos, some of which appeared more than once. Only four of the 68 had lyrics in Swedish, the rest were in English or were instrumentals.

The international promotional value of the SKY week was marginal according to local phonogram company staff. One producer told us that the project had 'little or no value for his company apart from the experience gained'. He described SKY's production of videos as 'rather pathetic – conveyor-belt production'. There had been no reaction from abroad after the week. 'I don't think SKY got any reaction either – they haven't done anything like it again' (Swedish record company producer interviewed in 1988).

The 'Switch on to Sweden' week was never repeated. Three years later,

SKY was reorganized, moved to the Astra satellite, and concentrated an increased number of channels on the UK market, buying up its only serious competitor, BSB and forming BSB-SKY with News, Sports, Entertainment and Feature Films.

SKY channel transmitting pan-European programmes came and went. So did the Music Box video channel – it disappeared into Super Channel (another satellite programme controlled by Italian interests). In 1988, MTV-Europe got off the ground, backed up by Viacom (makers of US TV series such as 'Dallas'), British Telecom and the UK newspaper owner, the late Robert Maxwell. US staff were brought over to set up the operation, one of whom, Brian Diamond, became Programme Director. He too came over to Sweden and indicated that he was clearly aware of the 'tribal' factor in Europe. No promises of a Swedish week on MTV were made, but he did express his interest in running Swedish videos, even those with lyrics in Swedish. Addressing a seminar at Gothenburg University on 14 September 1988, Brian Diamond was adamant that:

> 'People said: "You're an American company. You're going to steamroll through Europe and not pay any attention to what's going on." I think on the contrary that we have paid attention to what's going on. The only misfortune for me is that I wish we could get more European videos. . . . The challenge is to programme a channel for an area that has so many languages. The beauty of a music channel is – without sounding corny – that music is the international language. I don't mind if [a song is] sung in a local language. That matters not to me – it comes down to, is it geared to our audience, in terms of the 16–34 market?'
>
> (Diamond, TI 28/09/88)

MTV's Programme Director also explained that his channel adhered to a '5-minute rule':

> 'We try to satisfy people – if you don't like what you're watching now, wait 5 minutes and something else will come along. I try to look at European music as objectively as possible, saying, this is music. It's either good or it's not good. Or, even if it's not something that we think warrants getting on the air, if it does have some chart action somewhere, we'll put it on. Give it some action. Give it that shot!'
>
> (Diamond, TI 28/09/88)

The desire to satisfy as many listeners as possible in different European countries has led, not surprisingly, to a scarcity of videos featuring smaller European languages on MTV-Europe. MTV's early promises of an output featuring a wide variety of music styles/languages were similar to those given by SKY. The actual results were also similar with output becoming more mainstream, Anglo-American in character. Few, if any Swedish-language videos are featured any longer on MTV-Europe.

At the same Gothenburg seminar addressed by MTV's Brian Diamond, media researcher Simon Frith also commented on the music satellite channel phenomenon. Frith noted that the MTV Programme Director's description of his station's apparent prime interest in supporting European music differed somewhat from the statement of intent distributed by MTV's advertising department.

> 'MTV Europe delivers the audiences advertisers want to reach. Now advertisers can hit the 16–24 year-olds with MTV's laser-sharp targeting, not scattered buckshot. This audience's discretionary income is not in piggy banks or pension funds. MTV reaches its viewers all over Europe with a consistent clarity. It's about the cars they drive, the clothes they wear, the foods they fuel themselves with. MTV is their choice.'
>
> (Frith, TI 28/09/88)

Whilst the MTV Programme Director's aim in 1988 was to reflect the styles and traditions of European popular music culture, his advertising department's aim was to identify and reach an affluent group of Europeans in their twenties who like the same material goods. It seems hardly likely that these two aims can be regarded as compatible.

SWEDEN'S TWO 'UNOFFICIAL' CHANNELS

At the start of this chapter we mentioned how commercial TV channels were reaching the Swedes despite their government's unwillingness to act on this issue. With a somewhat vague law governing what could be fed into Swedish cable systems, there were few legal problems for the Scansat company to start up TV3 broadcasting out of London via satellite and selling advertising time. Owned by a wealthy Swedish financier resident in the USA, TV3 filled its output, not only with relatively cheap US series, but also with some of the Swedes' favourites. TV3 used its cash supply to purchase rights for traditional Swedish TV highlights such as the Wimbledon tennis tournament, or the World Ice Hockey Championships. Public TV in Sweden then experienced the humiliation of having to repurchase the right to show these sporting fixtures, generally several hours after TV3 had run them live. Scansat's owner (Jan Stenbeck), in other words, had used his capital and entrepreneurial ability to redirect contributions from Swedish licence-payers into his own pocket.

It is quite clear that had the Swedish government realized in 1987 that the advent of commercial TV was inevitable, then the act of giving a national, terrestrial franchise (with public service features as in the case of British ITV) would have effectively taken the market away from TV3. But this did not happen until 1991 – by which time TV3 was well established through cable. In effect, by sitting on the fence for too long, Sweden's politicians abdicated their ability to implement an important part of national media policy.

With TV3 enjoying a growing audience for an output containing mainly international material, yet another commercial channel appeared on the Swedish scene, TV4, run by the Nordic Television company. TV4's goal from a faltering start in 1986 with limited cable transmissions, was to win a franchise for a third terrestrial net alongside Swedish TV's existing two channels. The policy involved heavy lobbying of politicians coupled with a programme strategy promising a large percentage of nationally produced programme material. TV4's original financiers included Sweden's largest industrial empire (the Wallenberg conglomerate who dominate Ericsson, ASEA, Astra and other major corporations), the Farmers' confederation as well as a book publishing company. The station went on air in September 1990 using the Tele-X direct broadcasting satellite (owned by the Swedish government's Space Corporation!). The satellite-fed newcomer, however, soon ran into financial difficulties. Advertisers already into satellite TV preferred the established TV3 channel which used Luxembourg's Astra satellite and which already existed in all cable systems and most private dishes.

All through its build-up period, from 1986 through to 1990, TV4 was actively lobbying not only the political establishment but also the Swedish artistic community. At the same 1986 seminar organized by the Swedish Music Centre (see above) where representatives for Rupert Murdoch's SKY channel described their dedication to Swedish music, one of the founder members of TV4 gave a similar message:

'If you are going to build up an advertising-financed TV channel in Sweden, then one should concentrate first and foremost on Swedish-language programmes, programmes that have their origin in the reality of Sweden, Swedish culture, Swedish music. A Swedish audience wants to see its own actors, musicians and artists. Such a channel as we are intending to create needs Swedish music – we believe that Swedish music also needs such a channel to find its audience.'

(Lejonborg, TI 18/03/86)

This TV4 spokesman went on to give details of how the new station would link up with different groups playing different types of music (jazz, troubadours, etc.), with different clubs and venues which could feature regularly in output. At this time (March 1986) TV4 – then known as Nordisk Television – had already started producing some pilot programmes, paid for by sponsorship money. They were then distributed in video cassette form via cable systems in major cities. One such series consisted of music videos – only half of these, however, were of Swedish origin! At the 1986 seminar on Swedish music and television, the same TV4 founding father (a TV producer who left a top management position at Swedish TV to start his own channel) proposed some interesting observations about the development of media technology, activities and policies in Sweden. Little ever happened as the result of policy initiatives, according to his analysis. Radio's third national popular music channel in the 1960s was a response to an entrepreneur's activities from a pirate ship. The introduction of colour TV around 1970, he claimed, was also the direct result of an earlier experimental programme within state TV showing what it could offer, not as a consequence of political media-policy foresight regarding desirable or even inevitable developments. TV4 would be such a 'cutting edge' activity, which would force the government to award one or more franchises for terrestrial commercial TV networks. Test productions were coupled with an extensive lobbying and advertising campaign. A TV4 document distributed in 1988 emphasized further the Swedish national angle:

> In competition with American and Pan-European channels, our high percentage of attractive, national programmes will make us the dominant channel. . . . We will be the Swedish TV-channel for Swedish viewers. This will give us a clear and dominant profile within a speedily-growing international output of programmes.
>
> (Nordisk Television 1988)

In 1986, these operators still believed that a Swedish government decision on the formal introduction of commercial TV would be forthcoming within a year. In actual fact, the process took all of five years. In March of 1991, the Social Democrats and the major opposition parties agreed on the terms. The existing two state channels, TV1 and TV2, would remain public service and licence-financed. The franchise for a third channel would be granted. The terms were made public on 28 March 1991, and applications had to be in by 31 May, a short period in which to form and finance such a billion-kronor operation. Would-be franchise operators were also expected to be on-air within six to eight months. After years of sitting on the fence, a total about-turn in policy involved getting the problem out of the way as soon as possible (probably a pending general election in September 1991 was the explanation).

The rules for Sweden's TV franchise application form an interesting document. They specify that would-be programme operators must include news, information and entertainment in a 'varied output of high quality'. As regards national content, the formulation indicates a somewhat vague direction of intent:

> Transmissions should include, to a considerable extent, programmes in the Swedish language and programmes which feature Swedish artists

and works by Swedish copyright holders. Foreign programmes should reflect different cultures.

(Swedish Ministry of Education 1991, section 2.2.1)

The franchise announcement attracted some ten applicants including TV Plus with French interests. The latter and some seven others were soon rejected by a vetting committee (TV Plus because the government would not allow a majority foreign share-holding and the others because of doubts about financial muscle). The first screening left two of the original applicants, the existing semi-legal operators TV3 and TV4. A parliamentary committee voted for the TV3 application – the company had promised to set up a regionally based operation in Sweden which would satisfy the content demands of the tender. Two prominent regional Social Democratic politicians were featured on the Board of the new company. TV3 had also promised to discontinue its satellite/cable channel into Sweden if granted the terrestrial franchise.

A decision to give the channel, in effect, to the Manhattan-based Swedish entrepreneur, Jan Stenbeck, was a sensitive one (bearing in mind that this was in July 1991, only two months before a general election). TV4 would certainly have gone bankrupt. The leadership of the ruling Social Democrats overruled the recommendation and delayed the decision until after the election. Sweden's September election ousted the Social Democrats and put a centre-right coalition in charge. One of their first tasks was to sort out the TV franchise mess. However, before a decision could be made, and with TV4's finances getting worse by the hour, TV3 owner Stenbeck produced a trump card. He offered to pull back his own application if TV4 allowed him to become their largest shareholder (for an undisclosed fee believed to be very small). They were cornered and had but one way out. TV4, under the control of TV3's owner, became the sole remaining applicant for a Swedish commercial TV channel. Stenbeck could keep his TV3 satellite channel going (by now it was out of the red) and he also gained total control of all sales of advertising for both the new channel and his existing TV3, i.e. a virtual monopoly on TV advertising sales in Sweden. The politicians claimed they could do nothing but accept the new situation. Entrepreneur and media mogul Jan Stenbeck, who prefers to call himself a 'media mongrel', had got the best of all possible business worlds.

The contract for Sweden's first, fully legal commercial channel included many of the conditions which had been suggested in the franchise application. The loose term 'a considerable amount', was still used to refer to the content of works by Swedish copyright-holders, without any attempt to define what was meant by 'considerable'. By contrast, the rules for children's programmes (five hours weekly with the exception of the summer months) decree that 'the major part shall be produced in Sweden or in the other Nordic countries'. Overall the new channel promises to maintain a 50 per cent domestic production level (including sports and news) which is 20 per cent less than the original aims of TV4's founders. The agreement also stipulates the size of an annual franchise fee, consisting of a fixed sum (app. US$8 million) plus a percentage in the region of 15 per cent of advertising income. This combined fee will, in effect, be used to support the running costs of Sweden's two existing public service, licence-financed TV channels, i.e the new channel's main competitor. The more money the new channel earns, the more it has to pay to the former Swedish broadcasting monopoly (a strange form of 'market economy' regulation). If the new channel makes a loss, then Stenbeck can let it collapse without losing too much, and concentrate once again on his satellite channels, outside the constraints of Swedish content regulation and bound only by the looser terms of the 1987 European convention on transborder television transmissions.

Jan Stenbeck's rise to fame as Scandinavia's new media mogul has followed a path that is not unknown in European media history, as we shall note in our concluding section. Stenbeck utilized the combination of deregulation and new technology to get access to a new TV channel and fill it with low-cost programmes, and then proceeded to expand by swallowing others. But his involvement is not only in television, far from it. The growth of his various media and electronic operations (all of which end in the suffix '-vik', in English, 'creek') involves a network of cases of formal and informal integration. Stenbeck owns a private analogue mobile phone network in Scandinavia. His Kinnevik parent company controls 10 per cent of the shares in the Luxembourg company that owns the two Astra medium-powered satellites and has a contract for four transponders on Astra A and B; these are used to send language versions of TV3 to Denmark and Norway as well as a scrambled subscription film channel TV1000. Stenbeck has a book publishing company (Brombergs), a video production house (Strix) and a newly started record company (Z-Records) in Sweden together with Time-Warner. While TV4, under the control of Stenbeck, was signing the agreement regulating the content of the new terrestrial commercial TV channel, another part of Stenbeck's organization was distributing commercially funded radio programmes via satellite to small neighbourhood radio stations, encouraging them to break the law which still forbade commercial radio on land-based transmitters.

If Sweden's media politicians had been more aware of the history of the commercial growth of broadcasting in Europe, then they would at least have known what to expect. Maybe they would have reacted in a very different way much earlier. But this was not the case – they had preferred to sit on the fence too long. Party politics was also involved. Whilst in opposition, the centre-right parties had accused the Social Democrats of stalling on the important issue of 'free' radio and television, inferring that the then ruling party wanted to retain the monopoly of the former Sveriges

Radio for its own propaganda purposes (the possibility of this actually happening is something most staff at Sveriges Radio would vehemently deny). When a non-socialist coalition was voted in, in September 1991, their previous rhetoric forced them to act, even if the outcome was hardly what anyone wanted. The new Minister of Culture summed up the dilemma perfectly in terms of political expediency: 'We had the choice of doing something or doing nothing. There would have been an awful row if we had done nothing.'

By way of a postscript, we should mention one other aspect of the Stenbeck-Swedish saga. Students of Swedish political life will be aware of an interesting coincidence; Jan Stenbeck just happens to be the brother of Sweden's Foreign Minister in the government that took office in September 1991. However, we do not believe this has any relevance in his media empire building; the two have not been on speaking terms since a feud in the 1970s involving their inheritance from the family estate (the very resources which gave Stenbeck the power to buy media technology and software to fill it). Such relationships can be expected to turn up in small countries where the power hierarchy is very small at the top.

THE SWEDISH PHONOGRAM INDUSTRY: GENERAL STATISTICS

Statistics show that the Swedes are still buying phonograms. The CD, after a relatively slow start in Sweden compared to some other industrial countries, overtook the vinyl LP in May 1991. Company spokesmen credit CD sluggishness to the fact that Swedes invested heavily in audio systems in the late 1970s and early 1980s which made vinyl software more attractive.

The early 1980s also saw a general stagnation of phonogram sales. That is definitely a thing of the past (Nylöf 1990: 89). From 1989 to 1990 total units sold, according to combined statistics for both members and non-members of IFPI, rose from 25.6 to 27.3 million. Sales of CDs and pre-recorded cassettes accounted for the net increase despite a drop of 1.5 million units in shipments of vinyl LPs. The 1990 statistics suggest that the 8.5 million Swedes purchased annually an average of 3.2 phonograms per person. If taxes (25 per cent VAT) and retail margins are added to the wholesale value, then one can arrive at an estimated per capita outlay in 1990 of around US$31 per annum (on a par with the USA). This amounted to an increase of $3.5 or around 12 per cent over the 1989 figures. In 1991 the number of units sold decreased slightly to 26 million, but total *retail* sales continued to rise, putting per capita expenditure above that of the USA. One possible reason is that the local industry has been able to keep CD prices at an artificially high level (approximately US$25) through blocking cheap imports from the USA.

In international terms, of course, the Swedish phonogram market is just as marginal as those of the other small countries in this study. The total wholesale value in 1990 was approximately US$170 million – that's about 5

178   Media Policy and Music Activity

Table 8.4   Sales of pre-recorded music, 1991

Country	Retail sales (US$m)	Per capita
Sweden	334	38
USA	7,716	32
UK	2,202	38
Germany	2,270	29
Japan	3,300	26

Source: IFPI

per cent of the annual turnover of one of the giant transnationals, Polygram. Industry statistics, however, show an interesting history of ups and downs. They also illustrate the problems of describing developments via conversions of local currencies to US dollars – the dollar itself has fluctuated so widely against other currencies throughout the past decades.

THE MAJORS INCREASE THEIR INFLUENCE

The past two decades have seen a steady increase in the Big Five phonogram companies' dominance of the Swedish phonogram industry. This applies both to market shares for their own productions as well as to their control over distribution. Manufacturing, too, has been affected via the movement of disc and cassette production to large facilities primarily in Holland and Germany.

EMI, formerly known as 'The Gramophone Company' have been important actors since the 1920s (Gronow 1983: 60ff.). CBS purchased a local distribution and production company in 1969. WEA created a local subsidiary via the same method in 1979. Polygram amalgamated its two local subsidiaries (Polydor and Phonogram) in the early 1970s and created a joint distribution company with a local national independent, Sonet. When BMG bought the RCA record division and adopted a strategy of global expansion in the late 1980s, it established a footing in Sweden not by taking over its former local distributor (a locally owned Swedish company called Electra) but by starting its own operation. The result was that Electra went bankrupt in 1990, leaving many small local phonogram producers who used its distribution facilities in dire straits.

Soramäki and Harma estimated that the Big Five accounted for 70 per cent of sales of LPs and 77 per cent of singles sold in Sweden in 1977 (Soramäki and Harma 1978). EMI enjoyed a dominant position with over 30 per cent of album sales. A problem with these figures is that they probably do not include sales of companies not organized within the Swedish branch of the IFPI – such statistics were hard to come by in the late 1970s. More exact estimates of market share have been collected and made public since 1989 (Table 8.5). They show Virgin (then part-owned by

Table 8.5 Phonogram industry statistics in Sweden, 1965–91

Year	1965	1970	1975	1980	1982	1984	1986	1988	1990	1991
Units (millions)										
Singles	NA	3.5	1.4	1.9	2.7	3.9	4.7	4.3	4.7	3.7
LPs	NA	6.1	10.7	10.5	8.9	8.9	10.0	10.4	9.1	6.1
Cassettes	–	0.4	2.0	2.6	1.7	2.8	4.6	4.7	5.7	4.9
CD	–	–	–	–	–	0.0	0.8	3.2	7.5	11.2
TOTAL	5.0	10.0	14.1	15.0	13.3	15.6	20.1	22.6	27.0	25.8
Wholesale values SEK	NA	108	268	285	294	386	559	750	1,024	1,162
Retail value US$m excl. VAT	NA	70	125	138	89	82	154	189	208	276

Sources: Kulturrådet 1979: 1, chapter 5; Swedish IFPI.
Note: Dollar figures are based on average annual exchange rates.

Japanese Fuji) on the threshold of transnational status with almost 8 per cent of the Swedish market and a repertoire consisting of 75 per cent of international imports. (Virgin, of course, became part of EMI in 1992.)

Table 8.6 is not entirely self-explanatory, particularly as regards the Big Five's dominance over distribution. Warner's Swedish subsidiary controlled the distribution of both Virgin and Sonet (in the early 1970s, Sonet owned a distribution outfit together with, amongst others, Polygram). Warner, Polygram and BMG also distribute a number of smaller Swedish labels. Sonet's recent history is of particular interest as regards the fate of national, independent phonogram companies. Up to 1989, some 30 per cent of Sonet's phonogram income came from their licence to sell records on the Island, Chrysalis and Polar labels – Polar is the Swedish phonogram company built up around the ABBA group in the 1970s. Polygram bought Polar in 1988 as well as Island a year later. Chrysalis was absorbed by EMI. This led Sonet executive and part-owner, Dag Häggkvist, to admit in a speech to the International Music and Media Conference (Amsterdam, 1990) that the loss of the Scandinavian distribution for Island and Chrysalis was 'the severest blow we have ever suffered'. Häggkvist also described how 'Sonet intended to maintain its independent role at a time when almost all of its European counterparts have been swallowed up by WEA, EMI or Polygram'. He said that 'in the Nineties, the niche to be occupied by European indies was an audio-visual one' (*Europe* 1990: 9).

Sonet's survival strategy was twofold. Through formal and informal integration the company expanded film and video interests to cut dependency on the phonogram business and thereby replace the stability which

Table 8.6 Market shares for different companies and groups of phonogram producers in Sweden

Market share (%/annum)	1977	1989	1990
BMG (1977=RCA)	2.0	8.0	12.1
EMI	31.5	15.6	15.0
Polygram	13.0	11.9	12.6
SONY (formerly CBS)	12.0	15.6	15.6
Warner (WEA)	11.0	18.7	17.5
Virgin	–	7.7	7.6
TOTAL %	69.5	77.5	80.4
Sonet	NA	7.3	6.7
SGA	–	4.9	3.4
SOM	appr. 3%	3.7	4.2
Others	–	6.5	5.3

Sources: Soramäki and Haarma 1978; IFPI Sweden

had previously been provided by a steady flow of releases from well-known artists on Island and Chrysalis. The other strategy adopted by Sonet in 1990 was to put more funds into domestic repertoire, both for the home and the international market. Indeed, Sonet's turnover actually rose from 65 to 68 million SEK from 1989 to 1990, despite the loss of major labels. But within a year, Sonet's management came to the conclusion that it is virtually impossible to run a large, national phonogram company without other related media interests because of the majors' increased control of distribution, coupled with a lack of attractive international labels available for local licence deals. Without a steady flow of income from international repertoire which can serve to even out the dips in income between important domestic releases, a national phonogram company of Sonet's size was deemed not to be a going proposition. In July 1991, the announcement was made that Sonet's phonogram and very lucrative publishing business (with an impressive array of Swedish repertoire) had gone the same way as Polar, sold to Polygram.

The Big Five plus Virgin were now controlling almost 90 per cent of the Swedish phonogram market, an increase of 20 per cent over the estimate from the mid-1970s.

Even more interesting facts emerge from a closer scrutiny of Table 8.6. SGA built up a market niche selling primarily Swedish 'dance band' music – combos which entertain a young to middle-aged audience in hotels and dance halls. It went bankrupt in 1990 and the operation was later taken over by a Dutch company. SOM stands for Swedish Independent Music Producers, a group of phonogram producers who emerged from the so-called Swedish music movement of the 1970s, producers who referred to themselves then as 'non-commercial'. They work primarily with local repertoire but have also distributed material from smaller companies in other countries. Some of SOM's members who emerged from the radical student and music movements of the late 1960s have now celebrated twenty years of operations. Their impact in terms of market share, however, remains around the same level as estimated by a Swedish government report in 1979, namely 4 per cent. SOM account, of course, for a far higher percentage of total releases of Swedish music, as we shall see shortly.

SWEDISH OR INTERNATIONAL REPERTOIRE

About 10 per cent of annual LP/CD/MC releases contain music recorded in Sweden – these account for approximately 30 per cent of total sales. The distribution amongst companies of different size is far from even. As on the international level, larger companies with impressive distribution capacity attract the most popular local artists; the smaller operators take the risks in the market that go with a large number of new products. Thus we find an artist such as Thomas Ledin, singing pop ballads mainly in Swedish, selling over 450,000 phonograms between June 1990 and March 1991 for BMG's 'Swedish' label, Record Station. Record Station releases on average only eight LPs per annum but account for 37 per cent of BMG Sweden's turnover (though 60 per cent of the company's costs!).

Whilst the majors' income from sales of Swedish phonograms ranges from 25 per cent (Polygram, Virgin) through 31 per cent (EMI) to 37 per cent in the case of BMG, the independents organized within the SOM group earn no less than 80 per cent of their income from Swedish sales. Comprehensive statistics concerning new releases of domestic artists have been hard to come by in Sweden, especially regarding singles. From 1987 onwards, however, the Swedish branch of the IFPI has collected data on releases in the LP format. In the following table, an LP which is also available as CD and/or MC is regarded as one new release. Rereleases are not included, unless they comprise new compilations of older material. Singles are excluded from the new release count.

Table 8.7 shows that the transnationals have *not* merely used their stronger position to concentrate on importing international hit songs and material by superstars. Their output of new Swedish releases, however, would seem to have decreased since the last available data were collected in 1977. Then they accounted for 65 per cent of pop and dance music and 55 per cent of classical releases (Kulturrådet 1979: 55).

Table 8.8 shows a drop in religious records as well as recordings of simpler styles of pop songs (schlager music). Classical releases showed a marked increase in 1990 which can be attributed to the breakthrough of the CD as a medium for recordings of music with a large dynamic range. The drop in 1991 suggests that this phase was over. The number of Swedish releases increased

Table 8.7 New releases of international/Swedish phonograms in LP format, and market shares for different groups of producers

	1986	1987	1988	1989	1990	1991
% Swedish sales	*30*	*30*	*34*	*29*	*32*	*28*
Total releases	3,486	6,780	5,163	6,667	7,332	7,270
Swedish releases	NA	540	670	585	779	644
Big Five + Sonet, Virgin, SGA						
% Total releases	*77*	*53*	*61*	*64*	*58*	*58*
Total releases	2,656	3,584	3,135	4,260	4,264	4,263
% Market share	*90*	*92*	*91*	*90*	*91*	*92*
% Swedish releases	NA	*48*	*48*	*49*	*30*	*31*
Swedish releases	NA	260	322	286	230	208
% Market share (Swedish recordings)	*85*	*87*	*88*	*76*	*79*	*72*
SOM						
% Swedish releases	NA	*18*	*32*	*19*	*17*	*30*
Swedish releases	NA	95	213	110	134	204
% Market share (Swedish recordings)	*11*	*8*	*9*	*10*	*11*	*11*
Others						
% Swedish releases	NA	*34*	*20*	*32*	*53*	*37*
Swedish releases	NA	185	135	189	415	252
% Market share (Swedish recordings)	*4*	*5*	*3*	*13*	*10*	*16*

Source: IFPI, Sweden 1991
Note: Percentage shown in italics

Table 8.8 Releases of phonograms with Swedish recordings, by style

	No. of releases			
Year	*1977*	*1987*	*1990*	*1991*
Jazz	35	26	15	16
Religious	100	17	6	4
Folk music	25	22	19	29
Children's music	40	60	72	77
Classical	100	159	334	139
Pop/rock/schlager	450	249	324	394
Other styles	50	7	9	5
TOTAL	800	540	779	664

Sources: 1977 SPK in Kulturrådet 1979: 55; IFPI Stockholm, 1991: 13.

Case Study: Sweden 183

from around 500 to 800 per annum in the latter half of the 1980s, dropping back to around 660 in 1991. The major companies, however, maintained a market share in the region of 80 per cent for sales of Swedish phonograms. BMG alone accounted for 14 per cent of sales of phonograms with Swedish music with less than ten LP releases (1 per cent of Swedish releases).

The BMG example quoted here highlights the important role of successful national artists in offsetting the risks that go with superstar dependence for major transnationals. That the transnationals play an important role in promoting young artists, however, is not entirely true, at least in a Swedish perspective. Often the national stars with successes on transnational labels are those who established themselves first through smaller independent companies.

The transnationals' involvement in producing, distributing and selling phonograms with Swedish music and artists can be attributed to a number of factors:

1 The need to continually seek new talent combined with the existence of a demand for a number of national stars in domestic markets.
2 The tendency for successful local artists to gravitate towards companies with larger financial resources as they achieve fame. Smaller phonogram companies find it difficult to invest the necessary capital in videos and other marketing operations. The transnationals' control over efficient distribution resources makes them a more attractive proposition than smaller, locally based companies.
3 The public debate on music in the media in the 1980s has concentrated on the role of Swedish music in the broadcast media, not on the need to support nationally and locally owned phonogram companies which can form the backbone of a local music industry. The latter was the case in the 1970s, when big selling groups such Hoola Bandoola or Nationalteatern were selling between 100,000 and 200,000 copies of LPs but were still content to stay with small companies for political reasons – the transnationals showed little interest at this time in local repertoire. Now one finds numerous artists and groups who started off within small companies which were often controlled by the musicians, moving to the subsidiaries of the international giants in their search for better marketing resources (e.g. Eldkvarn, Wilmer X, Eric Gadd).
4 The financial ability of the transnationals to give immediate and long-term financial support to groups and artists. Small companies cannot pay large advances on royalties. BMG could use its resources for a long-term involvement in Swedish music by purchasing a successful local company, Record Station, complete with a collection of established phonogram artists, shortly after it bought its way into Sweden in 1988.

The figures in Table 8.7 above demonstrate the dilemma facing smaller phonogram companies. In 1990, the SOM group, together with a variety of smaller operators categorized as 'Others', accounted for 70 per cent of all releases of Swedish music – specialist classical releases accounted for no less than 329 of the 'other' releases that year. The combined share of the market for Swedish phonograms was a mere 21 per cent. A spokesman for one of the original 'music movement' companies, MNW, gave this warning in 1989:

> There is a risk that everyone with any ideas in Sweden will rush off to Polygram, CBS or BMG just to get a royalty advance. Independent companies with sound finances which can afford to make different and creative decisions must exist. You need hundreds of thousands of kronor to market a record today. The most elementary video costs 50,000 (US$8,000). . . . The structural changes we are witnessing in Sweden are merely a reflection of the international competitive race between Bertelsmann and Warners.
>
> On the manufacturing side things are happening, too. When BMG bought up Record Station, manufacturing of discs and sleeves was moved to Germany. Two of three Swedish pressing plants are about to be closed down.
>
> The same applies to distribution. Soon the whole of Scandinavia will be distributed from Hamburg. What sort of conditions can Swedes expect in Hamburg? This is a very dangerous development.
>
> (Sjöström 1989: 9–10)

FROM PRIMARY TO SECONDARY INCOME: PAST THE 50/50 POINT

The availability of statistics makes Sweden one of the few territories where it is possible to estimate the important shift from primary to secondary incomes within the phonogram industry. Data indicate that Sweden has just about reached the critical point where as much or more of the phonogram industry's income comes from secondary sources, such as performance and publishing rights.

Secondary income sources are of three kinds. In countries which have signed the Rome Convention, phonogram companies have the right to collect dues when phonograms are performed in public (on radio/TV but also in some cases in shops, bars and other places where the public can hear recorded music). The other two sources are related to publishing activities. By buying music publishers, and making sure that composers sign away publishing rights to such publishers, phonogram companies can augment their income from both performing and mechanical rights. Of the 8 per cent or so of the price of a CD which goes to copyright-holders, between 33 and 50 per cent would be retained by publishers. Thirty-three per cent of incomes from performances on radio/TV or in other public contexts also go

Table 8.9 Estimate of secondary incomes to Swedish phonogram industry, 1990

	SEK (millions)
Wholesale value of phonogram market	1,000
Estimated profit 10%	100
Secondary income sources:	
Rome income (radio/TV/public performance)	
SEK 40m. 50% musicians. 50% IFPI	20
Performing rights, radio/TV/cable	
SEK 60m. Publishers (1/3)	20
Mechanical rights, NCB total Sweden	150
Publishers' share (33–50%)	50–75

to the same recipients. As the figures in Table 8.9 indicate, assuming a 10 per cent profit on wholesale value, phonogram companies are now earning just about as much from such secondary sources. Selling pieces of plastic is no longer the overriding source of income. This, in its turn, is likely to have a significant influence on forms of informal integration in the future.

STATE CULTURAL POLICY AND MUSIC ACTIVITY IN SWEDEN

Much official cultural policy during the past two decades can be related to a set of cultural goals which the Swedish parliament unanimously endorsed in 1974. Neighbouring Denmark followed another path, introducing a Music Law which stipulated minimum requirements for what the state and local authorities were expected to achieve in the field of music. But those were times of economic expansion in Sweden, which is probably why Swedish policymakers chose to formulate 'sky is the limit' goals rather than minimum standards. A phrase often used in the process was one of formulating a 'social environment policy'.

The cultural goals covered areas such as the decentralization of culture, involving support for measures to increase access to the arts in rural areas. In practice this led to the formation of regional theatre companies and music ensembles. A system of press subsidies, loosely coupled to a tax on advertising in the print media, was introduced. The aim was not only to support cultural publications with a small circulation, subsidies were also to be used to keep ailing local newspapers alive, if not well.

Sweden's ambitious cultural goals soon were richly reflected in state and municipal budgets. These showed an average annual increase of 19 per cent throughout the 1970s, with an all-time high of 25 per cent in 1975, the year after the goals passed parliament. In the 1980s, however, economic reality took its toll; the cultural budgets' average annual increase dropped from 19 to under 2.6 per cent. At present (1991/2) around 1 per cent of the state budget goes to the culture account, and of this, some 30 per cent (SEK 600m or around US$1m) is spent on musical activities. The lion's share goes to traditional recipients of arts grants. The Stockholm Opera, the country's twelve symphony orchestras and a number of regional chamber ensembles receive almost 80 per cent of state music subsidies.

Another much-discussed 1974 goal involved the difficult concept of 'commercialism'. Cultural policy should aim to decrease the 'negative effects of commercialism', an aim which gradually led policymakers into the area of popular and mass culture. In a prelude to the 1974 government Bill on state cultural policy, the then Minister of Education wrote:

> The pursuit of profits leads to efforts, via advertising or other means of manipulation, to influence consumption without regard for the importance of various needs. . . . This leads to a cultural content which neither provokes nor furthers critical attitudes and which demands passivity on the part of the consumer. Another consequence of commercial production or distribution is that even products of a serious nature have difficulty meeting the demands made by society: activities are concentrated into areas yielding the highest profit, thus discouraging variety and innovation.
>
> (Malm 1982: 45)

The commercialism debate at this early stage sought to find, or at least create, a magic dividing line between commercial culture (a commodity to be sold, a product to be consumed) and non-commercial culture (an activity serving to strengthen communicative potential). An assumption was that large transnational companies which had been swallowing up local Swedish phonogram producers would inevitably cause the market to be more commercial in a negative sense, with a greater concentration on international hits, favourites of Western 'Art music' and disco music. Such perceived negative effects of commercialization were seen as a major threat to Swedish musical activities. Much attention was focused on the workings of the Swedish phonogram industry.

The first indication of official Swedish concern about such matters can be found in a government report published in 1971, 'Fonogrammen i Musiklivet' (The Phonogram in Music Life) (SOU 1971). This study noted the increasing dominance of imported music, and the increasing difficulties experienced by those producing Swedish phonograms. The latter included some subsidiaries of the big transnationals such as EMI Sweden, but their limited activities with Swedish music and performers invariably depended on subsidies from organizations such as Swedish Radio or the Composers' Copyright Organization, STIM. The report was solely concerned with the so-called 'serious' music sector; the structure of and problems faced by phonogram companies outside the world of 'Art music' received no comment. The 1971 report recommended the setting up of a state-owned phonogram company (Caprice) attached organizationally to the state-supported concert organization, Rikskonserter.

Eight years later, in 1979, another Swedish report on the phonogram industry was published, this time by the National Council for Cultural Affairs (Kulturrådet 1979: 1). Entitled 'The Phonogram in Cultural Policy', this second official Swedish study had as its starting point the anti-'negative effects of commercialism' goal.

This second report noted that the Swedish phonogram industry was experiencing both internationalization and localization. The majors were concentrating on importing international hits. At the same time, as we have observed in a previous section, local groups of enthusiasts were starting their own local phonogram companies, working almost exclusively with Swedish music.

The situation of the Swedish 'popular' music industry was not ignored by the 1979 committee report. It noted the need to support all forms of music activity (art, folk, jazz, rock, etc. in both live performance and recordings), arguing that all played an important role in the maintenance and development of a national music heritage. This change of attitude as regards the importance of popular music forms and music activities from the point of view of cultural policy is a clear result of the 1974 Cultural Policy Bill and its smooth flow through the Swedish parliament. The underlying message in both reports, and indeed in the writings of many other commentators (Hellqvist 1977; Karlsson 1980) was that Sweden, despite the high standard of living of its citizens, was experiencing ever-increasing effects of cultural imperialism (although such a term was seldom used in official reports). Cheap imports of music, primarily from Anglo-American transnationals, were slowly killing Swedish music, and were also responsible for a growing outflow of funds which citizens spent on musical entertainment. It was becoming harder to work profitably with phonograms featuring Swedish creators and performers because of the relatively small quantities which could be sold compared to international phonograms with which domestic products had to compete. State involvement was needed to break this trend, and such involvement should not only apply to traditional areas of patronage in the arts, but should cover the commercial sector as well.

The focus in these official Swedish reports had been mainly on the Swedish phonogram industry (contra its international counterpart), and not so much on its growing degree of interdependence with other sectors of the music industry. The question of the local/national broadcasting industry in Sweden and its duty or role in promoting Swedish music was only parenthetically covered (Kulturrådet 1979: 154–8), mainly because those responsible for arts policy had no jurisdiction over broadcasting.

The 1979 committee report resulted in a call for some form of intervention by the government to ensure the continued release of phonograms with Swedish music and Swedish artists. Concrete suggestions included continued support for the government-subsidized phonogram company, Caprice. The idea was also mooted of general subsidies, linked loosely to a levy on blank sound and video cassette tapes and available to any phonogram producer working with Swedish music. The government accepted the spirit of these recommendations and a state-supported system for funding phonogram productions was set in motion in 1982.

The Swedish phonogram production subsidy system is administered by the National Council for Cultural Affairs. Grant applications from phonogram producers have averaged around 400 per annum. The council's phonogram committee, consisting mainly of musicians, musicologists, critics and cultural bureaucrats, distributes subsidies to some 25 per cent of the applicants. The order of magnitude averages around 40 per cent of total production costs. The committee's 1991 budget amounted to SEK4.5m (US$700,000); another SEK5.5m from the public purse was used to run the state phonogram company, Caprice.

With almost a decade's experience of such phonogram subsidies, an obvious question is: how valuable has the exercise been? Has it served to make a broader repertoire available to more people in more places? Fifteen per cent of new releases have received phonogram production grants. They cover a wide range of genres. But distribution, both in terms of physical sales and radio plays has been minimal. The highest average sales noted in a group of 344 subsidies phonograms can be found in the 'children's records' genre – and then only a meagre 3,000 during the first year on the market (Table 8.10).

Table 8.10 demonstrates a stronger leaning towards jazz and folk genres amongst gatekeepers on the grants committee than is apparent in the market as a whole. A curious anomaly is provided by the 'children's' genre – here the percentage receiving grants was smaller than the percentage of releases in the market as a whole. Official statements have frequently stressed the need to provide extra support for children's culture as a means of combating the negative effects of commercialism. The figures above say nothing, of course, about the relative qualitative virtues of state-supported children's phonograms and those from the commercial industry as a whole. It merely indicates that the phonogram grants committee may have different standards than the gatekeepers at the phonogram companies.

Most of the subsidies have been received by small Swedish phonogram companies – local subsidiaries of the majors have only rarely applied for grants. Both musicians and phonogram producers claim that the poor sales figures are the result, not of poor quality, but of lack of media exposure. A small study by the Swedish Association of Popular Music Composers showed that 54 per cent of a sample of 281 works recorded with phonogram subsidies were not performed at all on Swedish radio during the two years

Table 8.10 Distribution of subsidized phonograms (applications, grants in numbers and percentages)

Genre	Applications no.	% (86/8)	Grants (% of total)	Market comparison	Average sales phongr/	units
Western Art music	176	20	24	29	61	1,489
Electro-acoustic	–	–	–	–	7	203
Pop/rock	328	37	28	46	96	2,359
Jazz	132	15	15	5	74	675
Folk	97	11	14	4	49	935
Ballads	62	7	7	NA	21	920
Children	35	4	8	11	16	3,035
Others	53	6	4	1	21	576

Notes: Sales refer to a sample of 344 subsidized phonograms which had been on the market for more than one year in March 1989. Figures for 'units' refer to sales during first year in the market. 'Others' are mainly rereleases of older material. The 'market comparison' column shows the total spread amongst all releases on the market in 1987.

1986/87. Producers at Swedish National Radio present a variety of responses to the accusations of lack of support for subsidized phonograms. These range from claims that phonograms from small phonogram companies don't find their way to radio producers, to assertions that the music is either of poor quality or of the type that would appeal only to a very small minority in the audience.

We will now attempt to sum up the net result of almost ten years of phonogram production subsidies in Sweden.

Positive aspects

— increased availability of new Swedish music and artists on phonograms;
— documentation of creative activities which would have been impossible otherwise;
— support for small local phonogram companies working with local artists/composers allowing them to survive some of the ups and downs of trade cycles;
— an indirect positive effect on live music activities. A phonogram release gives artists more status when negotiating with those promoting concerts.

Less positive aspects

— Physical distribution has been limited despite the creation of a state-supported distribution organization, CDA. The decreasing number of

specialist music stores results in difficulties for new music to reach a 'browsing' public.
— Promotion has been limited. Production grants cannot be augmented with funds for publicity in the form of videos or extensive printed matter.
— Media exposure has been limited. Swedish Radio's formal 'independence' *vis-à-vis* the phonogram industry makes it impossible to guarantee promotion through radio plays. Gatekeepers on the phonogram grant committee are mainly musicians or cultural bureaucrats, whereas gatekeepers in radio/TV/print media tend to be non-performing music critics or commercial entrepreneurs – this can lead to a discrepancy which does not enhance exposure.

By 1982, the commercialism debate in Sweden had begun to mellow. The derogatory connotation of the term 'commercial' was no longer at the forefront of the ideological debate. In a tract entitled 'Five Researchers on Cultural Commercialism', published by the National Council for Cultural Affairs, one could find admissions that increased commercialization of the cultural sector had identifiable positive effects:

> Duke Ellington is an artist who probably would have been less well-known in our nation if he had not been launched commercially. . . . Reggae music from Jamaica is [another] example. An awaking interest has been followed up by the commercial system.
>
> (Nylöf 1982: 157)

The same author goes on to note several undesirable consequences related to the increased power of the profitability goal in so many areas. Indeed, the 1980s involved a rethink in terms of cultural policy activities dictated to a large extent by economic realities. Whilst sponsoring was regarded with great suspicion in the 1970s, in the 1980s gifts from those who could afford them were often seen as a saving grace. Thus the Volvo company started paying for second violins in the Gothenburg Symphony Orchestra and a paper company contributed generously to Swedish Radio's Symphony Orchestra so that it could go on tour.

Attitudes also changed as regards the sort of music activities which can be embraced within the concept of 'edifying culture'. Tommy Steele playing Shakespeare would be a historical analogy to the process we are describing. As Nylöf observed in 1990: 'The realm of "edifying culture" has expanded since the 1950s and 1960s, when only classical and contemporary concert music was considered "fine art" ' (Nylöf 1990: 99).

This change of attitudes has been reflected not only via spectacular events, such as rock guitarists performing with symphony orchestras, but also in state cultural policy regarding the division of available funds. Jazz, folk and rock groups get state grants totalling around US$1m per annum.

The music of the angry young men and women who were so anti-establishment in the 1970s has become clean and accepted. Some might say they have become the victims of repressive tolerance.

MUSIC ACTIVITY IN SWEDEN

The increasing degree of commercialism and industrialization of culture has not led to a marked decrease in music activity in Sweden. Yet there are few signs of an increase in the numbers of performing individuals and groups, despite all the funds that have been directed towards supportive actions. On the other hand, non-performance activity seems to have shown the greatest growth, presumably as a result of the rising presence of music in the media environment.

> Between 1975 and 1986, the share of the population who say they are very interested in music has increased from 14 to 19 per cent . . . the greatest changes have occurred with respect to interest in popular music. . . . The share of the population who, when asked to name their favourite artists and/or composers, mentioned at least one person in the category of pop/rock, rose from slightly over 40 per cent in 1975 to 60 per cent in 1986.
>
> (Nylöf 1990: 87–8)

As regards performance activities in the pop/rock field, two different factors are of interest. One is the number actually involved and the other is the language used for vocals. In the 1960s, Beatles fever inspired several thousand Swedish pop groups to establish themselves, singing in English (Wallis and Malm 1987: 113). By the early 1970s this wave had died down and equally many new groups appeared singing in Swedish. A growing interest in matters pertaining to cultural identity also inspired a folk music revival with literally thousands of musicians and listeners regularly congregating at traditional 'fiddlers' conventions', open-air gatherings out in the countryside during the short hectic Swedish summer. A significant observation concerns the renaissance enjoyed by a traditional folk instrument threatened with extinction, the *nyckelharpa* (keyed fiddle). A few enthusiasts started study circles in the mid-1970s where those who wished could make their own *nyckelharpa*. This activity spread over the country. Fifteen years later, the *nyckelharpa* was no longer a curio performed on by a few aged gentlemen. It had become very much an instrument played by young persons, male and female. One can trace this development to the combination of enthusiasm, a general interest in national culture, and the administrative structure in the form of subsidized study circles (part of the cultural budget). With the exception of one or two television programmes, the electronic media seem to have played only a minor role in stimulating this form of performance activity.

Plate 8.1 The Swedish *nyckelharpa* (keyed fiddle): once almost extinct, it is now kept alive by enthusiasts who build their own instruments.

In 1990 a national Year of Folk Music and Dance was proclaimed by a number of organizations and institutions involved in this cultural area. The aim of the manifestation was to improve the low status of folk music and dance. Committees were formed on national, regional and local levels. Thousands of concerts, dance shows and other activities were organized locally with very modest financial resources. Gradually the politicians and the mass media began to take note of the campaign. There was a marked increase in the folk music and dance content of TV and radio programming. A change of attitude could be noted in the press. Instead of journalists merely filing nostalgic reports on exotic fiddlers' gatherings, folk music events began to be the focus of more serious reviews (Schäfer et al. 1991). The year-long campaign can be seen as an example of a conscious effort by representatives of a non-mass media music form to get access to the media without having to change or adapt their art to the media too much. Mediaization of Swedish folk music, however, is certainly taking place with several media-oriented groups incorporating synthesizers in their instrumental line-up.

Choral activity is another area where Swedes excel. Almost half a million actively participate – a figure which has remained stable since the mid-1970s. On the whole, Swedish music life has become very diversified during the past few decades. This is partly owing to the increased availability of different music styles through the media, and partly to the immigration of peoples from other parts of the world. Examples of the media influx are provided by the existence of groups that specialize in big band jazz from the New York 1928–9 era, or French Creole music from Guadeloupe of the 1930s: musical styles that are virtually never performed any more in their countries of origin. The influence of immigrants can be noted in the Stockholm subway with its variety of buskers, or at clubs with salsa or music from the Balkan countries. This diversity, however, is rarely reflected in the broadcasting media, who tend to shun 'odd' styles of music.

Increased availability and the lower pricing of music machines, synthesizers, home studios, etc. has probably led to more semi-professional recording activities. This is reflected in applications for phonogram grants. In 1982/3 the grant committee received only three applications concerning works where the music had been created by one person using electro-acoustic devices in a studio. They were all in the category of electronic Art music. In 1989/90, however, the number had increased from three to nineteen. Only one application was in the Art category – the remaining eighteen were categorized as popular or experimental popular music (equivalent to an increase from 1 to 6 per cent of total annual grant requests). Although these figures amount to a clear trend, they hardly represent the total number of home studios using digital samplers and PC programmes – hundreds have been sold and much music-making undoubtedly occurs in such individual environments.

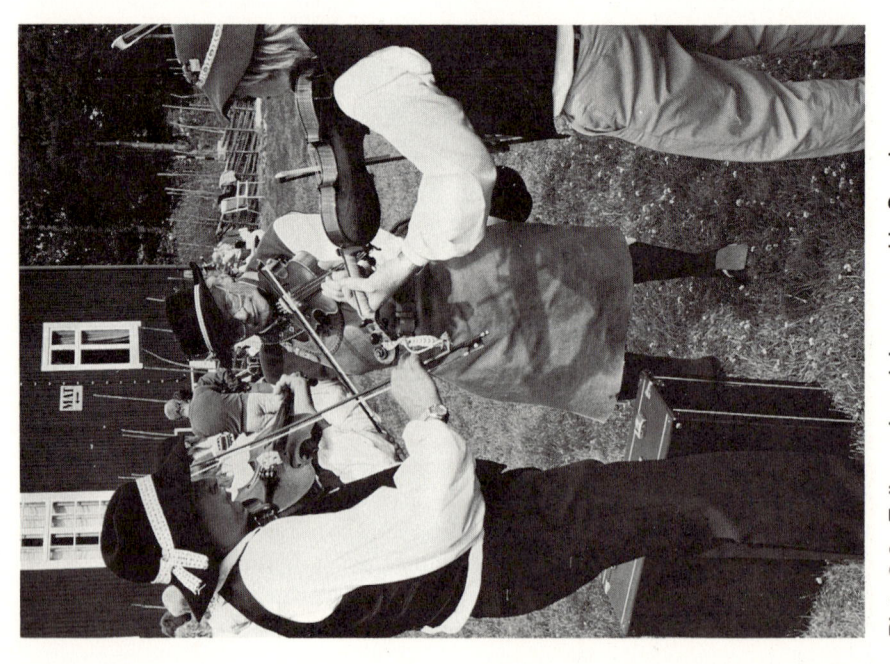

Plate 8.2 Folk music gaining ground in Sweden.

As we enter the 1990s, Sweden still has several thousand artists and groups in the pop/rock genres which emerge from time to time. When the national Post Office sponsored a Swedish rock championship in 1990, the organizers received 4,200 cassettes from would-be finalists. Only one of the ten finalists sang in Swedish. This observation would seem to stand in contrast to the findings of a study commissioned by the Swedish Composers' Association (SKAP) in 1987 and repeated in 1991. A sample of 1,000 Swedes was asked how many would prefer more than half of the music played on the national pop music channel (P3) to have lyrics in Swedish. In 1987, 31 per cent answered affirmatively. In 1991 the figure rose to 39 per cent, with an even spread across all age groups, even including the 16–29 year olds which make up the core listeners to Sweden's many new pop radio stations which play mainly Anglo-American hits. That many of the groups aspiring to win the 1990 Swedish rock championships sang in English might be the result of the fact that the last such extravaganza, organized in 1982, was won by a little-known group from a Stockholm suburb. The group was 'Europe', which went on to win international fame with hits such as 'The Final Countdown'.

Chapter 9
Conclusions

AS WE ENTER THE 1990s

'One of the great worries about music these days is that when one walks down the streets of any capital in Europe, one hears, for example in pop music terms, the same music coming out from discos, from boutiques and so on. I think throughout the world, particularly with the television industry moving so quickly as it is, you could develop a situation whereby only a dozen superstars in music were acceptable to television, sponsorship, to broadcasting companies, to record companies. I fear that the local, but very worthy and very good artist could suffer increasingly from this very high selling power'.
(Huw Tregellis Williams, Head of Music, BBC Wales, 23/07/83)

This statement was made in a filmed interview for Swedish television in 1983. The sentiments are perfectly understandable in the early 1990s. If anything, his limitation to Europe could be extended beyond this continent; Huw Williams was not too aware of MTV at that time and neither were the Swedes, nor the Jamaicans.

In the 1970s, fears were expressed that the transnational phonogram companies could squeeze local music industries and activities out of existence. The 1980s were characterized by the growth of even bigger global media conglomorates where recording, manufacturing and distributing musical products were only divisions of a larger totality. On the other hand, size, we presume, was the curse of the dinosaurs. The Small are still around, with enthusiasts coming and going, doing 'their own thing', relying on access to affordable, available technology, and not infrequently helping the Big with sources of new artistic and creative talent.

With broadcasting and narrowcasting showing an explosive development in virtually all nations (apart from the very poorest), it has been natural for us to focus on questions of access to secondary music media. Our six case studies have been full of examples of musicians, lobbyists and pressure groups and even the occasional politician or senior decisionmaker expressing favourable opinions of local forms of music and their rights in the media. Not infrequently this has been accompanied by a wealth of policy rhetoric which has had little if any effect either on enhancing status in the media or on stimulating music activity. All too often, technological and economic variables have decided the rules of the game, with policymaking tagging along behind, regretting developments that have been unfortunate but apparently inevitable.

In many nations, music and particularly recorded music has simply not been regarded as an area worthy of detailed policy considerations. Canada, for instance, is a nation which has gone further than many by introducing specific rules for Canadian music content on radio stations. A Canadian government report in 1982 noted, however, that the very industry which was a prerequisite for a supply of local music to broadcasting, the Canadian phonogram industry, had been more or less ignored by the policymakers (not unlike the case of Kenya's various attempts to change music policy on national radio).

The Canadian report noted:

> Clearly sound recording is one of the seminal cultural influences of our times, making much music happen 'on demand'. Yet, paradoxically, the sound recording industry has not usually been included among other cultural industries when major support policies were being considered by . . . government. The government has devised policy tools to assist in other cultural industries – book publishing, magazine publishing and film – which have produced demonstrable cultural gains. But in the case of sound recordings, such measures have been very few.
>
> (Government of Canada 1982: 235–6)

The same applies more or less to all the nations in our sample. All too often, policies in one cultural, industrial or social area do not tally with policies in another; more examples will follow.

At this point, it seems wise to return again to consider the three significant music industry variables proposed in our introduction; technology, economy and organization. A number of important media phenomena in the 1980s can be viewed in relation to these variables. Digital technology, satellites and the expansion of broadcasting are important developments, as is the continued dichotomy of the Big and the Small. The growth of global conglomerates represents the Big; the Small appear in various guises amongst the rich area of local music activity.

SUMMARIZING THE MAIN PHENOMENA OF THE 1980s

By the mid-1980s, the analogue cassette and associated cheap playback equipment was firmly established virtually everywhere. Then the world got a new sound carrier, the CD. Manufacturing CDs is more complex than copying analogue cassettes and requires a higher investment. Playback machines for analogue cassettes are fairly simple mechanical devices (which is another reason why they have replaced vinyl discs in many tropical countries). Thus our data shows CDs firmly established in industrialized Sweden (overtaking the LP in 1991), and just beginning to be used for pop and rock in Wales. A few CD imports have appeared in Jamaica and some can be bought as tourist souvenirs in Trinidad. CDs are virtually absent in Kenya and Tanzania; the likelihood of CD manufacturing facilities appearing within the immediate future in either our Caribbean or our East African sample would seem to be remote. With the concentration of CD manufacturing in a handful of large centralized factories in Europe, Sweden – which used to boast any number of vinyl record plants – now only has two small locally based CD factories, both of which are barely breaking even.

That CD players and some international software will turn up in the homes of wealthier citizens in the poorer nations, on the other hand, seems more likely. Some of this software might even include variants of local African or Caribbean music recorded and manufactured in Europe or the USA. The relevance of the CD as a sound carrier for local musicmaking activities in these poorer nations will be limited. The same will apply to the next generations of digital sound carriers (Digital Audio Tape) which also are associated with a higher degree of precision than conventional analogue cassettes.

Another reason for a slower spread of such manufacturing technology can be found in the growth of business conglomerates in the consumer electronics and entertainment fields. We have already referred to the significance of hardware manufacturers such as Sony purchasing the software producer, CBS records. Sony have a different degree of interest in protecting intellectual property from piracy than during the 1970s, when the Asian hardware manufacturers were spreading analogue cassette technology around the world (made possible in part by Philips's decision not to protect the patent of their analogue 'music cassette' or MC). With Philips and Sony jointly controlling the CD patent, they have a mutual interest in controlling the spread of this technology in such a way as to avoid piracy. Sony had also learnt from their experiences with the Betamax video format (which lost the battle in the marketplace to VHS) that new hardware standards cannot be launched without access to suitable software.

Centralizing manufacturing to large, strategically placed centres in Europe has been one way to control the spread of CDs – this also has the added advantages of scale. With the formal integration of hardware and software manufacturers, the phonogram industry has even been able to vet plans for selling CD manufacturing technology to the newly emerging democracies of Eastern Europe, even though these countries have provided so much of the classical music repertoire which fills many low-price

CDs on sale in the industrialized Western nations. The likelihood, in other words, of Philips-Polygram opening up a CD plant in Kenya is remote, despite low wage costs; the risk of local music activities deemed to be illegal would be regarded as too high. Here we can note an important difference from the 1970s, where the presence of pirate manufacturers also provided local musicians with an opportunity to use new manufacturing resources. Such considerations support our postulate concerning a growing technological gap between the developed and the developing nations in the late 1980s.

We have already noted in the case of Wales how local musicians who reproduce themselves only on cassette can have problems gaining access to the media. Such a phenomenon could be aggravated if the expansion of broadcasting is associated with a policy move towards playing only CDs, for quality reasons. Even if the recordable CD (WORM) is a way around such difficulties, this solution is hardly likely to present a practical or affordable alternative for musicmakers in the poorer nations.

The spread of electronic musical instruments, many with digital circuits allowing for synthesized or sampled sounds, is likely to become more widespread. The example from Trinidad, where hundreds of DX7 synthesizers had been sold even before the first CD appeared, is a good illustration of this. Musicians tend to travel and, wherever possible, buy the latest sound gadgets. Even the 'Tanzanites' playing at a hotel in Dar es Salaam had up-to-date synthesizers in 1988. An important point is that such instruments are manufactured at a few factories around the world and require little in the way of service locally as long as their circuits hold. Pirate manufacture is hard to conceive even if piracy of memory cards with digitally sampled sounds is beginning to become a software problem.

Satellites

Satellites were a prerequisite for the conception of non-stop music television (MTV), non-stop news TV (CNN), non-stop sports channels, etc. The MTV notion of 'One Planet, One Music' (Roe and Wallis 1989: 35–40), however, assumes a global market with peoples in every nation capable of receiving the signals, willing to subscribe for a cable connection, and being potential customers for MTV's advertisers. In practice, of course, this is not the case.

The reasons for satellites sending TV signals to, say, the Caribbean are very different from the factors that have governed this phenomenon in Sweden. In the Caribbean, it was a question of technical spillover, with US satellites covering areas outside continental US. The primary aim was not to find new markets for American soaps in small, developing island states south of Miami. Local entrepreneurs tapped into domestic US satellites; after a while US copyright owners found this could be a source of extra revenue. Many Caribbean policymakers and media operators viewed this development with considerable apprehension and anxiety. The US authorities in the form of the United States Information Agency (responsible for US PR, including the Voice of America and related operations) seemed to view this as an excellent new way to 'communicate' with the developing world. The Motion Picture Association of America, on the other hand, representing copyright owners, was not too pleased when local Caribbean stations started relaying satellite signals over terrestrial transmitters as a cheap way of filling transmission time (Wallis and Baran 1990: 143–6).

The European satellite explosion definitely *was* part of a search for new markets. Rich entrepreneurs hoping to tap unexploited territories found they could avoid restrictions on terrestrial transmissions by going out via transponders on 'birds' poised over the Equator, and being bounced back again. There was little risk of governments trying to ban private individuals or organizations erecting satellite receiver dishes, and where cable was being installed, any qualms about content were usually overruled by industrial interests.

Europe, of course, is not nearly as homogeneous a market as the US or even the English-speaking Caribbean. There is no common language, even if MTV has found that 60 per cent of Europeans in the 15–34 age group can follow English programmes (presumably without turning off through linguistic incomprehension). The new satellite channels soon found that one could not simply purvey transnational mass culture and rely on a mass audience across Europe even hooking on to the novelty effect. Pan-European TV commercials were a problem because of traditions, different standards and norms in different European nations. Murdoch's SKY satellite channel soon found that tribalism is rife in Europe – they were trying to reach a group of tribes and subgroups of tribes (the Scandinavians, the Celts, etc.) with the same message. Our Swedish chapter described how SKY, and by and by, MTV, embarked on 'courting exercises' aimed at different tribes. Sometimes this took the form of presenters speaking minority languages such as Flemish in particular programmes. Sometimes the goals and related actions were more specific and local as in the case of the SKY 'Switch on to Sweden' week in 1985.

Entrepreneurs will pay for putting satellites in orbit and rent transponders for TV channels only if they believe there is a large enough potential market for cable subscribers or local broadcasters willing to retransmit programmes under controlled forms (i.e. paying copyright dues). The Caribbean experience shows that wealthier individuals will go to extraordinary lengths to erect receiving dishes where satellite signals are available. The same would probably occur amongst, say, sectors of the Indian business community in East Africa, if a wide range of satellite signals were aimed at the Indian Ocean. The likelihood of an organized national cable market appearing at all in Kenya or Tanzania is small;

without such a market, satellite distributors of software are less likely to provide signals (unless they are determined to achieve a total global reach for publicity reasons related to status).

Technological developments have also played an important role in the expansion of radio, providing the prerequisites for small-scale radio via cheaper transmission technology. The change-over from AM to FM broadcasting has been important in this respect. A Swedish government report on the technical aspects of the pending introduction of commercial radio presented this comparison of investments and running costs for AM and FM radio:

Table 9.1 Comparison of investment and variable costs for AM and FM radio (US$)

	Range 5km	Range > 100km
AM transmitter		
Investment	80,000	6.5 million
Running costs/annum	8,000	0.5 million
FM transmitter		
Investment	16,000	170,000
Running costs/annum	300	33,000

Source: Swedish Government Study, 'Tekniskt utrymme för reklamfinansierad radio', SOU 1991: 108. Ministry of Culture, Stockholm.

The figures in Table 9.1 tally with the observation from two researchers that:

> At its smallest, an effective radio station can be put on air for the price of a small car. It will give listeners in its primary service area a signal virtually indistinguishable in quality from that of the network station, with operating costs at a fraction of those incurred by the large-scale broadcaster. This is in sharp contrast to the costs of establishing a local newspaper.
>
> (Crookes and Vittet-Philippe 1986: 125)

The ease of technological access has encouraged many would-be radio broadcasters to clamour for access to frequencies. Once on air, many have also discovered that ambitious programme aims require funds. The result all too often has been 'multiclone broadcasting ... with essentially the same programme with no more than slight differences in the voices between the records' (ibid : 156).

The 'multiclone' development is also encouraged by another technological development, namely that of satellite-distributed digital music feeds, mostly originating from the USA. Numerous channels with different music formats are available via satellite; a broadcaster can subscribe to one or more and merely add a few local news, weather and traffic reports to produce a very cheap radio station that has the appearance of having local relevance. Another alternative is the totally automatic station based on multiple CD players with news and weather being fed from other sources. Neither of these solutions have any relevance for local music activities in a small nation; both are certainly attractive alternatives for entrepreneurs whose aim is solely to make money out of broadcasting whilst minimizing content obligations.

Economic and organizational changes

Economic and organizational changes during the 1980s have been characterized by the growth of giant conglomerates; the Time-Warner and CBS-Sony link-ups are two of the more significant cases of multi-media giants. Horizontal and vertical integration has continued within sectors of these new media conglomerates. The major phonogram companies have consolidated their control over manufacturing and distribution in the industrialized world (thus indirectly affecting local enthusiasts' musicmaking activities by removing locally based manufacturing and distribution resources). On the artistic side, larger independent phonogram companies such as Island and Chrysalis have been swallowed up by the majors. Often such deals have been related to the acquisition of rights and established acts, rather than having the aim of buying up a creative entity; that the Island deal with Polygram included the Irish group U2 was probably its most attractive aspect for the new owner. Polygram's purchase of the last remaining Swedish national phonogram company of any size, Sonet, included a large publishing catalogue of Swedish songs which is likely to go on earning money locally in Sweden for many years to come.

With the growth of the conglomerates, their focus on informal integration, and thereby the search for sources of secondary income, have also gained more attention. This has often occurred in conjunction with lobbying or negotiating exercises involving a variety of trade organizations and governmental agencies. It is hardly surprising to note that the most serious issue hampering trade talks between the USA and China at the end of 1991 concerned copyright issues and piracy (for films, computer programmes, chemical formulae, etc.).

Moves within Europe to strengthen local audio and audio-visual production and its access to the broadcasting media (via quotas) have met with heavy lobbying from US organizations such as the Motion Picture Association of America or the music copyright society ASCAP. It is important to note that such lobbying does not primarily represent individual American creators, but rather the wider concept of 'Hollywood'

ANNOUNCED SERVICES

...PUTER SERVICES

...N MARKETWATCH
(703) 790-3570

8300 Old Courthouse Rd. Suite 200
Vienna, VA 22182
Parent Company: Financial News Network (Data Broadcasting Corp. division)
Personnel: Ed Happ, General Manager; Ed Anderson, Senior VP Marketing/Sales; Fred McEnony, Sales Manager
Program Hours: 24 Hours
Program Format: Business information and stock quotes
Satellite: Satcom IIIR/22
Subscriber Information:
Affiliates: 900 as of 03/23/90;
Subscribers: 4,000; Price/sub: $110

CD-18/THE DIGITAL MUSIC NETWORK
(212) 983-3300

342 Madison Ave.
Suite 505
New York, NY 10173
Parent Company: International Cablecasting Technologies
Personnel: Jerold Rubinstein, Chairman; W. Thomas Oliver, President; Molly Seagra.., VP Communications; John Flanne.., Director, Affiliate Sales & Marketing; Mike Davis, Network Operations

DIGITAL CABLE RADIO:

THE HIT LIST
THE COUNTRY CHANNEL
SOLID GOLD OLDIES
ROCK OF AGES
SOFT ROCK
NEW AGE/CONTEMPORARY JAZZ
THE URBAN BEAT
CLASSICAL CHANNEL
BIG BAND NOSTALGIA
EASY LISTENING
LOVE SONGS
ROCK 2000
THE LATIN CHANNEL
THE GOSPEL CHANNEL
CHILDREN'S CHANNEL
HARD AND HEAVY ROCK
TRADITIONAL JAZZ
OPERA
FOLK MUSIC
SHOW TUNES

THE DIGITAL RADIO CHANNEL
(213) 513-1630

22010 S. Wilmington Ave.
Carson, CA 90745
Parent Company: Digital Radio Laboratories Inc.
Personnel: William Delany, President; Douglas Talley, CEO; Robert Aten, CFO; Marianne Seiler, VP Marketing; Michael Hanafee, Senior VP Affiliate Sales
Program Hours: 24 Hours
...am Format: Various-91 audio
...ite: TBA; VideoCipher
...ted
...ted launch: 6/90

DIGITAL CABLE RADIO
(215) 957-8290

220. Byberry Road
.atboro, PA 19040
Parent Company: Jerrold Communications
Personnel: David Del Beccaro, General Manager; Paul Clough, Director, Marketing
Regional Offices: Pamela Jensen, Director, Affiliate Relations, Central Region-1900 East Golf Rd., Suite #100M, Schaumburg, Il 60173-5011
Thomas Ferraro, Director, Affiliate Relations, Eastern Region, 2200 Byberry Rd., Hatboro, PA 19040
Terry Taylor, Director, Affiliate Relations, Western Region, 566 N. Diamond Bar, Diamond Bar 91765
Program Hours: 24 Hours
Program Format: 18 channels of commercial-free music. 10 channels of cable TV audio simulcasts
Satellite: TBA; VideoCipher encrypted
Projected launch: 2nd Quarter 1990

X*PRESS INFORMATION SERVICES
(303) 721-1062

Regency Plaza One/4643 S Ulster
Suite 340
Denver, CO 80237
Parent Company: Tele-Communications Inc.
Personnel: Gerald Bennington, President; George Backer, VP Technical; Gary Clark, VP Affiliate Relations; Judy Spurgeon, VP Customer Sales & Support; Tomec Smith, VP Marketing
Program Hours: 24 Hours
Program Format: News, information features and children's material
Satellite: Galaxy I/7, 18 VideoCipher encrypted
Subscriber Information:
Affiliates: 550 as of 01/01/90;
Subscribers: N.A.

Plate 9.1 Digital Satellite music feeds. Not only TV but any number of music channels available in different satellite footprints.

(which is heavily Japanese-owned) or US-registered copyright holders (who could also be controlled by Japanese or German interests). ASCAP has even issued veiled threats to bypass Europe's traditional national copyright organizations, with which it has always had reciprocal agreements, threatening to sell performance rights for phonograms from the USA separately to European radio stations. Such a move could lead to a price war not unlike the one Europe (and indeed the USA) has experienced in the field of textile imports from low-wage countries. If local radio stations can play US music at cheap preferential rates, then local music activity is likely to suffer a decrease of access to the media.

This is already a policy dilemma in Europe where many nations have signed the Rome Convention which allows for royalty payment to producers and performers when phonograms are performed publicly; records produced in non-Rome USA already cost sometimes as little as half as much per play for a broadcaster than phonograms resulting from local music activity. This could have a discriminatory effect on local phonogram producers whose financial survival depends just as much on secondary incomes for radio plays as on record/cassette sales.

If US interests are concerned about a decrease in the use of American-produced audio- and audio-visual software in European broadcasting then such fears are surely exaggerated. In actual fact, deregulation of the broadcasting media in Europe appears to have led to an increase in the output of US-produced materials, even if the stated aims of initial European media policies were exactly the opposite (Tunstall and Palmer 1991; Dyson and Humphreys 1988).

Deregulation

Deregulation, sometimes coupled with privatization, has been a popular political war cry in Europe throughout the 1980s:

> American rhetoric about the 'technological inevitability' of more channels and less regulation drifted across the Atlantic after 1980 and became in some respects a self-fulfilling prophecy. This 'inevitability' was somewhat naively accepted in western Europe.
>
> (Tunstall and Palmer 1991: 3)

That developments in Sweden such as the introduction of commercial TV came much later than in the rest of Europe cannot be explained in terms of non-participation in the Common Market and the EC's media deliberations. Sweden was in the throes of its own media deregulation, in radio via the 'Neighbourhood Radio' experiment, and in TV via the entrepreneurial efforts of wealthy operators using satellites and cable. Delays in formulating media policy in Sweden allowed a budding entrepreneur (Jan Stenbeck and his Medvik conglomerate) to build up a new

ASCAP Threatens Europe With BMI Joint Venture

Messinger says that, even if ASCAP were to expand into Europe, it would license only broadcasters, which supply the lion's share of performing rights income, ies claiming they do not have sufficient information to credit U.S. works in the same way as they treat local copyrights.

Another problem, says Mes- savings there."

In addition, Messinger told the IFPMP attendees at MIDEM that she opposes moves in some countries toward stringent local content

European Assns. Stung By ASCAP Criticism
Say Messinger Off Target On Overhead, Quota Complaints

■ BY MIKE HENNESSEY

LONDON—Authors' rights societies in the European countries have reacted with a mixture of skepticism, dis- costs, "subtle" discrimination against foreign repertoire, and moves in some European countries toward stringent local content laws.

An angry reaction has come from "Everybody knows it is very common in the game between ASCAP and BMI to play tricks on each other at any given moment," he says. "This is the result of the pointless competi-

ASCAP No to Euro radio quotas

The possible introduction of French-style broadcasting quotas in the European Single Market is under attack from Frans de Wit, European Director of US rights body ASCAP.

"The audience alone should decide what they want to watch and listen to" he says. "We don't want any favours for US repertoire, but we do want fair treatment".

Dutch-born de Wit became ASCAP's first continental European official in 1989 after 17 years in music pub- lishing with Intersong, Warner Bros Music and EMI Music Publishing.

ASCAP is barred by reciprocal agreements from an active role in European rights. But de Wit may lobby directly if there is a risk of airplay for US repertoire being limited by the European Commission.

NIGEL HUNTER

Plate 9.2 The music press heralding the ASCAP assault on Europe in early 1990: 'Don't discriminate against US songs on European radio or else . . .'.

regional media empire, using virtually the same methods as had been practised by another European media mogul, Silvio Berlosconi, in the early 1980s. After waiting up to three years after Stenbeck had started satellite broadcasting to Sweden before granting the first commercial terrestrial TV franchise, Swedish media policymakers virtually abdicated any ability or duty to force operators to observe obligations regarding music activity in the ouptut of a national commercial TV channel.

Sponsors

Another growing phenomenon of the media during the 1980s has been the extended role of sponsors following from a growth of informal integration. Organizations and companies seeking to identify the music and performers which can enhance their product images have been providing financial input to the music industry, requiring of course a good return in the form of good publicity. Sponsors who usually are also advertisers on commercial radio/TV not only affect the output of broadcasters by deciding which programmes to sponsor. They even create dependency relations directly with artists and phonogram companies, sponsoring particular videos or using artists exclusively in particular product campaigns. This applies both to international superstars as well as to successful national or local stars. Such links of mutual dependency are becoming so tight that there is a theoretical possibility that someone like Michael Jackson might sign his next recording contract, not with a Big Five record company, but with Pepsi Cola. With sponsors putting money in, as it were, at 'both ends', supporting both artists and their musical activities as well as funding radio/TV operations, the resulting system of demand–reward relationships has become extremely complex. One can even reach a state where advertisers' and sponsors' demands regarding music content in the broadcasting media (based on their understanding of links between musical taste and product taste) dictate repertoire policies in the phonogram industry. Former President of Polygram Records USA, Dick Asher, claims that music in radio has become: 'the tent which gets you in where all the products of the advertisers are displayed . . . if the people who like certain sorts of music are not the people who want to buy soap, then their music won't get played' (Asher 1987).

Expanding our systems approach presented earlier to include the demand–reward relationships arising from the addition of sponsors, advertisers, terrestrial and satellite TV channels creates a system with several subsystems striving to achieve equilibrium, often at the expense of others.

The bonds between satellite channels, network and other TV channels and the phonogram industry (via video clip production) have particular significance. MTV, for instance, offers phonogram companies exclusivity deals, whereby MTV puts up some of the costs of videos in return for

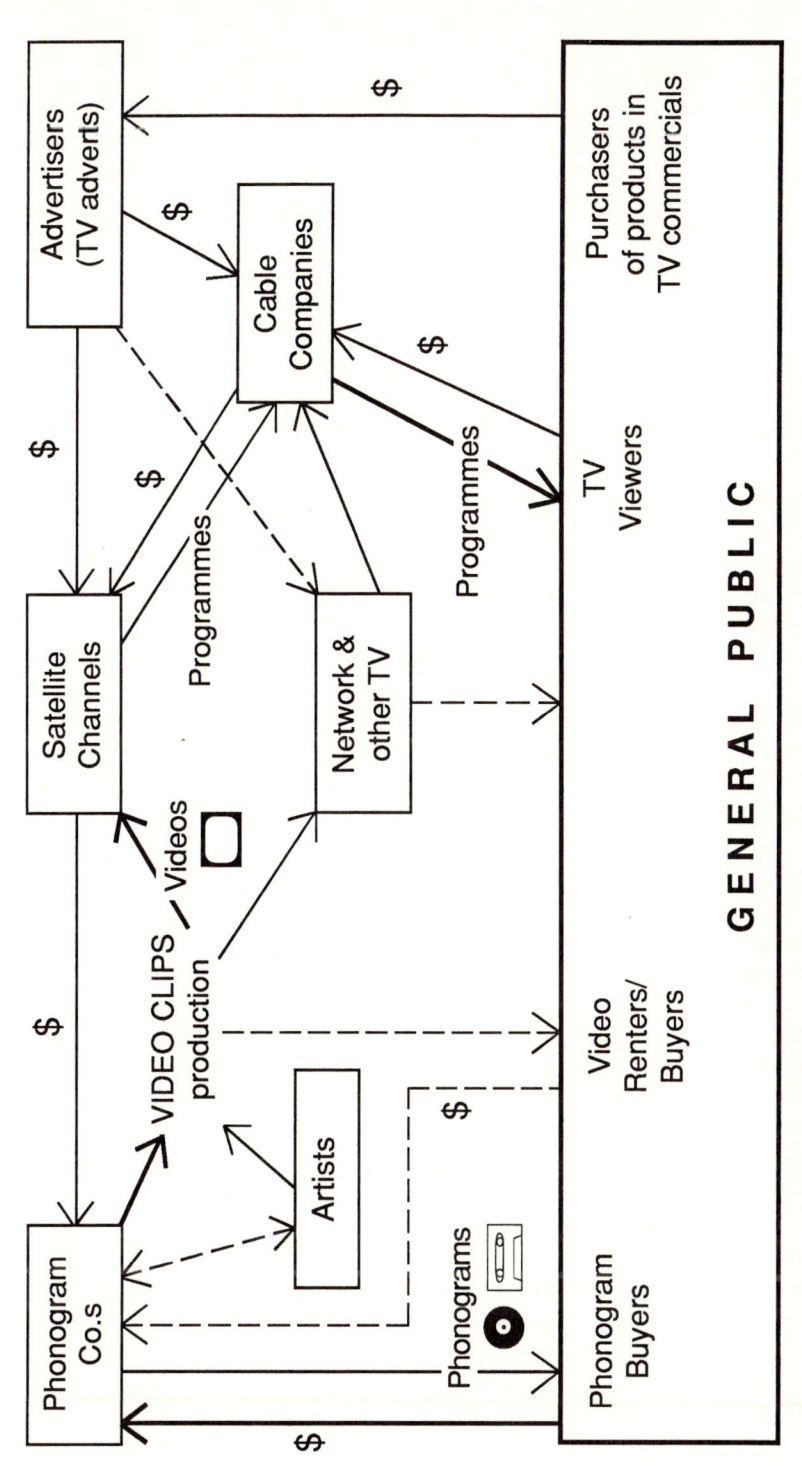

Figure 9.1 An extended system including sponsors, advertisers, terrestrial and satellite TV channels.

limited exclusive viewing rights. There are usually both positive and negative sides to increased informal integration for at least one of the parties involved. A deal with a TV station excluding publicity in others must involve a dilemma for the phonogram producer. Such phenomena are likely to increase as parties seek ways of cutting production costs. The new TV3–TV4 television group in Sweden with the franchise for Sweden's first terrestrial commercial TV service is already offering deals to local phonogram companies whereby TV3–TV4 records and broadcasts live concerts with popular artists in return for a share of the proceeds from the exploitation of the soundtracks from such programmes. Such an offer, as one might expect, is hardly popular amongst phonogram company staff – on the other hand, it could be 'an offer they cannot refuse'.

THE FLOW OF MUSIC BETWEEN PEOPLES AND NATIONS

Music activity in a society never occurs in a state of total isolation from outside influences. Different performers develop different modes of interpretation; these blend with others when musicians meet and exchange ideas or experiences. In our previous project, MISC, we suggested four ways in which music travels between countries, cultures and peoples: cultural exchange, cultural dominance, cultural imperialism and transculturation. All four categories continue to exist, affecting music activities in different ways. The extent to which they are affected by media policy also varies, as we shall note in the following pages.

Cultural exchange

The simplest and oldest mechanism by which music travels is that of cultural exchange; two minstrels meet and exchange songs on an equality basis in a give-and-take situation. No money passes hands, no individual property rights are established or asserted. As soon as musicians began to travel, such exchange began to take place. The process has continued and expanded with modern-day communications, allowing more and more musicians to meet face to face.

Such meetings often lead to the creation of networks linking musicians with similar interests in different countries. Networks can be formed as a result of musicians touring abroad, immigration or tourism. They can be fairly informal or they can depend on formal frameworks such as meetings taking place at international music festivals or within the scope of international organizations such as the ICTM (International Council for Traditional Music) which brings researchers and musicians together at conferences.

Nowadays primary music media play an important role in the exchange of music. Youth from different countries who meet up at the Ethno folk music camp each summer in Falun, Sweden, return home but keep in touch by exchanging tapes of local music. Members of samba groups and steelbands in Sweden get the latest news about these musical forms in Brazil and Trinidad through tapes sent by fellow musicians in those countries. In the same way, enthusiasts who play the Swedish *nyckelharpa* (keyed fiddle) in Belgium and France get tapes from friends in the heartland of *nyckelharpa* country, the province of Uppland, Sweden.

As a result of such exchange networks, musical styles and ideas can travel without ever entering secondary music mass media. Via old recordings, music forms which originally have been peculiar to a particular geographical place and time can influence music activity in quite a different place or time. Sweden, for instance, has a group specializing in French Creole music as it was played in Guadeloupe in the 1920s, a form which cannot be heard in Guadeloupe today. They picked up the style from old recordings.

Phonogram media such as cassettes and simple recording equipment appear to play an important role in musical exchange, keeping musical traditions and stylistic elements alive. However, we have come across no policy document which addresses this subject.

Cultural dominance

The second mechanism by which music travels, as noted by MISC, was that of cultural dominance, involving a dominant culture imposing its music and norms regarding music or culture on a subservient culture. It has often been associated with pressures to eradicate local music activity, pressures involving ridicule, threats or even physical sanctions. Our sample of nations in this study presents several examples:

> 'Folk music was almost killed off during the religious revival at the end of the last century. There has been a rejuvenation during the past few years. Possibly because of nationalist pride, possibly because of noting what the other Celtic countries have been doing to keep their traditions alive. In the last century, the church taught that music and dance was the invention of the devil. In the last few years, about twenty folk clubs have been set up.'
>
> (Gwyn Thomas, former Director of Welsh programmes, Swansea Sound radio, TI 01/08/81)

Similar stories could be told in Sweden concerning the Church and Swedish fiddle music, or the colonial administration in Trinidad and steelband music. The missionaries in Africa warned that drum music was in the service of the Devil. In Tanzania, as recently as the 1920s and 1930s, children who spoke Swahili at school were chastised. In Wales, a child overheard speaking Welsh in the playground would have to wear a 'Welsh Not' around his or her neck as a symbol of shame. Memories of such cultural dependence live on, stimulating feelings of antagonism and occasionally inferiority.

All five countries in this study show examples of a push in an opposite direction, with an intellectual, cultural and occasionally a political elite introducing musical activities into the education system which were previously on the receiving end of cultural dominance. We noted the examples of traditional music finding its way into educational syllabuses in Kenya and Wales. Steelbands are regular features in secondary schools in Trinidad. Folk music departments are becoming accepted or are even established at university level.

Cultural and media policies also show similar trends. That the 1990 'Swedish Folk Music and Dance Year' received not only government funds but also extensive coverage on radio/TV and in the press is an example of this development. It indicated a growing willingness to accommodate such music activity within the Establishment's view of cultural policy, even if enthusiasts played an important initiating role in getting it off the ground.

The official status of the annual Trinidad carnival can also be seen partly in terms of a reversal of years of cultural dominance. However, policy considerations in a variety of areas such as tourism, advertising or sponsoring, also play equally as vital a role in maintaining the carnival's importance as a national institution.

That these different signs of a resurgence of interest and respect for folk music and its traditions can be noted in the late 1980s (as opposed to the mid-1970s when the cultural policy debate in so many nations first started to focus on national identity) can be related to the time lag in the cultural factor. Rhetorical statements about the importance of national identity and the way it is or should be strengthened have little effect in practice before there is a groundswell of support on the local level. Maybe this is why so few of the policy recommendations of the Kenyan Presidential Commission on Music have been implemented in such a way as to produce any noticeable change in music activities.

Cultural imperialism

In common with many other writers, we have also identified cultural imperialism as a mechanism by which music travels (Wallis and Malm 1984: 299–301). Here, cultural dominance is augmented by the transfer of money and/or resources from dominated to dominating cultural group.

The term 'cultural imperialism', as we have already mentioned, was on the lips of many debaters when describing trends in Sweden during the 1970s. Observers feared a future where a few transnationals would control the Swedish music industry and merely import a small selection of popular phonograms featuring international superstars, thus killing off all support in the phonogram industry for local music activity. The Big Five have increased their control over manufacturing and distribution of phonograms in Sweden, but have not ceased to invest in Swedish artists and have the same average breakdown of sales as the market as a whole (66 per cent international/33 per cent Swedish). The larger companies, on the other hand, have concentrated on established artists. Small local companies representing the 'enthusiasts', of course, still account for the greater part of phonogram releases, many of which sell in small quantities; the same rules apply in all our sample countries.

So did the doomsday prophets of the 1970s get it all wrong? Yes and no. One problem in any judgement of the extent of cultural imperialism is that the very concept is vague, and has been used in many different contexts and featured in many conflicts. Most often, writers have used the term to refer to the role of the mass media in the poorer nations, focusing on either the telecommunications industry (Mattelart 1979), the news industry (McBride 1980) or mass media in general as part of and supporting the total transnational company sphere (Schiller 1976: 2–10; Nordenstreng and Schiller 1979). Boyd-Barrett has suggested that the term 'dependency' might be more appropriate because of the common association of 'imperialism' with the act of territorial annexation (Boyd-Barrett 1980). Cultural imperialism theorists have indeed tended to play down the ability of national sovereign states to control or regulate business activities within their own territories, or even of the need for subsidiaries of transnationals to improve their local status by showing some element of 'national' responsibility in the different countries where they operate. What's more, the focus on the industrialized/poorer nations dichotomy has ignored the cultural impact of transnational media corporations and their common denominators (e.g. Anglo-American hit songs) on the cultural life of nations and cultures which are small, even if their standard of living may be relatively high (for instance Sweden, Wales or even Trinidad during the oil boom).

A recurring problem with the notion of cultural imperialism is its inevitable tendency to invite thinking in terms of conspiracy theories. There is a plot, usually dreamed up by US government and business, to control the minds and the wallets of other peoples by selling them US media software in return for economic resources and an absolute minimum of cultural imports to the USA. Mattelart and Schiller are probably the fathers of the Early Warning Cultural Imperialism School. Mattelart's engagement is not surprising considering his close contacts with Chile, Allende and the pre-Pinochet period (where ITT is generally regarded as having played a role in the military coup). His and Schiller's message is that cultural imperialistic forces are all-pervasive. They are the backbone of the modern economic/industrial forms of colonialism that have replaced former brands of territorial imperialism as exhibited by the old colonial powers. Mattelart cites many examples from the spread and use of US satellite, audio and video technology, and the way in which dependence is created in the course of gaining access to such technologies.

Such authors constantly remind us of the US government's desire in collusion with big business to force cultural industries to adapt their products to the needs of export audiences so that certain American lifestyles and values can be triumphant when competing with other cultures and centres of power. Whether or not such intentions (often backed up by quotes from official documents) actually control policy implementation is not equally as clear. In a post-Cold War era where communism no longer appears as a major ideological threat to the American way of life, then the conspiracy theories become even more transparent. The fact that transnationals such as SONY-CBS, BMG and Polygram are not US controlled also forces us to question even more aspects of the cultural imperialism theories of the 1970s. Don't get us wrong! We are not doubting the postulate that transnational cultural industries are constantly exerting pressure on cultures and people all round the world, earning a buck or two (or three) wherever they can.

Much of the above argumentation assumes that the multinational media complex is essentially Anglo-American. But of late we have observed how both German and Japanese companies have taken over traditional US transnational cultural industries. Do they literally 'float up above' national boundaries (including the US) or do we see new nations controlling the flow of media software, gaining this power through economic achievements in other industrial areas?

Our previous analyses of developments during the 1970s viewed the Asian consumer electronics industry as more or less totally hardware orientated. Recent publications, however, have shown that Asian nations too can be heavily involved in the export of media software products.

In 1990, Mowlana and Rad published a number of studies on changes in the structure and content of Iranian television since the Khomeini revolution. Their research describes how, with the exodus of US software suppliers to TV stations after the fall of the Shah, the Japanese moved in providing a variety of programmes, including a number of their own variety of TV soap operas (Mowlana and Rad 1990). Throughout the Iran–Iraq war, Japan became one of the countries with the closest media ties with Iran. In 1988, Japan had eight newspaper, TV, radio and news agency reporters stationed in Tehran. Mowlana traces in detail some of the Japanese TV series that gained popularity, and maintains that their success depended on cultural background similarities. The long-running 'Oshin' soap, the tale of a young lady's life, included 'certain modes of behaviour, cultural cues and similarities well recognised by the Iranian audiences which, in turn, provided a common ground for sharing the experiences and events' in the series, 'despite tremendous cultural differences between Japan and Iran.'

The main point of this example is that cultural similarities are strong enough for the Iranians to accept and not reject imports from Japan, even after passing the religious filter. This ties up with Tunstall's views on cultural imperialism, written fifteen years earlier:

> Television is not necessarily the best example of the media imperialist thesis. . . . We must note both exporters' and importers' intentions – as well as recognizing that many social consequences are unintended. . . . Schiller attributes too many of this world's ills to television. He also has an unrealistic view of returning to cultures, many of which although authentic are also dead. In my view, *a non-American way out of the media box is difficult to discover because it is an American, or Anglo-American, built box.*
>
> (Tunstall 1977: 63)

Mowlana would argue that this is exactly what was underway in Iran, using a box the Japanese built with oriental wood and nails.

The case of US television via satellite footprints swamping the Caribbean is interesting in this context. The Caribbean nations didn't ask to get a new supply of programmes when US satellites were being put in orbit. The technology allowed for spill-over and both public broadcasters and private entrepreneurs discovered the new source of seemingly free software. Even state-controlled television stations received gratefully this new access to films, news, series and videos, presumably in accordance with the 'mango tree' school of thinking which states that the fruit on a branch of your mango tree which grows over the fence into my garden is my property. With the threatening might of the US administration promising retaliatory trade sanctions if payments were not made, Caribbean governments ordered their broadcasters to negotiate and pay. Local broadcasters and newspaper proprietors complained loudly about this 'attack on the culture and sovereignty' of the Caribbean nations:

> Neither our cultural identity nor our political sovereignty, nor indeed our territorial integrity should be eroded by any foreign power as a result of our location or size. We in the media take our responsibility seriously, and it is for this reason that we raise this issue rather than be spectators to our own cultural emasculation.
>
> (Hoyte 1986)

The mechanism involved in satellite transmissions to the Caribbean tallies closely with Schiller or Mattelart's description of cultural imperialism, but what effect, if any, has it had on musical activity? Our interviews and observations suggest that the impact is restricted mainly to a youth audience that is impressed by the lifestyles and ways of musicmaking presented in US MTV. One of our Jamaican interviewees referred to teenage musicians wanting the same synthesizers they saw on MTV. The growth of local radio in Jamaica and Trinidad, on the other hand, suggests a reaction against MTV-style content in the form of increased local music output on the media.

There is little evidence of MTV-Europe affecting music activity in Sweden. Those who have access to MTV get the programme via cable, in theory, twenty-four hours a day. It functions more as a radio programme, providing background sound with pictures which one occasionally views. In the Caribbean, MTV comes to most people in bursts when the local TV station decides to relay a portion of MTV-USA, usually in conjunction with a local sponsor.

Transculturation

In Tunstall's mid-1970s analysis of cultural imperialism referred to above, he linked Schiller and Adorno as two researchers who were both yearning for something called authenticity. Adorno had claimed that a symphony concert when broadcast on radio was drained of significance. Others had said hard things about large audiences that went to 'Westerns' and crime films in the 1930s. Tunstall notes that many such films have since been declared to be masterpieces 'after all'. He concluded that 'such a caricature illustrates that the real choice probably lies with hybrid forms' (Tunstall 1977: 59). In many countries we have observed examples of older musical forms which continue in vigorous existence, although modified by Western influences. Popular music frequently appears in such a guise.

Writing over a decade later, Frith has also focused on what actually emerges from the international and national activities of the music industry. Citing several of the phenomena we have noted in our data section (government support for phonogram production in particular countries; quotas for local music in the media; etc.), Frith concludes somewhat bluntly that: 'the resulting National music is, more often than not, just a local variant of global style; the real idea is that small countries will generate hits of their own' (Frith in Lull (ed.) 1992: 71).

Our data and conclusions regarding actual policies in the countries we have studied do not support the hypothesis that the aim of government policy anywhere is to provide musical equivalents of a local TV 'Dallas' which can be an international hit. On the other hand, that there is a continuous mixing of styles within the operations of the music industry on all levels is patently clear. 'Borrowing' (Kivikuru 1990) and the mixture of 'Indigenization/modernization' (Robinson *et al.* 1991: 262) are other ways researchers have chosen to describe such phenomena.

Researchers in this area have noted how cultural imperialism analyses tend to focus too one-sidedly on the 'external role' of transnationals whilst underestimating the effects of internal forces and activities within countries subjected to activities of transnationals (e.g. Fejes 1981). The transnational phonogram companies cannot totally manipulate and control public taste. Affordable and practical technology, together with outside and domestic musical influences, allow for a fourth process of music transfer, transculturation, to take place. This involves the combination of stylistic elements from several forms of local music taking place in the industrial environment. Thus transcultural music is an industrial product without roots in any one specific ethnic group. In the transculturation process, individual local music cultures pick up elements of the output of the international music industry.

A good example of transculturation is provided by this description of a new product from the French music industry:

> The Arab influence is now cropping up in the most unexpected places. Penfleps come from Brittany in the North-West of France, and their self-titled début on Lagon Bleu manages to switch from an accordion and acoustic guitar based on sub-Cajun sound to some altogether more exotic Arabic scales, and through all that they manage to sound like the same band. They sing in English for the most part and the songs show a definite slant towards folk rock, on the basis of material heard so far they are yet another French band with that all-important 'international sound'.
>
> (MBI 1991: 16–17)

Some of the numerous sounds and styles that emerge from the 'transculturation' process have been accorded their own category in the business terminology of the music industry: 'World Music'. The phenomenon was predicted by the MISC research (Frith and Goodwin 1990: 126) though the term emerged when the phonogram industry noticed it was selling considerable quantities of phonograms for which there was no established category, i.e. no section in a record store where you would find such phonograms. A name was needed and World Music/World Beat became the choices of the marketing men (Schnabel 1990).

The result of transculturation on the local level is any number of permutations and combinations of styles, providing for the time being a strong contender to any 'one world, one song' doomsday concept. In the long-term perspective, this could, of course, be only a stage of continued convergence of music styles (Wallis and Malm 1984: 300–4).

DEREGULATION AND THE FORMULATION AND IMPLEMENTATION OF MEDIA POLICIES

Supporters of deregulation in the electronic media have argued that small is beautiful, that the removal of restrictions governing operations and structures can only increase individual and group access to the media, guaranteeing a greater plurality of output. The introduction of scores, hundreds or even thousands of new radio stations, in other words, should ensure total access of local music activities to such new media elements. Deregulation has not infrequently involved a marked increase in the number of music-based commercial stations, but usually it has been a question of more of the same.

Writing after almost a decade of radio deregulation in the USA, during which the number of FM commercial stations increased by over one thousand, two researchers concluded:

> Commercial radio profoundly affects the style and content of popular music. This is due to . . . the repeated exposure of 'typical' or 'non-objectionable' songs. The [radio] industry's reliance on formats, trade journals, music industry promoters and consultants tends to reproduce the choices at station after station. In conjunction with the industry's obsession with profits and work routinization in the guise of efficiency, this means as a rule that contemporary commercial radio actively discourages significant stylistic innovation in popular music and the communication potential that such creative endeavours would produce.
> (Rothenbuhler and McCourt 1992: 113)

Our own data tend to suggest that the outcome of radio deregulation is remarkably similar, irrespective of the ideological forms or reasons for deregulation. Sweden produced the ultimate system for 'free radio' by providing frequencies for any non-profit-making association. Initially it did attract a large variety of programme producers, many of them representing local music activities. This category soon got tired or was ousted by other organizations or groups with bigger pecuniary resources as data from the regulatory Neighbourhood Radio Board illustrate (Table 9.2).

The figures in Table 9.2 show the largest increases for the categories 'political groups', 'trade unions' and 'others'. The dual increase for the first two of these categories reflects the link between the trade unions and the political labour movement who have co-ordinated their publicity activities in Neighbourhood Radio. The 'other' category, accounting for almost a quarter of all transmission time, includes a variety of groups with the resources and know-how needed for running a professional-sounding radio station (e.g. groups supported by the Swedish Employers' Federation).

Whilst music associations accounted for some 10 per cent of licences in the early 1980s, they have now shrunk to 2 per cent. Less groups have accounted for more transmission time, and the majority of output consists of non-stop popular music. Similar trends have been reported from France, Italy and the UK. In general, one can conclude that the results were not what the politicians expected and certainly not what the fans of 'free radio'

Table 9.2 The development of Neighbourhood Radio in Sweden during the 1980s: transmission time and distribution of licences by major categories

Licence category	% of transmission time						
	1982	1984	1986	1988	1989	1990	1991
Religious (churches)	55	59	45	36	22	29	28
Political groups	5	9	17	22	19	17	16
Music societies	8	3	2	2	3	2	3
Education groups	1	3	6	9	12	9	9
Trade unions			1	2	6	5	4
Student unions	6	8	8	7	8	6	7
Others	15	11	16	17	24	25	27
Licence category	% of total licences granted						
Religious (churches)	32	34	27	22	22	24	25
Political groups	16	19	29	28	27	26	26
Music societies	10	4	2	2	2	2	2
Education groups	2	5	6	7	7	6	6
Trade unions			2	4	5	5	6
Student unions	6	7	3	4	4	4	4
Others	19	18	18	21	22	20	20

Source: Swedish Neighbourhood Radio Board, based on measurements during one sample week per annum.
Note: Some categories are missing from this table, including sport, immigrant, handicap and teetotaller groups which show little change.

promised. One of the few counter-movements we have observed concerns the decision by the Swedish Association of Popular Music Composers to enter the Neighbourhood Radio fray in 1989 with Radio SKAP, playing non-stop Swedish music to provide an alternative to the excesses of international Top 40 formats.

A baffling fact is that as Sweden moves towards the formal introduction of commercial radio in 1993, media politicians appear to accept tacitly that such deregulation will probably merely fill the airwaves with similar-sounding pop stations, and second, to be unaware of the fact that thinking in the rest of Western Europe has moved from support for deregulation to an understanding of a need for some element of *reregulation* (Tunstall and Palmer 1991: 213ff.). Even though all are aware that recorded music will be the main filler of new radio channels, there is virtually no debate on its content or of the significance of this fact for the music industry in particular or for music activity as a whole. The Swedish government has even announced its intention to grant frequencies to highest bidders in a public auction, without any cultural thresholds, content regulation or even financial scrutiny of would-be operators' ability to survive. If this policy is actually applied when licences are awarded in 1993, then this would put Sweden far ahead of anything that has been tried, even in the USA.

Maybe the reason for this apparent naïvety lies in the fact that the fall from fame of the deregulation gospel is only just beginning to emerge. Throughout the first half of the 1980s, experts were producing a wealth of optimistic statements about the future for deregulated, small-scale radio in Europe (Partridge 1982). Even in 1986, Crisell prophesied: 'On a local scale, this opens up a truly exciting future for radio, pointing to a time when the medium will be subjected to fewer technological and political restrictions than ever before' (Crisell 1986: 40).

Crookes and Vittet-Philippe (1986: 155) stated boldly that: 'Local radio does not have to be boring, amateurish or trivial. Nor does it have to be a clone of the big-city network pumping out an endless supply of plastic music presented by plastic personalities.' Their study of 'Local Radio and Regional Development in Europe' envisaged a radio broadcasting environment where plurality of views and diversity of styles of content would be guaranteed, first, by ease of access to the media and second, by actual involvement of people and organizations on a community level. The fact that two spectacular experiments in this field from the early 1980s had failed (the co-operatively owned Radio Cardiff commercial local radio station in Wales which we have already described and Radio Delle Donne, a women's movement station in Rome) is explained in terms of the problems such endeavours face 'when initial money and enthusiasm run out'.

In 1988, another observer, Higham, concluded that Vittet/Crookes' optimism regarding a future for small-scale radio full of pluralism and diversification was premature. Local radio was rapidly being replaced by what amounted to a number of *de facto* deregulated commercial networks (Higham 1988: 29). In Britain, local stations were becoming more and more similar in music choice to their major competitors: BBC's national channels, Radio 1 (pop/rock) and Radio 2 (middle of the road) (Local Radio Workshop 1983). In many countries, local radio stations were admittedly still local in name, but a growing percentage of their content was produced centrally, often distributed via satellite networks. In some cases, an increasing number were being incorporated into the same sphere of ownership. This trend was more apparent in Europe than in, say, the USA, since Europe does not have the system of affiliation and limits of ownership (including restrictions on cross-ownership between different media) which still apply in the somewhat decimated US regulatory system. Dyson and Humphreys note that in Italy, '*Pluralism* soon revealed itself to be superficial. *De facto* national networks developed as local companies formed links and synchronised their programmes [thus] . . . circumventing Italian broadcasting law' (Dyson and Humphreys 1988: 24). The same authors conclude that regulation has changed from being a 'trusteeship for the national cultural heritage to regulation as an exercise in "international gamesmanship" . . . as a means of attracting investment and jobs, and thus generating tax revenue' (ibid.: 308).

In general, politicians with responsibility for media matters seem to have been fooled by those who have preached the message of technology's complete ablity to democratize.

Another observation from our data is that political decisions concerning deregulation tend to occur in leaps and bounds. Trinidad did nothing for years, despite the lobbying and court actions of various respected calypsonians. A high court reprimand for sluggishness opened the floodgates without any real consideration of the consequences. Who, for instance, could afford the entrance fee to the newly deregulated area? Those already established in the media, of course.

Jamaica privatized its slumbering local/regional radio stations, selling them off to groups who promised to stay local in their output. As soon as the new operators found that their signal reached other more densely populated areas, their policy changed from regional to semi-national. But the new stations did, at least initially, account for an increase in Jamaican music.

Deregulation is likely to come in Tanzania and Kenya, encouraged indirectly by demands from donors such as the World Bank that such nations move further towards a market economy. It is hard to conceive how new, local radio stations in, say, Tanzania could continue the music policies of Radio Tanzania, documenting local music activity. Even in Wales we have seen how deregulation has led to a removal of pressure on local commercial stations to record their own music or even include a token output of Welsh music.

The observations and postulates above do not only apply to a Swedish or a 'small country/small language area' phenomenon. Indeed, there is plenty of evidence to prove a common trend in the deregulation of broadcasting. An initial increase of available choices soon reverts, via a process of streamlining, into an output with relatively few choices, but with a regrouping of the power structure that control the media. As regards music output, this has not led to the great plethora of voices, sounds and styles which the fans of deregulation promised under the 'freedom of choice' umbrella.

Figure 9.2 below represents our attempt to chart the development of popular music output as channels increase, as formats come and go, and as ownership and control move from one power centre to others.

Figure 9.2 sums up the data we have collected within our sample of nations, other European countries and the USA. Deregulation fervour eats away at the protected status of traditional national broadcasters. The prime movers are not only market economists and entrepreneurs looking for new lucrative business areas – the record industry and even enthusiasts preferring the anarchistic route of pirate radio have hastened this trend (see Mulryan 1989; Wallis 1990). At times the public broadcasters themselves have probably contributed to the process through arrogance and aloofness.

The mode of expansion is affected by a number of variables. Access to

```
                Traditional Monopoly / Duopoly
                            ↓
                      (Deregulation)
Technology
Economy      ➡
Organization
                            ↓
                        Expansion
                            ↓
                  Fragmentation of output
```

Segmentation   Exclusion

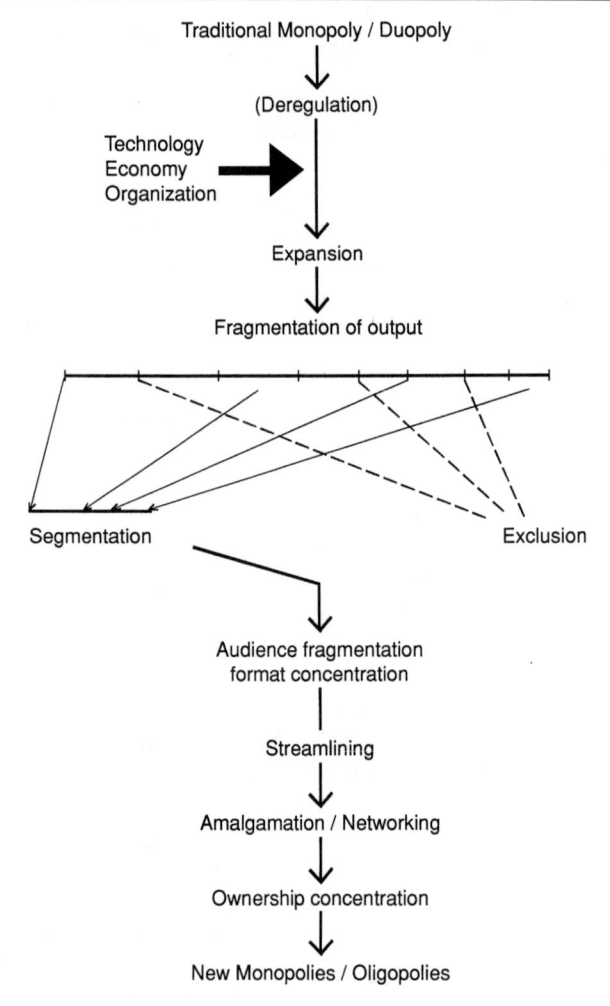

```
                            ↓
                  Audience fragmentation
                   format concentration
                            |
                       Streamlining
                            ↓
                  Amalgamation / Networking
                            ↓
                   Ownership concentration
                            ↓
                  New Monopolies / Oligopolies
```

Figure 9.2 Deregulation of existing monopolies, leading to new forms of ownership/format concentration.

technology and finance are the most important; legislation can limit the speed of expansion but only to a certain extent. In the absence of restricting legislation (such as franchise application procedures that place stiff demands on would-be operators seeking the more attractive frequencies), those with financial and technical resources decide the rules of the game. The same applies if legislation is out of date, for instance, by ignoring the technical realities of satellite distribution.

Expansion of services leads to a fragmentation of the audience as a large number of new and different programmes can be heard. Some become more popular than others, leading to a segmentation of services. Some programme styles and contents which are assumed to be more likely to attract listeners tend to dominate. Others die a quick death leading to exclusion of certain music styles (see Wallis and Malm 1988: 272).

As audience ratings come through, the process of format concentration (e.g. golden oldies/Top 40/middle of the road) increases. Streamlining of output continues as less commercially successful stations observe and copy more successful ones.

By and by, stations with high ratings generate a considerable economic worth and those with financial resources attempt to take control. This leads to a process of amalgamation through ownership concentration. In the European context, this brings us back more or less to square one. The monolithic, monopoly corporation has been replaced by a new, small group of commercial owners.

DIFFERENT ACTORS IN THE MEDIA POLICY ARENA AND THEIR RELEVANCE FOR MUSIC ACTIVITY

International level

Unesco

Unesco has constantly concerned itself with the mass media, usually on a global scale and focusing primarily on issues involving the flow of information between nations, human rights and moves to counter racism. Unesco's 1979 Declaration on the Mass Media does not mention music. The organization is only involved in programmes that directly affect music activity and media policy at a more decentralized level, via regional operations (providing video equipment in the Caribbean, and music education programmes in Africa, etc.), or via associated organizations such as the International Music Council or the Mediacult Research Centre in Vienna. Much of the material that emerges from Unesco's general assemblies has the character of ambitious rhetoric and aims. The twenty-sixth session in 1991 was asked to adopt a plan for a World Commission on Culture and Development. Such a commission would

> focus mainly on identifying, describing and analysing basic questions, concerns and challenges related to:
> a) the cultural and socio-cultural factors that affect development.
> b) the impact of social and economic development on culture.
> (Unesco 1991: 2)

The proposal ends somewhat despondently with a clause to the effect that if funds are not forthcoming through donations, then plans for a World Commission on Culture and Development will be scrapped. This is not an unlikely outcome bearing in mind the state of member nations' economies and the fact that important donor nations such as the USA and Great Britain left the organization in the early 1980s after differences of opinions over calls for a new World Communication Order and dissatisfaction with senior executives.

The US and British exodus from Unesco has been featured in a number of tracts. To understand this organization's trials and tribulations during the late 1970s and 1980s, however, it is important not to forget the developments of previous decades.

Writing in the mid-1970s, Tunstall noted that Unesco had constantly supported notions such as the 'free flow of information', notions which 'inevitably favour the major media exporting nation' (Tunstall 1977: 208). Tunstall traces how the first 'Anglo-American' Director Generals of Unesco moved the organization towards supporting imports of media technology and software into the developing world. This British researcher also presents a scathing attack on Wilbur Schramm's *Mass Media and National Development* (1964) which became 'a Unesco bible on the topic. . . . There are no real policy recommendations – just that more and more media are a good thing' (Tunstall 1977: 211). That the M'Bow period with the McBride report and all that that entailed should lead to a head-on collision between Unesco and the US is not surprising in this context.

Some more recent research work has focused on the implications of Tunstall's earlier analyses. Mowlana has analysed the Unesco programme 'Communication in the Service of Humanity' and has concluded that the organization has attempted to play down the global debate on the media, a debate which was so central to the New World Information and Communication Order discourse in the early 1980s (Mowlana 1990). He criticizes the US government stance, as it has developed since the US left Unesco, and he expresses concern over what he sees as a growing isolationist tendency in the US in the post-Cold War era.

An obvious question is: why can't Unesco balance what the US does (assuming the power of US-led media is so overwhelming)? Samarajiva (1990) concludes that the answer lies in the fact that 'Unesco, being an international organization has no coercive power of its own'. Unesco relies on member states to enforce recommendations, and this power is not strong enough to balance the economic and organizational momentum of the transnational communications industry.

The Council of Europe

The Council of Europe, representing states both in the former west and eastern parts of Europe, has also specialized in cultural matters. The Council organized a series of studies of the cultural industries in the early 1980s. The many reports that ensued had titles such as *Creative Artists and the Industrialization of Culture* (Gronow 1982), *The Place of Small Firms in the Record Industry and their Role in Creativity* (Hennion 1982) and *The Impact of New Technologies and the Strategies of the Music Industries* (Wal 1985). Such tracts covered a number of issues involving the music media but had little direct impact on national policies in sovereign member states. Their main value was to bring together policymakers, researchers and people from the music industry for the first time (thus one can expect long-term rather than short-term effects).

With euphoria regarding European unity and a single market at an all-time high, it was perhaps natural that the Council of Europe should begin to concern itself with matters of European *national* identity. Competition between the Council and the European Commission in Brussels regarding the media field can also have fuelled this urgency. A Council for Cultural Co-operation was created in 1987; its brief was to study the threat involved in 'the trend towards uniformity and the blurring of identities in Europe' (Council of Europe report COM (90) 1a, p. 2). Some, of course, would suggest that any such blurring was exactly the result of the deregulation policies advocated by the EC earlier on in the 1980s.

The Commission's report, presented in Strasbourg in September 1990 and formulated by the Mediacult Institute in Vienna, focuses on the problems facing cultural activities. It concludes that musicians cannot survive on the income from live performances (one can infer that this observation only refers to artists in the so-called 'serious' field, working with art music). The commission recommends extra governmental support for both 'the cultural mandate of public broadcasting organizations' and 'a system whereby commercial and private broadcasters can be compensated for losses incurred whenever they exceed their statutory or legal obligations in the production and dissemination of cultural goods.' The report also supports the introduction of a quota system which guarantees domestic audio-visual products an 'adequate' share of transmission time. What this means in terms of percentages is not specified (cf. the local content debate in Jamaica or the rules for commercial television in Sweden). The study also believes that incentives rather than regulations are the best means to get the private domain to produce and disseminate cultural goods. Here we have an example of the latent incompatabilities which tend to creep into such ambitious policy documents. Guaranteeing media access for national and local activities via a quota system (e.g. 40 per cent Swedish music on a national commercial channel as a franchise condition) would hardly seem to necessitate the offering of pecuniary incentives to the same operator to produce more recordings of Swedish musicians.

Both the European Commission and the Council of Europe have devoted attention to the problems of television broadcasting across frontiers (transborder *radio* broadcasting was excluded early on from the regulation arena because there was so much of it). The traditional EC view is that media and cultural products are like any other goods; they should be the subject of free competition and trade should not be hampered by discriminatory measures. In theory, at least, a member state cannot run its own national subsidized media or cultural programme and exclude cultural or media workers from other states from benefiting from it. Culture still does not have a specific place in the Rome Charter and the EC's free labour market requires the absence of any rules that can be interpreted as discriminatory. Thus any move to restrict subsidies to benefit nationals from one country (even if the activity concerns their own specific cultural identity) could be interpreted as contravening EC rules.

A similar conflict of interests exists in the field of European media policy. EC directives have tended to view audio-visual products as goods sold and distributed in a market (subject to free competition in the absence of restricting legislation or structures). Discussions in the Council of Europe, however, on matters such as transborder television transmissions, have tended to stress the *national* interests of member states and the role of media in legitimate activities aimed at strengthening cultural identity (Wallis and Baran 1990: 111; Duelund 1991: 14–20). The vested interests of states with particular financial interests in European satellite broadcasting (e.g. Luxembourg with its two Astra satellites) have also complicated the picture; Luxembourg has consistently opposed moves to introduce European content quotas as well as restrictions on advertising in commercial satellite transmissions.

The latent conflicts involved in such matters are likely to become more and more intense in a united, single labour-market Europe, leading possibly to different forms and expressions of antagonism. Professionals in arts and media can be expected to gravitate to centres where access to grants, subsidies and attractive working conditions are perceived to be the most generous. If the Welsh National Opera sees its most important goal as winning international, or at least European acclaim, then it will naturally seek to attract artistic talent from anywhere in Europe, especially if it can be obtained cheaper than at home in Wales. Such are the economic rules of a free labour market with total mobility. They do not always tally with individual nations' or groups' views of and aspirations concerning cultural identity.

Surprisingly, these problems are hardly touched upon in the EC's attempt to map out the cultural landscape at the turn of the century, namely in the 'Culture for the European Citizen of the Year 2000' proposal, presented to the EC in 1989. This report boldly expresses the belief that:

> The EC will gain credibility in its cultural actions if it takes its distance from . . . thinking influenced by 'economic determinism' which per-

vades more and more the social notions of culture and underestimates its dynamics with evident political and economic implications.
(Committee of Cultural Consultants 1989: 8)

The section on music and opera deals solely with Western art music and its performers' problems. Here, the thinking would seem to be similar to that in other EC contexts, where the aim is to produce European superstars (as opposed to, say, American or Japanese). In musical training, it calls for a 'broadly based musical pyramid within the Community', involving the early discovery of child prodigies: ('the identification of musically gifted children, particularly in the 5–11 years range, is very important' (ibid.: 29). The report does not even mention popular music genres such as jazz, folk, rock, let alone the exciting possibilities associated with immigrant cultures in a mobile, multi-ethnic labour market. On the media side, support for art films is recommended but no mention at all is made of the largest purveyor of music, namely radio. The only link between media policy and music activity can be found in the opera section where one finds a somewhat *ad hoc* suggestion for 'the production of a science-fiction TV-series playing in European opera-houses' (ibid.: 33).

The EC report on culture in the year 2,000 also makes no recommendations concerning the harmonization of copyrights in Europe and the question of whether or not more countries should be encouraged to sign the Rome Convention. Such an opinion, nevertheless, is expressed in a report delivered to both the Commission and the Council of Europe by the French Comité National de la Musique. This notes that: 'Phonograms are a basic element in radio and television companies' programmes. It is logical that producers are ensured reasonable remuneration for this contribution' (Comité National de la Musique, 1989: 8).

That the rights of performers are not mentioned in this sentence would indicate that the phonogram industry's trade organization (IFPI) has done a good job lobbying the French committee – the report also calls for a surcharge for phonogram producers to compensate for home-taping, obligatory circuits in digital tape recorders limiting the ability to make copies, a levy on blank tapes in the Community and the harmonization of taxes on phonograms in the EC.

This illustrates the importance of the IFPI as a player in the field of international policymaking. It is, however, very much a European affair with its HQ first in London and then in Geneva, Switzerland. The International Federation of Phonogram *and Videogram* Industries (as the IFPI now titles itself) has become deeply involved in two specific areas of media policy and music activity; anti-piracy operations and lobbying for more countries to sign the Rome Convention (thus encouraging the shift from primary to secondary incomes). The organization is notably weak in the USA, presumably because the broadcasting lobby is so strong in

America – one of the two US copyright organizations, BMI, which distributes radio dues to composers and publishers, is still formally owned by the US radio industry! We have already noted how the USA's absence from the Rome club can provide preferential advantages in some countries, thereby hindering local music from access to the radio media.

Media conglomerates

The large media conglomerates will presumably continue to grow through amalgamations involving different types of media. This must inevitably lead to a series of policy dilemmas. Consider the case of a conglomerate that owns both radio stations and phonogram companies. The broadcasters will wish to pay as little as possible for the use of phonograms (even those produced within the same corporation); the phonogram division will correspondingly wish to earn as much as possible from secondary sources. Even within phonogram companies, one finds a similar dilemma concerning the purchase of publishing rights; the publishing division will seek to maximize the dues phonogram companies have to pay for, say, mechanical rights to include specific songs on a phonogram; the phonogram division will have exactly the opposite aim. As formal and informal integration grow, such policy deliberations will become even more complex with the outcome harder to predict. We have no indication as to how the new transnational media giants intend to act in this area. Up to now, the industry has been happy to hand the matter over to other legal authorities for a decision; the phonogram industry in Britain and the music publishers had a long conflict regarding mechanical copyrights solved by a copyright tribunal in 1991; divisions from the same multinationals could be found on both sides of the courtroom!

Another important aspect of many new media conglomerates is the breadth of their operations, leading occasionally to conflicts of interests which can affect artistic freedom and even result in censorship. This is a problem area which many mass communications researchers studying the flow of news information through the media have highlighted (Chadwick 1989; Bagdikian 1990). If General Electric, a major supplier of defence equipment to the Pentagon, owns NBC TV, can one guarantee that any negative information about General Electric's military activities will find a place on the NBC Evening Network News? Experience indicates that similar problems exist in the music industry. Murdock has reported how Toshiba, one of Japan's leading nuclear contractors, withdrew in 1988 a record attacking Japan's nuclear programme which had been commissioned by its Toshiba-EMI music subsidiary (Murdock 1990). With the growth of conglomerates where music is only a small part of the whole, one can expect a further move away from the notion of total 'artistic freedom'.

A new conglomerate we presented was the Stenbeck media empire in

Scandinavia, with satellite television, terrestrial TV, publishing, radio and phonogram activities, alongside interests in mobile phones and paging systems. Stenbeck's expansion policy clearly assumes that strong common denominators exist between countries such as Norway, Sweden and Denmark, because they speak closely related languages. He therefore offers the same entertainment fare (with a few linguistic variations in the subtitling) in all three countries. This has occurred at a time when governments in these countries have tended to play down both the future importance of regional co-operation and the current significance of regional institutions such as the Nordic Council; their attention has been mainly on the larger EC perspective. It is interesting to note that, at the same time, sales of Danish artists and music in Sweden have shown a marked increase. Should we conclude that a media entrepreneur based in Manhattan is more in tune with the effects of sentiments regarding regional cohesion on media habits than politicians in individual Scandinavian countries?

Jan Stenbeck's rise to fame as Scandinavia's new media mogul has followed a path that is not unknown in European media history. Indeed, it tallies exactly with the growth of Italy's Silvio Berlusconi, though almost a decade later. Berlusconi used the combination of deregulation and new technology to get access to a new TV channel and fill it with low-cost programmes mainly from the USA. When competitors working with more expensive local production got into financial difficulties, Berlusconi would move in, purchase them and adapt their programme schedules to his own concept. Berlusconi sought to gain as much control as possible over the sales of TV commercials to available channels. Although Berlusconi always squeezed the law to suit his own intentions, he could utilize political support through his excellent network of contacts and friends. Berlusconi's power was only slightly restricted by regulations in the 1990 Italian Broadcasting Bill; on the other hand his activities were legitimized (Tunstall and Palmer 1990: 169–73).

The Big Five

The Big Five phonogram giants are also important international actors. They have bought virtually all the existing large independents that have been up for sale. Virgin was one of the few exceptions. Twenty-five per cent of its capital, however, was acquired by the Japanese media giant Fujisankei, and EMI made no secret of the fact that it was pursuing Virgin in 1991 – the chase resulted in a deal being clinched in early 1992. The new owners promised that Virgin would be allowed to continue to live a relatively independent life under the EMI corporate umbrella.

Our initial analysis assumed that the Big Five would follow a policy of restricting music activity to a small number of international superstars, producing music which can sell in as many territories as possible. On the face of it, this seems to be the case. EMI reported worldwide sales of 5.7 million albums for the Swedish group Roxette's 'Joyride' in 1991, that's a figure not far off the total annual sales of albums with Swedish music in Sweden. Most of the superstars are recruited from the USA and the UK, but a trickle of new talents has emerged via other national markets – Sweden has produced ABBA, Europe and more recently, Roxette.

Simple policies, however, do not always work out as expected; even superstars' productivity is unpredictable and a delay in the release of one or two such releases can cause considerable financial problems even for a recording giant. The alternative is to look for sales of nationally successful stars to compensate for superstars not delivering on time, as this quote from the BMG 1990 annual report illustrates:

> Bertelsmann Music Group achieved its results despite major challenges. The toughest of these stemmed from delays in the releases of new albums by some of the international superstars. However other BMG artists and their emergence on the Top charts offset the negative impact.
>
> Of particular noteworthiness are several BMG Ariola companies which were successful . . . in promoting stars in their national markets.

The Swedish artist Thomas Ledin, who sold over 450,000 phonograms with Swedish lyrics in a year for BMG, was one such example. Maybe we will see a move away from the strategy of multi-media packaging of a small number of international superstars, to a hunt for attractive propositions in national or language-based regional markets. If so, we could be witnessing a totally new phase in international phonogram company policy.

With so much international repertoire being selected according to performance on the UK or US market, the question of how such success is measured assumes relevance for media policy, even in smaller nations. Over the decades there has been a series of payola scandals concerning the ways in which records are promoted on US radio. Dannen's exposé of 'The Network', a group of so-called independent promoters controlled by the US mafia gives a fascinating insight into the extraordinary payments US majors were paying in the 1980s to get their records on the air (Dannen 1991). One of the more interesting cases concerns a record by the British group, Pink Floyd – 'Another Brick in the Wall'. Despite five sold-out concerts in Los Angeles, local stations were not playing the record; an executive at CBS had decided not to pay the promotion fee, assuming that Pink Floyd's presence in itself would generate enough radio station interest. Pressure was exerted on the executive and he backed down. Within hours of the payment being made, the song was being aired on all the local CHR (Contemporary Hit Radio) stations in LA. Many of Dannen's details of how the Network functions are confirmed in a series of articles by a

German researcher (Wicke 1988a, 1988b) as well as by conversations we have had with the former CBS executive referred to above.

Dannen chronicles the unsuccessful attempts of the US legal system to do anything about the network of independent promoters, and concludes that business continues as usual in the 1990s, simply because it suits the interests of all parties involved, with the exception, of course, of small phonogram companies and artists whose records do not get promoted. In other words, broadcasters anywhere in the world, who base their output on what is played and publicized in the US hitlists, are basing their music policy on a selection process that involves many shady, if not outright criminal activities.

The national level

It is on the national level that we have observed the greatest changes in the ability to implement media policies. Traditional institutions such as national broadcasters, national independent phonogram companies, musicians' unions, etc. have seen their power diminishing in most countries. With electronic signals coming in from outside and up above, governments have been presented with a whole new set of limitations on broadcasting policy.

States continue, of course, to follow a policy of supporting certain types of music activities with subsidies. In cash terms, the contribution is greatest, as one would expect, in the developed nations, though even here one can observe considerable differences.

Sweden and Wales are the two countries in our sample where the largest sums of public money are invested in the arts sector, with most public funds being channelled through an Arts Council, and with opera and symphony orchestras consuming the lion's share. An approximate comparison of available statistics, however, indicates that public spending per capita on the arts sector is several times higher in Sweden than in Wales (Table 9.3).

The comparison in Table 9.3 shows that far more is spent in Sweden than in Wales on supporting fine arts in general and music in particular. A media policy element usually consists of labour-intensive music activities such as symphony orchestras having an obligation to both tour and provide a certain number of concerts which may be broadcast on national radio.

Financial support for the production of phonograms with local music is given in Wales (exclusively to Art music projects) and in Sweden. In Sweden, as we have seen, this policy does not appear to be in tune with that of other media sectors such as broadcasting; the subsidized phonograms receive very few radio plays and can thus generate little consumer interest. The phonogram industry in Jamaica and Trinidad has to rely on the money it generates itself via exports, home sales and occasional

Table 9.3 A comparison of state support for arts and music in Wales and Sweden

	Sweden		Wales	
Category (1989/90)	Total (£m)	Per cap.	Total (£m)	Per cap.
Total arts funding				
arts + museums	200	23.0	21.0	7.0
Music (centrally funded)	13	1.5	0.8	0.3
Regional music support	30	3.5	5.0	1.7
Opera (centrally funded)	20	2.3	1.8	0.6

Sources: Swedish National Council for Cultural Affairs and Policy Studies Institute, London report *Cultural Trends 1991*.

Notes: Assumptions: SEK10=£1.
Population: Sweden 8.6 million; Wales 2.9 million

contributions from sponsors. The same applies in Kenya; Tanzania has no organized phonogram industry.

Government policy as regards broadcasting is confused in all our sample nations (with the possible exception of Tanzania). The notion of *public service* broadcasting has fallen into disrepute under the shadow of deregulation's many promises. Whilst paying lip service to the notion of a high content of local programme material, governments have been unwilling to specify exact levels: terms such as 'adequate' or a 'considerable' amount offering a 'proper balance of subject matter with a high standard of quality' tend to feature in policy statements and documents. In reality, as regards potential sanctions, such statements mean more or less nothing.

In some cases, overall media policy is directly the result of government political strategy. Radio Tanzania's Swahili jazz band output is linked to the government's notion of using the Swahili language to unite a country of so many different tribes and local languages. Radio Cymru and S4C in Wales are the result of pressure group activities combined with a strategy in London of providing media frameworks to keep such sympathizers occupied with less militant activities (rather than a burning interest in the cause of Welsh culture). Broadcasting policy in Sweden provides one of the best examples of governments' decreased ability to affect the course of events. Non-commercial Neighbourhood Radio was introduced in 1988; a decade later its output differed little from the form of radio that emerged in the USA in the wake of the Reagan deregulation era. Swedish media politicians have been very unwilling to suggest measures regulating media content for fear of being accused of meddling with citizens' rights, such as freedom of speech.

A universal problem afflicting nations that attempt to create cohesive media policies is that media matters often fall under the jurisdiction of different government agencies and ministries. An Education Ministry will support educational broadcasting programmes – usually these are the responsibility of a separate organization from the national radio or TV companies. Broadcasting might be under the wings of a Ministry of Information which functions more or less as a publicity organization for the party or politicians in power. Broadcasting can also be included in the portfolio of a Communications Ministry, whilst matters pertaining to music are the responsibility of a Ministry of Culture (with very little influence over broadcasting).

We have come across many different variations on these themes in our sample; in Kenya in the late 1980s, for instance, even though Kenya's VoK was under the formal control of a Ministry of Information, most edicts concerning its operation were coming from a new Ministry of National Guidance, created by President Daniel Arap Moi to oversee the implementation of his personal decisions. That many of the findings of the National Presidential Music Commission regarding music in the media led to little or no action can be related to the new ministry's primary concern with 'national security'.

Even Sweden offers telling examples of how different ministries can be out of phase. In 1989, the Ministry of Industry rented out a direct broadcasting satellite (Tele-X) to a company wishing to find a loophole in the laws governing commercial television (TV4), laws which the Ministry of Education and Culture were trying to defend. And when two Swedish companies which were world leaders in the chemical and mechanical process involved in disc pressing got into difficulties (the parent company of one of them went bankrupt), not a murmur was heard from the Ministry of Industry; this industrial segment wasn't regarded as being of significance.

National *broadcasters'* attitudes in the new media environment have often been characterized by sluggishness, complacency and no small measure of confusion as soon as competition has increased. We have only found one example of a written music policy in our sample, issued by the S4C TV channel in Wales in late 1991. It is very general in essence and appears mainly to be geared to establishing S4C as a force to be reckoned with in a European/World market context:

> It is the aim of S4C's music policy to enable the production of programmes of the highest quality which would stand proudly in the European and World markets . . . what must not happen is that S4C in its musical progrmming is left behind by the rest of the broadcasting industry.
>
> (S4C 1991)

The only statement in the S4C policy document which can be directly related to music activities concerns the choice of music for sound tracks in documentaries and dramas; here the aim is clearly to commission original music from local composers rather than use standard, international 'library music'.

Few national radio broadcasters appear to have noted that the ability to make live recordings of their own could provide a significant competitive advantage over small-scale competitors without such resources, as well as decreasing their growing mutual dependency on the commercial phonogram industry. The following statement from Danish Radio's Head of Live Music is a glaring exception:

> In accordance with the general demands for comprehensive coverage made by public service radio stations, programme policy must be *for* variety, *against* uniformity; to offer listeners as many musical experiences as possible. The consequence must be an ever-increasing focus on the areas the music industry ignores, so *one* complements the other, with variety as a result. In this context, live music on the radio is indispensable.
>
> Non-commercial radio must look more and more to *as yet unestablished talent* as a supplement to the record industry which primarily deals in established, famous names. Moreover, radio can create *combinations of musical talent* not to be found in commercial music, both nationally and internationally. In this context well-known names can also come into the picture, as they can contribute glory that will rub off on less well-known partners, thus indirectly helping unestablished talent and thereby being part of the programme policy.
>
> (Moseholm 1991)

This statement contains many interesting concepts, particularly the notion of radio stations with recording facilities functioning as mediator between better and less well-known artists, thus adding status to more local music activities. The paper also complains about the attitude of the musicians' union which, it maintains, hinders live music activities within Danish radio by placing an impossible burden of contractual demands.

Our own data contain a number of references to live music on the radio. The Kenyan Music Commission recommended the Voice of Kenya to engage in such activities. But with over a decade and a half having passed since the VoK last recorded its own music, such competence has been lost in the organization and is difficult to retrieve. The same applies to Swedish national radio. Radio Tanzania, on the other hand, has built its competence on its own recording activities – this gave it an advantage when signals could be heard in southern Kenya.

As competition in the airwaves and cables has increased, public service broadcasters have tended to react either by doing nothing or by adapting programme output to approach that of the new competitors. Sweden's two non-commercial, licence-financed TV channels, for instance, offer an output which is very similar to that of the new commercial terrestrial channel. Somewhat crudely, one can claim that competition has merely upped the price for the Swedes of an episode of 'Dallas' or the Wimbledon tennis tournament.

The sluggishness is also illustrated by the following data. Music output on Sweden's national light music radio channel, P3, remained remarkably stable during the mid-1980s, despite the amazing increase of international hit music in the environment thanks to second- and third-tier radio:

Table 9.4 Music output of Swedish national radio, P3, by country of origin and music genre

Country of origin of phonograms	% of phonograms played on P3			
	1984 March	1986 October	1987 October	1988 October
Sweden	29.1	35.1	35.5	33.9
rest of Scandinavia	3.4	3.2	2.6	2.2
UK	17.8	16.1	17.5	17.0
USA	33.9	32.0	32.3	34.8
W Germany	3.0	2.1	2.3	2.1
France	2.7	3.1	2.6	2.6
Italy	1.7	1.3	1.1	1.2
rest of Europe	5.8	3.5	2.4	2.8
rest of world	2.7	3.6	3.7	3.3
Genre of music played	*% of phonograms played on P3*			
General light music	33.6	39.1	36.0	36.9
Pop	25.9	28.9	34.6	29.6
Rock	16.1	11.3	10.8	12.4
Jazz/country	16.1	13.8	14.8	16.8
Easy classics	6.5	5.5	2.3	2.0
Signatures	1.4	1.4	1.5	1.3

Source: statistics from Sveriges Riksradio (Swedish National Radio) based on annual 3-week samples.

Note: Phonograms have accounted for approx. 90% of music output on P3 throughout this period. The Swedish figure refers not only to Swedish music, but to all phonograms recorded in Sweden.

Table 9.4 illustrates that little changed for five years as regards the Anglo-American content on phonograms in the output of P3. The only clear trend one can discern in the breakdown of genres is a move towards more pop and light music, possibly at the expense of popular classics. National Radio, in other words, has not markedly changed the character of its music output in response to the increased dissemination of Anglo-

American hits in Sweden resulting from the advent of Local or Neighbourhood Radio and satellite music television.

Swedish radio did not adjust to the new situation by choosing to increase output either from Sweden or from countries other than the major exporters (the USA and the UK). There was little awareness amongst management of the important status that publicity over a national channel can give to local music activities (for example, John Peel playing Welsh music on BBC national radio), and thus little support for any obligation to search out and give public performance opportunities to local music. One notes similar attitudes amongst national broadcasters in most countries. This is, of course, a recipe for disaster.

National broadcasters also show a regular desire to keep realism out of the area of popular music output, particularly if it is home-grown. Videos which suggest that there is any violence in Jamaican society (and there is plenty) are banned from the JBC; the same does not apply to international music videos. A song about people getting money and spending it was banned on Radio Tanzania but the group was able to defend itself in the local press. A song praising Nelson Mandela was banned on the Voice of Kenya, as was another one about the government's budget. In the 1970s, US country artists singing heroic songs about the Green Berets in Vietnam were played on Sweden's national light music channel; songs in Swedish questioning the Vietnam war were banned.

Examples of such censorship abound. They can rarely be seen as exact responses to specific media policies. More often one has to interpret them in terms of the different forces that mould a gatekeeper's world. With the government holding the ultimate purse strings, even in countries with licence fees which go straight to the broadcaster, then ministers must not be offended. National broadcasters also have to consider other parts of the establishment, for instance, the religious lobby which has been active in Jamaica condemning the many reggae texts containing smut or 'slack talk'. For popular musicians whose music activity often takes place in situations and environments where conditions can often be tough, far away from the bastions of power, it becomes hard to satisfy policies that demand one disregards what one sees and hears daily.

In the face of conflicting demands and obligations, and with the vexed question of what an unpredictable public wants, broadcasters often end up in the same quandary as phonogram producers. A common way out is to choose a non-adventurous solution involving safe horses, i.e. established artists and tuneful, memorable songs which annoy as few listeners as possible. The Golden Oldie format is ideal in this context since they've all been tried before – it also has the least degree of contact with current music activity.

Traditional musicians' organizations such as trade unions have also found that life changes radically with an increased amount of recorded music in society, particularly when deregulation winds are blowing at gale force in the political establishment. It becomes harder to retain restrictions on radio stations playing phonograms (needle-time regulations, cf. local stations in Wales), or to adhere to a strict dividing line between professionals (members of the union) and amateurs or semi-amateurs. Another problem facing such groups is the replacement of musicians by machines. ABBA's drummer was made redundant by a studio drum-machine in the early 1980s. New technology has also served to make professional divisions less obvious. Studio engineers become musicians as they learn to programme synthesizers, while musicians become engineers for similar reasons. All too often, musicians' unions have tried to cling on to closed-shop principles guaranteeing as much media work for their own professional members, even to the extent of hindering broadcasters from allowing amateurs or recordings by amateurs access to the airwaves.

National, locally owned phonogram companies also have experienced growing problems. Even a general move into other media areas could not save the financial day for Sweden's last, large independent, Sonet, purchased by Polygram in July 1991. National independents have been heavily affected by the concentration of manufacturing and distribution resources more and more under the control of the majors. Thus Kenya has lost its only pressing plant; the Welsh have to purchase manufacturing in England; Tanzania never got a record factory on line; Jamaica with all its traditional vinyl pressing plants does not look like getting a CD plant; and the same applies to Trinidad. Sweden, which used to be world leader in vinyl pressing plant technology, has only two CD plants, one of them owned by British interests. Subsidiaries of the Big Five in Sweden manufacture most of their Swedish productions in Holland or Germany.

Distribution policy for the majors is to centralize operations to a few central points for European operations (EMI, for instance, distributes all phonograms in Denmark from Hamburg in Germany). This in turn affects the operations of another group of national institutions, copyright societies. They traditionally use their local monopoly position not only to audit on a regular basis local manufacturing facilities, but also to subsidize local music and media activities via phonogram production, stipends, etc., occasionally attracting the wrath of the US copyright association ASCAP, when it isn't satisfied with the financial returns it gets from other parts of the world. With manufacturing resources being concentrated in a few countries, the individual copyright holder's ability, via a collecting society, to retain control over the use of his or her works becomes more remote. An imbalance is created between different copyright collection societies, with those in countries where manufacturing is concentrated (e.g. Holland) retaining most of the handling fees. Costs for copyright collection in non-manufacturing countries rise correspondingly, thus indirectly having a negative affect on the well-being of individual creators in such places.

As physical sales of phonograms become less important for access to recorded music, the shift from primary to secondary sources of income will continue to be of importance for phonogram companies. This will increase their mutual dependency on the broadcasters and others who use phonograms for public performance. This could put smaller phonogram companies in a disadvantageous position, since they are less capable of satisfying documentational demands on the registration of new recordings (a prerequisite for the distribution of secondary incomes) – some small phonogram companies that work only with cassettes don't even bother to give each new release an identification number.

Local level

On the local level we have found a rich variety of groups representing different music activities, often trying with varying degrees of success to affect policy in the music media. A feature of the 1980s has been the growth of music organizations representing particular cultural or professional interests. Often these have taken over the former role of national musicians' unions.

— In Sweden, the musicians' union has split into two halves, one representing members of symphony and chamber orchestras and the other representing freelance musicians in the jazz, rock and folk area as well as members of restaurant dance bands.
— The Trinidadian steelband organization, Pan Trinbago, is an important lobbying group advocating more media access for a music style which only a few decades ago was regarded as the lowest form of vulgarity by the colonial Establishment.
— Kenyan musicians have founded numerous organizations for lobbying the government and the VoK for resources and more media access (the excess of organizations in Kenya is also probably related to the country's tough restrictions on the right of assembly).
— The Swedish 1990 Folk and Dance Music Year would never have got off the ground without a strong grass-roots folk music organization taking the initiative with a little assistance from supporters higher up the cultural bureaucracy.
— Without the persistent tenacity of the Welsh Language Society, there would have been no such institutions as Radio Cymru, S4C and even the youth Eistedfodd (where rock and pop with Welsh lyrics were performed for the first time at the festival around 1979). The return of youth programmes with Welsh rock music in one of Radio Cymru's night spots has also been associated with the Society's activities.

We have already mentioned examples of individuals and local groups creating small networks for the exchange of media products such as cassette compilations of favourite recordings. Such networks often cross national borders without even involving any officials or organizations on the national level. Groups in the Caribbean seek 'back to the roots' links with groups in Africa. Cultural enthusiasts in Wales seek contacts both with other Celtic nations, producing a form of European regional cohesion, and with other smaller cultures such as the Basques. This involves a total bypassing of normal staging posts in the contact process, such as Cardiff or even London.

Access to broadcasting or phonogram media for local music activity requires some minimum level of investments or resources. Without functioning instruments it is hard for musicians to develop skills, a prerequisite for performing, let alone produce recordings for the media. Schools, churches or other organizations providing rehearsal facilities, instruments and sometimes even rudimentary recording equipment thus play a vital catalytic role in encouraging music activity. Experience from Sweden shows that where municipalities formulated and implemented policy decisions to provide places for rock musicians to rehearse (e.g. disused warehouses as in Stockholm) then activity has expanded by leaps and bounds. Such projects have the added advantage of providing entertainment and places to congregate for a youthful audience looking for 'action' and an evening out on the town (a better alternative than walking the streets).

THE LOCAL–INTERNATIONAL DICHOTOMY AND THE NATIONAL BYPASS

Our conclusions in the previous section show that the greatest changes in the conditions for policymaking on different levels can be found amongst *national* institutions and actors. Also, that links between the *international* and the *local* level have become much stronger, thereby bypassing the national level. In combination with access to technology on the local level, this leads us to modify our original MISC model which viewed the national level as a necessary intermediary between international and local levels, providing for two different types of local activities (see Figure 9.3).

Media and music activities on a local level no longer require a national intermediary (e.g. a national radio station or phonogram company) to get access to music from the international level. A new hit record can be acquired from MTV, a new calypso record by the Mighty Sparrow from Brooklyn, NY. Thus a small local radio station which wishes to play Anglo-American hit repertoire can compete with a traditional national channel to be first with the news (a 'local–international' operation). Satellite channels getting local coverage via cable are another example.

At the same time, however, access to cheap technology (recording, FM transmitting or sampling equipment) allows local enthusiasts to create their own music media filled with local content ('local–local' activities in the

238 Media Policy and Music Activity

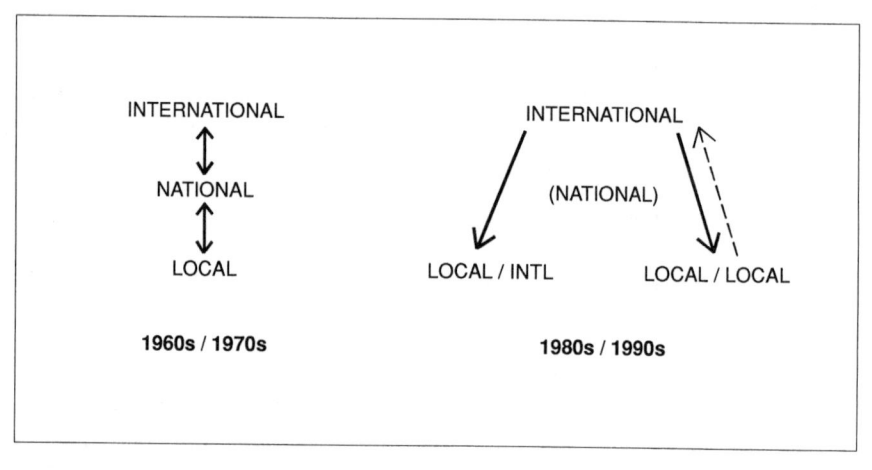

```
INTERNATIONAL           INTERNATIONAL
    ↑↓                   ╱         ↗╲
 NATIONAL              ╱  (NATIONAL) ╲
    ↑↓                ↙              ↘
  LOCAL          LOCAL / INTL    LOCAL / LOCAL

 1960s / 1970s          1980s / 1990s
```

Figure 9.3 The availability of cultural products on a local level changes the role of national institutions as intermediaries.

diagram above), or even with hybrids based on both local music and music or musical influences from other cultures. Variants of international Anglo-American popular genres created locally can also find their way to the international scene without going through a national intermediary. Sweden's Roxette achieved fame in the US not through a campaign engineered from the start by the Swedish subsidiary of EMI with which they have a contract, but thanks to an American exchange student taking a copy of 'The Look' back to his home town and getting it played on local radio stations – it was then accepted for US promotion by the US branch of EMI. A similar process has enabled Tanzanian artists visiting Kenya for recording purposes to have their works picked up by CBS or Virgin.

The national level gets bypassed in this way. Local interests can also build up their own contacts with local interests in other countries, still bypassing the established national institutions at home, but at the same time creating new international levels of media exchange and co-operation (e.g. Welsh enthusiasts creating media products together with musicians in other countries in the Celtic region).

The only alternative for the national level to recreate its importance as an intermediary, as far as we can see, involves a two-stage process:

1 Turning the focus of attention inwards, seeking musical activities at home and giving them national media prominence and thereby status.
2 Establishing bilateral or regional media exchanges that can provide programme material which differs from the standard international hit repertoire (in other words discovering new musical sounds).

The latter type of policy has been discussed at several meetings of

European radio producers convened by the EBU (European Broadcasting Union). As far as we know, the EBU has only achieved partial success in this area as far as folk music exchange is concerned.

THE GROWING TECHNOLOGICAL GAP

We have argued that access to music industry technology at an affordable price has brought about a general increase in the possibilities for producing music for the media. This was definitely the case in the 1970s and early 1980s as a result of the spread of audio cassette and related electronic technology. Frith's 1986 statement that 'technological change has been a source of resistance to corporate thinking' (Frith 1986: 272) suggests that the music machines have increased the artist's control over the shape and form of intellectual property. Goodwin (1992: 81) prefers a less technologically deterministic view, seeing access to technology as offering opportunities for people to play different roles in a creative process (artists become technicians, technicians contributing new things to art). This tendency seemed to be universal, thus resulting in a gradual closing of the technological gaps between different countries (small, large, rich, poor, etc.).

But things are changing. The data presented in this volume support the notion of a new gap appearing between industrialized and developing nations, with an analogue/digital hardware divide constituting a demarcation line that hardly existed a decade ago. Access to digital technology in different forms does not seem to be a part of any 'democratization' process in developing nations. At the same time, the flow of software (in our case recorded music) between nations, continents and peoples shows no sign of abating. And, as has always been the case throughout the music industry's history, the actual flow bears little relation to the distribution of the pecuniary rewards the industry generates through its various activities.

The analogue/digital hardware boundary, in other words, is osmotic by nature. It can temporarily be permeated when, for instance, recording engineers and artists from richer nations make field trips to capture genuine, exotic sounds from the peoples of poorer nations. The sounds are then processed in the industrialized world, and can often make their way back (on analogue cassettes, vinyl discs or via radio/TV transmissions) in a very different form to the source nations.

The worsening state of national economies can also add to the technological gap, and even affect small yet relatively wealthy industrialized nations. As debts increase, financial policy in many nations is to enforce strict fiscal mechanisms. This, for example, has even encouraged Swedish groups enjoying international success to move their business to other countries. Some of the ABBA members left STIM and took their copyright moneys elsewhere. The rock group Europe moved to the Bahamas. Such tendencies have been even more marked in the case of musicians from developing nations which often enforce rigid foreign exchange control regulations; Bob Marley joined the US copyright society ASCAP so that money his songs were earning went to the USA rather than directly to Jamaica. Jamaican film director, Perry Hensell, has given us a number of quotes expressing his feelings about the country's Central Bank.

With tougher currency restrictions in force and increased pressure on a country's economy through foreign debts, there is less likelihood of moneys earned abroad from music finding their way home. This in its turn decreases both the willingness and the ability to invest in new technology, thereby adding to a further widening of the technological gap.

MUSIC CONTENT IN THE MEDIA

Observations of music content also support the above bypass model. Our loggings of music content in Jamaica, Trinidad, Tanzania and Kenya, as well as data from Sweden and Wales, indicate a marked dichotomy between local and international music with a clear exclusion of other forms. Output consists of various quantities of domestic and Anglo-American hit music, with very small quantities of music from other cultures and countries. Relative amounts reflect the relative influences of local and international music. Other forms of music, if played at all, are usually featured in specialist programmes at non-peaktime hours, or, as is the case with art music in Sweden, in a special programme channel.

Table 9.5 Average share of music content on the radio for music of different origins in six sample nations

Music type	Jamaica	Trinidad	Kenya	Tanzania	Sweden	Wales
Local	40	51	84	85	34	70
Anglo-American	60	49	15	15	51	30
Others	–	–	1	10	15	–

Notes: Wales is a rough estimate of actual output (many programmes feature 100% Welsh music). Sweden is based on statistics from Swedish radio and the other four summarize our own loggings. When sampling the music content of Jamaican and Trinidadian radio, music from all English-speaking Caribbean countries has been logged as local. Likewise, all East African music has been logged as local in the Kenyan and Tanzanian samples.

Table 9.5 shows surprisingly low figures for the category 'Others'. This category didn't even show up in the samples in Jamaica and Trinidad. The rich popular music of the Latin American neighbours of these countries leaves no traces in radio programming. The 'other' music on Tanzanian radio was mainly South African music related to the struggle against apartheid and one or two reggae hits. Almost no West African popular music could be heard on Kenyan or Tanzanian radio. Sweden shows the highest content of 'other' music. Still it is surprising that more music isn't played from other Scandinavian (only 2–3 per cent) or central European countries (see Table 9.4). The European Broadcasting Union has discussed on a number of occasions the possibility of bringing more music from smaller cultures to the ears of European radio listeners. An EBU World Music Workshop was even created for this purpose, but seems to have achieved little, possibly because of institutional problems besetting traditional national public service broadcasters. News and music, for instance, enjoy very different priorities:

> Public radio has somehow decided that the public has to be informed on guerrilla war in the Philippines or political bribery in Japan, but I just don't see any radio station that expressly decided that its public should be introduced to the cultural heritage of say Myanmar, the former Burma, or the music of the griots in Western Africa. . . .
>
> Public radio in Europe is today still very dependent on the output of the multinationals. We have a programme staff which is a mix of generalists and experts. In some countries we have recommendations on national music. But in its music policy no public radio is dealing specifically with recommendations on world music.
>
> (Reitov 1990)

Data from our sample of nations show that concentration on local music is highest in the East African countries, which are also the countries with the greatest cultural distance to the base countries of the international music industry. These countries are also the least industrialized. One can assume that the more different a specific country's culture is to Anglo-American culture and the lesser industrialized it is, the harder it is for international hit music to penetrate the media of that country.

Considering the closeness of Jamaican and Trinidadian culture to US Afro-American culture, and the intense communications with the US, it is surprising that US music does not have a higher percentage of airtime. Jamaican radio has an average of 60 per cent Anglo-American music, but a closer look reveals that the Anglo-American content is concentrated mainly in the two FM stations. Trinidad radio plays less Anglo-American music than does Swedish radio!

MEDIA MUSIC AND LIVE MUSIC

We have previously introduced the concept of mediaization to refer to the changes that occur to music when it goes through the music industry pipeline, producing sounds that differ from traditional ones. From the

1960s up to the late 1980s, it appears that the mediaization process continued to gather momentum. More and more traditional forms of music were drawn into the sphere of the mass media. We have previously described the details of this process using Sri Lankan baila music and Trinidadian calypso as examples (Malm and Wallis 1985).

One common feature of the mediaization process is that the content of lyrics often change. This process has two main components. If the performers of a traditional music form desire access to the broadcasting media, then gatekeepers in these media usually require the lyrics to comply with what they regard as generally accepted norms of public speech. This means a minimum of offensive language or smut, no extreme political statements, etc.

The other component is the ambition of record producers to reach an international audience. Thus all allusions to local incidents and conditions in the lyrics have to go. A notable case is the calypso of Trinidad that used to have texts with an exclusively local content. As long as calypso for the international market was just second-hand copies made by people like Harry Belafonte, the original texts were only slightly adapted to be more comprehensible to an international audience. This did not affect the style of calypso in Trinidad. When some of the original Trinidadian calypsonians (such as four-times calypso monarch The Mighty Duke) were launched on the international market, it immediately affected both the musical style and the content of the text. The calypso beat was influenced by soul music and changed into soca, that is soul calypso. The tempo increased. The local content of the lyrics was substituted by simple exclamations about the thrill of being at a party. The most common word in soca texts of the 1980s must have been 'party', and it certainly did not refer to the political sort!

The record business itself also became an important subject for calypso and soca lyrics, thus mirroring the new situation. Quite a few calypsos have been sung on casette piracy and on the fact that there are no more record pressing plants in Trinidad. Texts referring to the life and conditions of the singer himself are also a sign of the gradual isolation of the professionalized performer from everyday life that comes with mediaization.

Another prominent effect of the mediaization process is that more music industry equipment is required when artists and groups give live performances (i.e. to achieve the same sounds as on their studio-recorded phonograms). Some major artists even elaborate with instruments or sections of instruments pre-recorded on tape, which have to be synchronized with their stage shows. With computer technology it is now possible to trigger ready-made musical structures from conventional instruments.

In the mid-1980s, Swedish popular dance bands discovered that computers could do a lot of their work. These bands play at dance halls, restaurants and hotels. Sometimes they have to work every night of the week for long periods, which is quite strenuous and demanding. Their musical style developed during the early 1960s and has not changed very much since. It contains a number of standard melodic phrases, sounds and rhythmical patterns. Now such bands have all these basic patterns along with gimmicks for specific tunes programmed into a computer. They still hold their guitars and horns, but no longer do they play them in the traditional way. They merely use them to feed the computer with information on how to execute the computer sound files. This means they set the tempo, some of the phrasing, etc. The singing is still live performance. The musicians can thus concentrate more on the singing since they don't have to do as much with their hands as in the past.

The technological know-how created and refined via the demands of the traditional Swedish dance bands for computer support, laid part of the foundation of the music of the Swedish group Roxette. This group is a very efficient industrial musicmaking unit with only two members and a lot of computer power. At some point, one reaches a stage where the whole point of a live performance is lost.

Reggae has reached the point where it is virtually no longer a live form of music. The professional division between a DJ and an artist has also been more or less wiped out, with 'sing-jays' improvizing on backing tracks or dubs. The musicians who record backing tracks also lose control of their creative works – a saxophone riff can turn up anywhere. The use of sampling machines has also produced a similar development in many parts of the world. In a sense, we have reached the ultimate state of mediaization with the sampling machine. The copyright dilemma of where to draw the dividing line between legitimate artistic experiment and financial rip-offs has not been solved.

Both Jamaica and Tanzania can boast high local music content on radio, yet the mediaization process has not come as far in Tanzania. This suggests that radio output alone is not a deciding factor in this process. The lack of studios equipped with up-to-date electronics and local phonogram manufacturing facilities in Tanzania is probably a more critical factor. Swahili jazz band music, though played regularly over the East African airwaves, is still primarily a live form of music rather than a mediaized form.

This is possibly a situation that could change, as the following intriguing mediaization incident illustrates. A Tanzanian musician came to Sweden on his own in May 1991. He belongs to the Wagogo people of central Tanzania. Some twenty years ago he was still in the village of Buigiri in Dodoma region. He was a young boy well versed in traditional music.

This Tanzanian musician started to play Swahili pop music in the mid-1970s, learning to handle electric guitars and simple keyboards. He also made a few recordings in rudimentary studios in Nairobi. He was confronted for the first time with a modern studio and its equipment in Sweden but picked up the possibilities of this environment at an amazing pace. In just a matter of two days he had recorded five tunes applying the potential

Plate 9.3 The old and the new. Modern 'midi' technology, synthesizers and other music machines allowing one musician to do the job of ten.

of the studio to his Tanzanian musical heritage, singing and playing all the parts himself. He was quite happy to be able to put together music that in a traditional context would have required quite a large group of performers. The result was a music that is basically structured like traditional Wagogo music, but with a new sound.

This goes to show that musicians who are given the opportunity can adapt quickly to the modern studio environment. One reason why musicians wish to do this is that having one's musical performances featured by the media gives high status. It also functions as an advertisement, bringing more work to the musician concerned. And, of course, the dream of becoming an international star makes a lot of young musicians do almost anything for an opportunity to get into the media.

Mediaization means that many traditional forms of music are subjected to a process whereby they can compete and maybe survive in the media environment. At the same time they run the risk of being drawn into the transculturation process and losing their specific identities. They could thus merely end up as a component of some 'World Music' combination.

In the 1990s there are indications, however, that the mediaization process is slowing down. We have found an increasing amount of live music activity which exists with virtually no contact with or dependence on either the broadcasting or phonogram industries. Often, as we have noted earlier, such musicians can be linked internationally via a variety of networks, independent of either the broadcasting or print media.

Another area which seems to live a life of its own, with little contact with mass media, is that of formal music education. As we have seen, grand plans for syllabuses are drawn up and implemented. School-children learn about their traditional instruments, schools start their own steelbands in Trinidad, thousands of children learn instruments in municipal music schools in Sweden. Some of this uses specific educational broadcasting media. There is little or no link to mainstream music media or to the leisure-time activities of the same pupils. Investigations in Sweden on leisure-time activities and interests show that 70–80 per cent of young Swedes claim to have a high interest in music. When asked about music as a subject in school only 4–6 per cent indicate a comparable degree of interest. It is not surprising that support for the kind of musical activities learnt at school soon starts to wane amongst school-leavers.

PERFORMANCE AND NON-PERFORMANCE ACTIVITIES

In the introduction we described the dual terms of performance and non-performance activities. The latter was defined as any music activity that is not an actual performance. Regardless of policy regarding content, the mere introduction of mass media into a music culture has the effect of increasing the amount of time devoted to music. This has been the case in

Nepal, where until recently virtually no foreign music was played in the media (Grandin 1989) as well as in Sweden with its wholehearted adoption of international hit music. The time Swedes spend listening to music increased fivefold during the 1970s alone. This was a result of the rapid penetration of new music mass media such as audio cassettes into Swedish homes during this decade.

Fears have often been expressed that the music media would create a massive shift from performance to non-performance activities resulting in less live music. These assumptions seem to postulate that if a music performance through mass media reaches more people than previously, the need for performances of music would decrease. The media would create a passive audience consuming the music of a few elite performers. Traditional forms of musicmaking would die. There are few if any data to support such theories.

Neither is there any proof that traditional forms of music disappear as a result of the implementation of a specific music policy for the media. Performance of traditional Swedish music, as well as of music from Latin America and Africa, has increased markedly during the past two decades in Sweden, despite the fact that these kinds of music are very rarely featured in broadcasting media. Of course, traditional forms of music do disappear, but in such cases this is generally owing to factors other than mass media (e.g. the destruction of the traditional physical environment of a certain ethnic group, or massive oppression including cultural dominance). Such eradication of living cultures has afflicted most Amerindian peoples; there are also several examples of this in the Third and Fourth Worlds. Media policy can play a role in combination with other factors in such processes. On the other hand, there are also examples of media policy counteracting the forces that kill off cultures. The Swedish government has supported the production of phonograms with music sung in the three distinct Saami (Lapp) languages, each one spoken by only one or two thousand people.

In previous sections we have noted a number of cases where forms of traditional music have been transformed by the media. There are also numerous examples of new styles of music being introduced to music cultures via the media. In the 1960s and early 1970s rock music played on electric guitars spread like wildfire through music media.

The influence of mass media and media policy on non-performance activities has been enormous. Before the advent of media there were a limited number of non-performance music activities in each community. These were completely dependent on the availability of local musicians. In many traditional cultures, most people present at a music event were more or less involved in the performance. In some music cultures the very phenomenon of non-performance music activities did not exist before the advent of music media. The most conspicuous non-performance music activity is, of course, the enormous number of hours spent listening to music. This has partly been made possible by the fact that one can listen to music while doing other things. Unless one is merely assaulted by music in the public environment (in a bar, shop, lift or from a neighbour's radio), the listener has to make a choice before listening. This choice can consist of selecting a radio channel, purchasing a record, selecting from the menu of available music on the stall of a cassette pirate, or copying borrowed recordings with equipment at home. In all our sample countries, some of the most popular music programmes are those where listeners write or phone to the DJ and request specific tunes. The morning programme on Radio Tanzania and the important Barry G Show in Jamaica are such programmes.

Artists' fan clubs, community radio music programmes and the kind of networking activities represented by Cytgord in Wales are also examples of non-performance activities by members of the public at large. If we add the large sector of activities involving professionals in media music administration (publishing, production, copyright societies, etc.), it is evident that more people than ever before are involved in non-performance activities.

Through electronic interaction games and instruments that produce partly prefabricated musical structures, we can observe a growing area of music activities that fall somewhere in between the clear-cut categories of performance and non-performance. There are predictions by the Roland Co-operation that 10 per cent of the population in industrialized countries in a few years' time will be regularly involved in such kinds of 'semi-performance' of music. Related to this category is the Jamaican 'sing-jay', international hip-hop styles, and the originally Japanese karaoke phenomenon (the singing in clubs, homes and even taxis of popular songs to a pre-recorded soundtrack or video). Karaoke clubs are presently opening up all over the world. The sing-jay and karaoke pre-recorded backgrounds do not include the text or melody of the song performed, merely harmonies and rhythm. This kind of media product is not covered by existing copyright legislation: composers and other copyright owners receive no remuneration from these activities. We have found no examples of official policies that try to influence developments in this grey zone of 'semi-performance'.

The conclusion we can draw from our data as well as from other research, is that the influence of the media leads to an increase of both performance and non-performance activities. The proportions between these two kinds of music activities have been changed, since non-performance activities show the greatest relative increase.

Every activity, non-performance as well as performance, demands certain musical skills, such as a knowledge of available music forms and music media, a knowledge of how to operate different music machines, etc. Musical knowledge in society seems to be more and more a product of the total effect of implemented music policies by different actors in mass media, and less and less the result of the activities of traditional authorities such as music teachers. Thus media policies play a vital role in deciding the kind of music activity taking place in the society of today.

FINAL THOUGHTS: RAYS OF HOPE AND SIGNS OF PENDING DISASTERS

Writing in a magazine published by Unesco in early 1991, an American journalist Joseph Fitchett of the *International Herald Tribune* suggested that the global media conglomerates were 'a necessary evil' (Fitchett 1990). According to his dinosaur theory, the new media giants are incompetent and wasteful monsters lacking any clear purpose and direction. But, without them, the world would not have got the available electronic technology that allows individuals to create their own media products. Fitchett maintains that only the conglomerates had the necessary capital to develop such technology. He concludes with the sweeping statement that the same technology will once again 'return the media to authors and publishers' whose duty it is, above all, to serve the public.

Throughout our final section we have highlighted several areas where the conglomerates will find problems with policy direction in the music media field. Numerous illustrations of local music activity utilizing music industry technology have also been quoted. Representatives for the developing world, too, have seen technology as offering bright rays of hope in a crusade to break smaller and poorer nations' dependency on an ever-increasing flow of external cultural imports. Representatives of fourteen Caribbean island states concluded after a meeting in 1987 that the best example of new technologies furthering media production:

> comes from the music industry, where certain instruments are selected utilizing forms of technology in order to improve on the music and expand production and sales. In a sense, technology which paradoxically serves cultural penetration, can be used for cultural production ... research should address how technology is appropriated for unleashing cultural production, that is, for culture that one can live by.
> (Brown and Sanatan 1987: 37)

This statement too infers a type of 'necessary evil' role for technology. But the argument also assumes that the resulting cultural production has access to distributing media, i.e. radio, television, cable, phonograms, videograms. Making television programmes that no one has a chance to see would hardly satisfy the goals and hopes expressed above. The commonly chosen policy of deregulation and privatization does not automatically provide a greater number of people and products access to the media.

Summing up our findings on the media policies that are carried out today, we can see that the major music industry conglomerates are concentrating on a small number of high-cost audio and video productions. This involves developing forms of music that can be produced only in a studio with multi-million dollar equipment. One reason for this policy is the urge to edge out less powerful competitors from the marketplace, a policy which can also be achieved through the use of shady methods such as the independent promoter network described by Dannen (Dannen 1991). The aim is, as the slogan goes, 'One Planet, One Music', and ultimately probably one music corporation. Through the increased importance of incomes from copyrights and neighbouring rights, the major conglomerates put more and more effort into getting their products into secondary music media, and less on the direct interaction with the phonogram-buying public at large.

The result of this process is music that cannot be performed live. In the future, we will probably not see many more tours by international recording stars such as Michael Jackson or Madonna. The majors try to contain music production to *studios*; this allows them to strive for a total control of music production with a few performers and technicians doing the music-making. The rest of the world's population are seen merely as music consumers. Such total control, of course, will never be achieved, since the activities of the majors initiate at the same time an increasing amount of local music activity which does not solely involve outright purchases of music hardware and software. The principles of cultural creation are not the same as the economic laws of the market. The policy of the international conglomerates, however, creates shockwaves through the world of national and local media and music life.

On the national level, we can see two main trends in policy. The first is a relatively firm central music policy such as in Tanzania, Kenya and Wales: the music in the media are used to 'build the nation'. In Tanzania, policies aim for national music conformity with the media favouring neo-traditional ngoma and swahili pop music. Behind this policy may lurk the concept of 'One Nation, One Music'.

In the case of Kenya, the policy is more ambivalent in dealing with the variety of musical styles. Where Tanzanian media policy is integrating, Kenyan is segregating, keeping different types of music in different radio channels, with Anglo-American music in the English service, tribal music in the Vernacular Services, etc. In Kenya, the local music industry sector is left to private entrepreneurs who also specialize in specific musical genres. This polarization is also mirrored in actions taken by different parties to influence media policies in Kenya. Wales could be compared to one of the tribal areas served by the Vernacular Service in Kenya. If Kenya were wealthier, the country would probably have radio and TV stations such as Radio Cymru and S4C. The strong central policies tend to limit the influence of the international majors.

The second main national policy trend we have observed is almost the complete opposite, comprising a lack of or at least a very vague, at times bewildered, central policy as in Jamaica, Trinidad and Sweden. This means that policy decisions are taken on the level of the national record company or broadcasting Programme Director. Media tend to focus public attention on those who present its content, the disc jockeys and presenters. A vague, non-existent or non-implemented overall policy makes the presenters the *de facto* policymakers. Popular presenters enjoy enormous status, status which can be used to encourage listeners/viewers to have an open mind to new experiences. Barry G in Jamaica is an example from our case studies; not only could he raise semi-controversial issues whilst broadcasting on a state-controlled channel, he could also present much new Jamaican music. Unlike many European broadcasters, Barry G does not appear to have the need to portray himself as the listener's link with the international superstars. On the contrary, he chooses to be the mirror of what is going on in Jamaican society.

This makes actual policy very dependent on the kind of people who are employed by broadcasting and other media, a thought, no doubt, which had occurred to the Chairman of the EBU's World Music Group, when he stated that:

> Music policy is not only a question of balancing the output of different types of music. Music policy is in particular the recruiting of staff. One of the essential questions of the Nineties in public broadcasting is: who are you going to recruit? . . . Do we need staff who are themselves conscious policymakers, who not only know what that means in practice but who are equally willing to take the fight over it?
>
> (Reitov 1990)

In nations involved in a decolonialization process and with strong, fairly young and non-institutionalized popular music cultures it appears that local music can get a fair share of media output even in a *laissez-faire* policy climate. This is the case in Jamaica and Trinidad. In a country like Sweden with a long-standing traditional, institutionalized music life which can function to a great extent without the mass media, the music of the major music corporations gradually becomes the content norm in the national phonogram industry and broadcasting media. This leads to a separation between national media, which concentrate on music that only exists in mediaized forms, and large sections of the music life in the country. One can even speak of national media isolating themselves from activities in the community at large. Live forms of music nurtured by powerful but very small groups (e.g. Western Art music) are given special channels. Such a channel is Sweden's so-called Music Radio (P2), which really should be renamed Art Music Radio. Probably the policy trend governing the national media in Sweden will lead to a severe crisis or to collapse.

On the local level we have witnessed a number of policies, but here too we can observe two main trends: policies that link media output to that of the major international corporations, and policies that link up to local music life. The latter means that local forms of music that are not represented in the output of larger media conglomerates get the chance to reach a bigger audience than they could meet at, say, a live music event.

Policies themselves, of course, are not enough to guarantee support for creative activity in society. Perry Hensell in Jamaica reminded us that 'when everything's in place, things happen'. This is true up to a point. Without a minimum of financial and technological resources, and without the necessary enthusiasts, they *don't* – at least not as far as music media activities on the local level are concerned.

Consider an example from Sweden. Each year, composers of popular music are invited to apply for scholarships from the copyright society, STIM. As a rule, about 150 of the 25,000 registered composers in Sweden apply. In 1991, the number of applicants rose sharply to 270. The reason was easy to deduce from reading the application forms; creative artists were experiencing hard times. Average incomes had dropped radically, even for singer/songwriters who usually enjoyed success. A number of factors in Swedish society had contributed to this decline: a new tax system, for instance, had added 25 per cent Valued Added Tax to rents as well as to entrance fees to various locales where live music is performed. But there was another interesting difference. Never before had the scholarship committee received so many demonstration tapes of high quality, indicating that even lesser-known composers had access either to their own semi-professional recording equipment or to a simple studio. Many of these tapes were from 'unknown quantities' who had never made commercial phonograms.

Such observations about performance activity and music media in Swedish society of the 1990s raise a number of interesting questions. One is as follows: if so much music activity is being recorded and documented by musicians and composers, why is it not being heard on more mainstream media such as, say, Swedish radio's national channels? After all, Sveriges Radio's franchise from the state clearly specifies a duty to reflect activities in Swedish society. In the early 1970s, Swedish public service radio even had a regular weekly programme called 'The Tape's Rolling', to which budding artists and composers could send recorded material. The programme was taken off because of doubts about the technical quality of contributions. Even though hundreds if not thousands have access to studios (if not their own equipment), Swedish radio has not considered reinstating the old programme.

We have lingered on this example because it highlights a major policy dilemma for secondary music media, namely their public service role in society, and more specifically, their ability to pick up feedback from music activity in their domestic environment, feedback which can affect policymaking.

The public service debate in Europe has often been blurred by a concentration on matters pertaining to the financing of media rather than their content. It is often assumed that licence-financed, 'non-commercial' broadcasting can, should and does devote its resources to widening listeners' horizons, presenting media output for minority listeners, and *never* seeking lowest common denominator solutions. Friends of the public service ethos see commercial counterparts as failing to fulfil any cultural obligations unless ruthlessly forced to, via tough regulatory measures. Neither of these extreme views is correct, a fact that media policymakers seldom seem to be aware of. Often policy has involved blind faith in a notion of healthy competition between a public and a private sector: 'While policy has been directed towards the overall system, its execution has interfered precious little with the economic progress of the private sector but has hindered the social development of the public sector' (Raboy 1990: 9).

Raboy is referring to Canada in this statement, a country known for its various policy attempts to encourage local music in the media. The same author concludes, some 300 pages later, that broadcasting policies in Canada have done little to increase media access. Government policies have continued: 'to inhibit the emergence of alternatives to both state and market conceptions of a "mass" public, alternatives that could be the basis for democratic uses of broadcasting and communications' (ibid.: 335). This comment has relevance in most countries that have come some way down the deregulation road. For deregulation to make any democratic contribution, in the sense of broadening media output and giving more groups in society access to it, then the public service concept must be expanded to apply across the board.

The broadcasting media are not the same as the print media. As long as a person or organization has access to paper, printing machines, writers, necessary capital and means of distribution, then it is possible to start up a newspaper. Frequencies, on the other hand, are finite resources; the total spectrum and individual broadcasting bands are limited in extent. Although the cost of entry into, say, radio broadcasting, is much cheaper than starting a newspaper, someone has to portion out frequencies amongst would-be broadcasters, decide transmitter power, and spell out which demands society places on those who are awarded operating licences. A *laissez-faire* alternative was tried in Italy, and it led to total confusion.

If the above argument is correct, it follows that any debate which categorizes broadcasters into those who have a duty to perform in the public interest, as opposed to those who do not, is illogical. One can hardly conceive a system whereby frequencies are allotted to broadcasters whose output is *against* the public interest. And we all know that any notion of communication being neutral is a complete myth. Our conclusion is that some form of public contribution should be demanded of all who are allowed to use the finite resources of the broadcasting frequencies.

Some nations have been content to regard a franchise fee as a fair contribution. Others have even elaborated with systems whereby frequencies are auctioned off; Britain did this with television franchises in 1991, despite the evidence from Australia of the negative consequences of such a procedure (Hindell 1991). We consider that the aim of any such franchise-award process must be not to put some extra revenue in the state coffers, but to maximize creative media activity in society; in this respect every would-be operator should incorporate or be encouraged to incorporate an element of public service (irrespective of whether the broadcaster is formally state-controlled, an independent non-profit organization or a purely private contractor). Some franchise systems do include a loose element of control, but as we have seen, this usually involves fairly meaningless statements regarding aims of quality and content.

In the field of music media policy, operators could be given a financial incentive to encourage performance activity, for instance by being charged a franchise fee from which costs for recording and stimulating local music activity could be deducted. This would effectively make life less financially attractive for operators wishing to make a quick buck on a lowest-common denominator output (e.g. a satellite feed of international hits). It would encourage broadcasters to be more independent of the phonogram industry – this would be good for both industries.

The above proposal is but one example of how those who are given the opportunity to use finite resources can and should be made publicly accountable. In the case of commercial channels fed in from abroad via satellites and distributed by cable, it seems reasonable that they should also make a contribution to creative activities in the countries where they earn money. The Swedish TV3/TV4 débâcle, allowing the same operator to run both a regulated terrestrial and an unregulated satellite channel (with the opportunity to play one off against the other) must be a classic case of how *not* to conduct media policy. Just as the music industry clamours for a levy on blank tapes to offset the losses from home-taping, so a levy should be put on cable systems distributing foreign commercial channels; funds generated in this fashion should be used to support local media activities. Such moneys, however, must be distributed in a decentralized fashion so that they encourage performance and creation on the most local level; they must not be eaten up by either a cumbersome central bureaucracy or by a small number of high status, national projects which only involve a small professional elite. Neither should they be merely transferred as a lump sum to some existing national operator.

Where licence-financed, non-commercial broadcasting sytems still operate, as in Sweden and Wales, then the only motivation for their continued existence would seem to be a different output from their commercial counterparts. Trying to achieve some sort of 'balance' between nominally public and private sectors, whereby a national music channel offers virtually the same music content as a commercial rival is pointless. It is also doubtful whether the public will continue to be willing to pay a licence fee for such a fare.

Wales, of course, is slightly different from Sweden in this respect. Whilst English-language BBC Radio Wales continues with a policy of playing music that annoys as few listeners as possible, its Welsh-language counterpart, Radio Cymru, and indeed S4C television, have very clear briefs. They have to base their own output on existing creative resources in their own local environments. The same applies to Radio Tanzania's brief. Welsh media are constantly under pressure to find more local activity, within a base of half a million Welsh-speakers, which can be reflected in the media. A clear music media policy which sets the sights high is apparently the type that is most likely to be implemented; it is also the one most likely to initiate the greatest amount of local music activity.

Most of our six sample nations are either about to embark on, or are already wandering down the tricky deregulation road. With the World Bank and the IMF calling for a liberalization of the economy as a general condition for loans, it can only be a matter of time before broadcasting is offered to private contractors even in Kenya and Tanzania. The types of financiers that consider entering these markets will depend, of course, on analyses of potential markets in these countries. So far, deregulation policy in the Caribbean would seem to be loosely based on recommendations made by the 1987 gathering of island states referred to above. Consensus at this meeting was that state ownership of the media had not been particularly effective in furthering the goals of 'recovering, preserving and advancing cultural sovereignty'. A proposal was formulated for: 'The deregulation of radio to allow for more public access to and local control of the medium. To increase, through legislation and active public policy, the extent of local and regional programming in the electronic media' (Brown and Sanatan 1987: 12).

Many would endorse the virtue of such aims. Achieving them is harder. Local stations in Jamaica have left their local obligations as soon as they found their signals could reach a larger audience in the capital, Kingston – Jamaica, after all, is so small as to make the whole concept of local radio somewhat diffuse. After years of inactivity in broadcasting media policy in Trinidad and Tobago, everything was put up for grabs. The only would-be operators who could take on the challenge were existing heavyweights in the media field. Small-scale Neighbourhood Radio in Sweden was more or less taken over after a few years by a small number of large operators offering virtually the same music-based output.

On the other hand, local music output over radio has not decreased in either Jamaica or Trinidad – there has actually been an increase which we have suggested could reflect a reaction to the influx of international cultural products via US satellites, notably MTV. This highlights another observation worth remembering, that nowhere have citizens become passive consumers of a few superstars whose music is globally distributed by a handful of giant media conglomerates. The increase in non-performance music activity has provided a guarantee against this happening.

But local music activity is still suffering from lack of policy co-ordination among different institutions in society. The Caribbean media report quoted above, which incidentally is provocatively titled 'Talking with Whom?', also confirmed a resolve to:

> Develop and seek to have instituted at all educational levels, formal and informal programmes for study of the media and their effects. . . . There needs to be meaningful co-ordination between the media and education systems in the interests of cultural sovereignty.
>
> (Brown and Sanatan 1987: 11–12)

We have found little evidence of this happening anywhere, even if there are some signs of activity. The establishment of a folk music studies department at Bangor University in Wales included the building of a state-of-the-art recording studio where music could be documented, arranged, modernized, etc. Some of this output has begun to flow into the broadcasting media.

Modern music machines such as synthesizers, samplers and sequencers are now part of the syllabus for music teacher training courses in Sweden. As new groups of qualified teachers enter education, it seems likely that such knowledge will colour their mode of tuition.

Even closer links are needed between the media and education systems. One important task at all levels of education is to demystify the media by giving at least an elementary introduction to how media function; how video and phonogram technology creates certain effects – in short, the functioning of the mediaization process. It should be a basic element of human rights for citizens to know what they are being subjected to when video clips and even commercials or news broadcasts emerge from their receiving equipment.

Education programmes geared at increasing performance activities must also have a link to the media, since the media can assist in giving that extra little bit of status to such activities. In a highly decentralized media system with small-scale radio/TV stations and public-access channels on cable, then even a local evening of music activities at a school could benefit from media access. This rarely happens. Forms of regulation, incentives and even support from the public purse could be used to encourage it.

The more international music media content becomes, the more we can expect feedback links from music activity to media policy to weaken. The examples of networks of musicians working with certain forms of music independently of broadcasting and print media is an indication of this process. For national and local broadcasters who have an inscribed duty in their operating licences to reflect, support and develop music activity in the society around them, identifying and establishing such feedback channels is of paramount importance. Only in such a way can media policy achieve what must be its primary societal goal, namely the maximization of both performance and non-performance music activities, even on the most local level.

Policies, of course, are no better than the people who formulate and implement them. Many politicians pay generous lip-service to ideals of national and/or ethnic cultural identity and the importance of access to the media in building up such an identity. Not so many hasten the implementation of such policies. Politicians hesitate before opening the media to thoughts and statements which could weaken their own position, and musical expression by virtue of its popular appeal can do just that. Politicians also usually have a secret desire to retain guarantees for their own access to the media, desires which inevitably conflict with open-door access policies. It is no coincidence that deregulation has often led to friends of leading politicians being allowed to buy or retain attractive pieces of the media business cake.

Technologies, conglomerates, organizations, governments and policy-makers will come and go. Humans will continue to engage in creative activity based both on traditions and on impulses from the surrounding environment. Such activity can be thwarted and supported by the policies that are actually applied by the music media. The goal, we reiterate, must be to maximize music activity. Media policy can be both friend and enemy of this goal.

References

Adorno, T.W. (1941) 'On popular music' in *Studies in Philosophy and Social Science*, reprinted in S. Frith and A. Goodwin (eds) (1990) *On Record*, New York: Pantheon.
Adorno, T.W. and Horkheimer, M. (1977) 'The culture industry: enlightenment as mass deception', in J. Curran (ed.) *Mass Communication and Society*, London: Edward Arnold.
Aho, W. (1987) 'Steelband music in Trinidad and Tobago: the creation of a people's music', in *Latin American Music Review* 8 (1): 26–58.
Aldrich, H.E. (1979) *Organizations and Environments*, Englewood Cliffs, NJ: Prentice-Hall.
Asher, R. (1987) 'The record industry', address to seminar at San Jose University, California, March.
Bagdikian, B. (1990) *The Media Monopoly*, 3rd edn, Boston: Beacon Press.
Barnard, C. (1938) *The Functions of the Executive*, Cambridge, Mass.: Harvard University Press.
Becker, H.S. (1976) 'Art worlds and social types' in R.A. Peterson (ed.) *The Production of Culture*, Beverly Hills: Sage Books.
Blaukopf, K. (1974) 'Towards a new type of research', in I. Bontinck (ed.) *New Patterns of Musical Behaviour*, Vienna: Universal Edition.
—— (1976) 'Youth as an agent of cultural change', in K. Blaukopf and D. Mark (eds) *The Cultural Behaviour of Youth*, Vienna: Universal Edition, pp. 121–30.
—— (1977) *Massmedium Schallplatte*, Vienna: Mediacult.
—— (1982a) *The phonogram in Cultural Communication*, Vienna: Springer Verlag.
—— (1982b) *The Strategies of the Record Industries*, Report CC–GP 11 (82) 16, Strasbourg: Council of Europe.
Bohana, R. (1977) 'The Welsh Arts Council's sponsorship of recordings of contemporary Welsh music', in *Welsh Music*, pp. 23–8.
Bontinck, I. (1974) *New Patterns of Musical Behaviour*, Vienna: Universal Edition.
Boyd-Barrett, O. (1980) *The International News Agencies*, London: Constable.
Brown, A. and Sanatan, R. (1987) *Talking with Whom*, Kingston: CARIMAC.
Burnett, R. (1990) *Concentration and Diversity in the Popular Music Industry*, Unit of Mass Communication, Gothenburg University: Nordicom.
Burnett, R. and Weber, R.P. (1987) 'Concentration and diversity in the popular music industry', draft paper, Unit of Mass Communication, Gothenburg: Nordicom.
Carlsson, U. and Anshelm, M. (1991) *Media Sverige '91*, Gothenburg University: Nordicom.
Chadwick, P. (1989) *Media Mates*, Melbourne: Macmillan.

Chapple, S. and Garofalo, R. (1977) *Rock 'n Roll is Here to Pay*, Chicago: Nelson-Hall.
Cohen, S. and Young, J. (1981) *The Manufacture of News*, London: Constable.
Comité National de la Musique (1989) *Musique et C.E.E.*, Report AD.SG.89.1, Paris: CNM.
Committee of Cultural Consultants (1989) *Culture for the European Citizen of the Year 2000*, Report CCC 15.11.89(E), Brussels: EC.
Council of Europe (1990) *The Role of Communication Technologies in the Safeguarding and Enhancing of European Unity and Cultural Diversity*, Council for Cultural Co-operation, report COM (90) 1a, Strasbourg.
Cox, P. (1985) *Broadcasting Policies in the EEC*, report from the European Institute for the Media, Manchester, 24–5 Jan, pp. 14–34.
Crisell, A. (1986) *Understanding Radio*, London: Methuen.
Crookes, P. and Vittet-Philippe, P. (1986) *Local Radio and Regional Development in Europe*, Manchester: European Institute for the Media.
Curran, J. (1991) 'Mass media and democracy: a reappraisal', in J. Curran and Gurevitch (eds) *Mass Media and Society*, New York: Routledge.
Dannen, F. (1991) *Hit Men*, New York: Vintage Books/Random House.
Dean, J. (1951) *Managerial Economics*, Englewood Cliffs, NJ: Prentice-Hall.
De Coster, M. (1976) *Le Disc, Art ou Affaires?*, Grenoble.
De Fleur, M.L. and Ball-Rokeach, S. (1989) *Theories of Mass Communication*, 5th edn, White Plains, NY: Longman.
Denisoff, R.S. (1975) *Solid Gold: The Popular Record Industry*, New Brunswick: Transaction Books.
DiMaggio, D. and Hirsch, P.M. (1976) 'Production organization in the arts', *American Behavioural Scientist* 19: 735–49.
Duelund, P. (1991) 'Kan svensk musik og identitet overleve inom gemenskapen?' (Can Swedish music and identity survive within the Common Market?), in H. Karlsson (ed.) *Sverige, Musiken och EG*, Stockholm: Musikaliska Akademien.
Dyson, K. and Humphreys, P. (1988) *Broadcast and New Media Policies in Western Europe*, London: Routledge.
Edström, O. (1989) *Schlager i Sverige* (Popular Songs in Sweden), Gothenburg University: Dept of Musicology.
Etzkorn, P. (1982) 'On the sociology of musical practice and social groups', *International Social Science Journal* XXXIV (4): 555–71, Paris: Unesco.
Europe (1990) 'Radio debate puts conference spotlight on media', *Music Week* supplement, London.
Fayol, H. (1916) 'Administration industrielle et générale', in *Bulletin de la Société de l'Industrie Minérale*, Paris.
Fejes, F. (1981) 'Media imperialism: an assessment', in *Media, Culture and Society* 3: 281–9.
Financial Times (1989) 'Time-Warner deal takes US back to the future', 6 March, London.
Fitchett, J. (1990) 'Are the media giants a necessary evil?', *Unesco Courier*, Jan.
Fornäs, J. (1979) *Musikrörelsen en Motoffentlighet* (The Anti-Establishment Music Movement), Gothenburg: Rödabokförlaget.
Frith, S. (1978) *The Sociology of Rock*, London: Constable.
—— (1981) *Sound Effects: Youth, Leisure and the Politics of Rock'n'Roll*, New York: Pantheon.
—— (1986) 'Art versus technology', in *Media, Culture and Society* 8 (3).
—— (1987) 'Copyright and the music business', in *Popular Music* 7 (1): 57–75.
—— (1992) 'The industrialization of popular music', in J. Lull (ed.) *Popular Music and Communication*, 2nd edn, London: Sage, pp. 49–74.

Frith, S. and Goodwin, A. (eds) (1990) *On Record*, New York: Pantheon.
Fuglesang, M. (1990) 'Film som romantikens verktyg. Om medialisering i staden Lamu, Kenya' ('Film as a tool for romance. On medialisation in the town of Lamu, Kenya'), in U. Hannerz (ed.) *Medier och kulturer*, Stockholm: Carlssons.
Golwg (1988) 'A crack in the record', no. 60–88, Cardiff.
Goodwin, A. (1992) 'Rationalisation and democratisation in the new technologies of popular music', in J. Lull (ed.) *Popular Music and Communication*, 2nd edn, London, Sage, pp. 75–100.
Government of Canada (1982) *Report of the Federal Cultural Policy Review Committee*, Ottawa: Ministry of Supply and Services.
Grandin, I. (1989) *Music and Media in Local Life: Music Practice in a Newar Neighbourhood in Nepal*, Linköping University, Sweden: Dept of Communication.
Gröndal, T. (1983) 'The record industry, growth of a mass medium', in Popular Music Yearbook, vol. 3, Cambridge: Cambridge University Press, pp. 53–77.
—— (1986) *Strategies of Music Industries and Broadcasting Industries*, report CC–GP 11 (85) 29, Strasbourg: Council of Europe.
—— (1986) *Massmediers Utvecklingsförlopp* (Stages of Mass Media Development), Report 13, Gothenburg University Business School.
Gronow, P. (1980) *Statistics in the Field of Sound Recordings*, report C–21, Division of Statistics on Culture and Communication, Paris: Unesco.
—— (1982) *Creative Artists and the Industrialisation of Culture*, report CC–GP 11 (82) 17, Strasbourg: Council of Europe.
Hamm, C. (1979) *Yesterdays: Popular Song in America*, New York: Norton.
Hedman, L. and Strid, I. (1990) 'Radioutvecklingen i Sverige' (Radio development in Sweden), *Medianotiser*, nr 1/90, Gothenburg: Nordicom.
Hellqvist, P.-A. (1977) *Ljudspåren Förskräcker*, Stockholm: Forum.
Hennion, A. (1982) *The Place of the Small Firms in the Record Industry and Their Role in Music Creativity*, Report CC–GP 11 (82), Strasbourg: Council of Europe.
Hennion, A. and Vignolle, T.P. (1978) *L'Economie du Disque en France*, Paris: La Documentation Française.
Higham, N. (1988) 'Will satellites save European radio?', in *Broadcast*, 1 July, pp. 29–30.
Hindell, K. (1991) 'The auctioning of UK TV licences', in 'Media Watch' (radio programme), London: BBC World Service.
Hirsch, P.M. (1969) *The Structure of the Popular Music Industry*, University of Michigan: Ann Arbor.
—— (1972) 'Processing fads and fashions: an organization-set analysis of cultural industry systems', in *American Journal of Sociology* 77, Chicago: Chicago University Press.
Holmes, S. (1990) 'Liberal constraints on private power', in Lichtenberg (ed.) *Mass Media and Democracy*, New York: Cambridge University Press.
Hoyte, M. (1986) *Influence of Foreign Television on Caribbean People*, Port of Spain: CPBA.
Hutt, J. (1980) 'Whose voice is it anyway?', stencil, Cardiff Radio Trust.
IFPI Sweden (1986/7/8/9) *Musik på Fonogram* (Music on Phonogram), Stockholm: IFPI.
Karlsson, H. (1980) *Musikspelet*, Gothenburg University: Institute of Musicology.
Kealy, E.R. (1979) 'From craft to art: the case of sound mixers and popular music', in *Sociology of Work and Occupations* 6: 3–29.

Kenya Arts Co-operative Society (1988) *Introduction to Five Years' Budget*, Nairobi.
Kenya Institute of Education (1985) *Music Syllabus for Kenya Certificate of Secondary Education*, Nairobi.
Kivikuru, U. (1990) *Tinned Novelties or Creative Culture*, Dept of Communication, Helsinki University.
Kulturrådet (1979) *Fonogrammen i Kulturpolitiken* (Phonograms and Cultural Policy), Report 1979: 1, Stockholm.
—— (1988) *Utveckling och prognos för den statliga kulturpolitiken 1982/83–1986/87*, (Development and Predictions for State Cultural Policy), Report 1988: C5.
—— (1989) *Musik på Fonogram* (Music on Phonograms) ed. Schöld, Report 1989: 1.
Laird, C. (1987) *Inside the People TV: Television for National Development*, Port of Spain, Banyan.
Lawrence, P.R. and Lorsch, J.W. (1967) *Organization and Environment*, Boston: Harvard University Press.
Local Radio Workshop (1983) *Capital Radio: Local Radio and Private Profit*, London: Comedia.
Lokalradio (1990) 'Local funding request', Stockholm: Swedish Local Radio.
Lönsmann, L. (1990) *Radio ifölge Burns* (Radio according to Burns), Copenhagen: Danish Radio Development Department.
Lull, J. (ed.) (1992) *Popular Music and Communication* (1st edn 1987), Beverly Hills: Sage.
Lull, J. and Wallis, R. (1991) 'The best of West Vietnam', in J. Lull (ed.) *Popular Music and Communication*, 2nd edn, Beverly Hills: Sage, pp. 207–36.
Malm, K. (1978) 'The parang music of Trinidad', in *Anthropological Studies* 25/6: 42–50.
—— (1982) 'Phonograms and cultural policy in Sweden', in K. Blaukopf (ed.) *The Phonogram in Cultural Communication*, Vienna: Springer Verlag, pp. 43–73.
Malm, K. and Wallis, R. (1985) 'The baila of Sri Lanka and the calypso of Trinidad', in *Communication Research* 12 (3): 277–300.
Marcuse, H. (1970) *One-Dimensional Man*, London: Sphere Books.
Mark, D. (ed.) (1981) *Stock-taking of Musical Life*, Vienna/Munich: Ludwig Doblinger.
Mattelart, A. (1979) *Multinational Corporations and the Control of Culture*, Brighton: Harvester Press.
MBI (1991) 'Exotic Cajun sound from accordion and guitar', December, pp. 16–17.
McBride, S. (1980) *Many Voices, One World*, New York: Unipub.
McQuail, D. (1969) *Towards a Sociology of Mass Communication*, London: Collier Macmillan.
—— (1983) *Mass Communication Theory*, London: Sage.
McQuail, D. and the Euromedia Research Group (1990) 'Caging the beast: constructing a framework for the analysis of media change in Western Europe', in *European Journal of Communication* 5, pp. 313–31.
Mohammed, S. (1982) 'Masthana Bahar and Indian culture in Trinidad and Tobago', PhD thesis, Port of Spain: University of the West Indies.
Moseholm, E. (1991) 'Live music, its role and future prospects on the radio', address to the EBU Light Music Seminar, 6–7 Sept., Rome.
Mowlana, H. (1990) 'Old wine in new bottles: NWICO and the democratisation of communication', in *Media Development* 3: 25–37.
Mowlana, H. and Rad, M. (1990) *Japanese Programmes on Iranian TV*, Washington: ICP.
Mulryan, P. (1988) *Radio, Radio – the Story of Independent, Local, Community*

and Pirate Radio in Ireland, Dublin: Borderline Publications.
Murdock, G. (1990) 'Redrawing the map of the communications industries: concentration and ownership in the era of privatisation', in Ferguson (ed.) *Public communication*, London: Sage.
Music Week (1985) 'Music Video Feature' special supplement, 6 Oct.
Nordenstreng, K. and Schiller, H.I. (1979) *National Sovereignty and International Communication*, Norwood: Ablex Publishing.
Nordisk Television (1988) 'En ny kanal för svenska folket' (A new channel for the Swedish people), publicity handout, Stockholm: Nordisk TV.
Nordström, B. (1991) *Hem Elektroniken* (Home Electronics), Report SR/PUB 9–1991, Stockholm: Swedish Radio Audience Research Dept.
Nylöf, G. (1975) *Svenska ungdomars attityder till och kontakter med musik* (Swedish youth – attitudes to and contact with music), Stockholm: Institutet för Rikskonserter.
—— (1977) 'Musik politik for schlager – ar det nadvöndigt?' (A music policy for hits – do we need it?), stencil, Stockholm: Kulturrådet.
—— (1982) 'Vad kan man göra?' (What can one do?), in *Fem Forskare om Kulturkommersialismen* (Five Researchers on Cultural Commercialism), Stockholm: Kulturrådet. pp. 147–93.
—— (1990) 'Trends in popular music preferences in Sweden, 1960–1988', in K. Roe and U. Carlsson (eds) *Popular Music Research*, Gothenburg: Nordicom.
Omondi, W. (1984) *Report of the Presidential National Music Commission*, Nairobi: Govt of Kenya.
O'Neill, A. (1991) *A Music Policy for S4C*, Cardiff: S4C.
Pan Trinbago (1981) *Report from the Pan Trinbago Convention*, 6–7 Dec., Port of Spain.
Partridge, S. (1982) *Not the BBC/IBA: The Case for Community Radio*, London: Comedia.
Pearsall, R. (1975) *Edwardian Popular Music*, Rutherford, NJ: David Charles.
Peterson, R.A. (1982) 'Five constraints on the production of culture', in *Journal of Popular Culture* 16: 158–73.
—— (1985) 'Six constraints on the production of literary works', in *Poetis* 14: 45–67.
Peterson, R.A. and Berger, D.G. (1971) 'Entrepreneurship in organizations: evidence from the popular music industry', in *Administrative Science Quarterly* 16: 97–107.
PSI (1991) *Cultural Trends 1991*, ed. Feist and Eckstein, London: Policy Research Institute.
Raboy, M. (1990) *Missed Opportunities: the Story of Canada's Broadcasting Policy*, Montreal: McGill-Queen's University Press.
Reitov, O. (1990) 'Can new things be done?', address to the EBU workshop on young people's programmes, 2 Oct., Helsinki.
Rhenman, E. (1964) 'Organizational goals: from contributions to the theories of organizations', ed. Agersnap, T. 75–86 *Interdisciplinary Studies from the Scandinavian Summer University*, Munksgaard, Copenhagen.
Rhenman, E. and Stymmne, B. (1965) *Företagsledning i en föränderlig Varld*, (Business Management in a Changing World), Stockholm: Aldus/Bonniers.
Robinson, D., Buck, E. and Cuthbert, M. (1991) *Music at the Margins*, London: Sage.
Roe, K. (1985) *The Programme Output of Seven Cable-TV Channels*, report from the project 'The Advent of Cable-TV in Sweden', Uppsala- Lund universities.
—— (ed.) (1986) *Music as Communication*, issue of *Communications Research* 12 (3), Beverly Hills: Sage.
Roe, K. and Carlsson, U. (eds) (1990) *Popular Music Research*, Gothenburg: Nordicom.

Roe, K. and Löfgren, M. (1988) 'Music video use and educational achievement', in *Popular Music* 7 (3): 303–15.
Roe, K. and Wallis, R. (1989) 'One planet, one music: The development of music television in Western Europe', *Nordicom Review* 1: 35–41.
Rothenbuhler, E. and McCourt, T. (1992) 'Commercial radio and popular music', in J. Lull (ed.) *Popular Music and Communication*, 2nd edn, London: Sage, pp. 101–6.
Ryan, J. and Peterson, R.A. (1982) 'The product image: the fate of creativity in country music songwriting', in *Sage Annual Reviews of Communication Research* 10: 11–32.
Samarajiva, R. (1990) 'Without any obstacle: Unesco's conundrum', in *Media Development* 3: 31.
Schäfer, J. (ed.) (1991) *Folkmusik och dansåret utvärderat* (Folk Music and Dance Year Evaluated), Stockholm: Musikmuseet.
Schiller, H.I. (1976) *Communication and Cultural Domination*, White Plains, NY: M.E. Sharpe.
Schlesinger, P. (1987) *Putting Reality Together*, London: Methuen.
Schnabel, T. (1990) 'International Bandstand', *Los Angeles Times Magazine*, 7 Jan., pp. 20ff.
Schramm, W. (1964) *Mass Media and National Development*, Paris: Unesco.
Sjöström, J. (1989) 'Strukturella forandringar i musikindustrin' (Structural changes in the music industry), interview in *STIMNYTT* 4 (3): 9–10.
Soramäki, M. and Haarma, J. (1978) *The International Music Industry*, Helsinki: Finnish Broadcasting Co.
Stepp, C. (1990) 'Access in a post-responsibility age', in Lichtenberg (ed.) *Mass Media and Democracy*, New York: Cambridge University Press.
Strid, I. and Weibull, L. (1988) *Media Sverige 1988*, Report 14, Unit of Mass Communications, Gothenburg University.
SCB (1991) *Media Usage in Sweden*, annual statistics, Stockholm: SCB.
SOU (1971) *Fonogrammen i Musiklivet* (The Phonogram in Music Life), Report 1971: 73, Stockholm: Swedish Government.
—— (1991) *Tekniskt Utrymme för Reklamfinansierad Radio* (Technical Limitations for Commercial Radio), Report 1991: 108, Stockholm: Swedish Govt.
Sweden Now (1989) 'Sweden strikes the right note', no. 2, Stockholm.
Swedish Government (1978) *Temporary Neighbourhood Radio Bill*, no. 978: 479, Stockholm.
—— (1981) *Permanent Neighbourhood Radio Bill*, no. 1981/2: 127, Stockholm.
—— (1985) *Radio propositionen* (Broadcasting Bill), no. 1985/6: 99, Stockholm.
Swedish Ministry of Education (1991), *Franchise Application for a Commercial TV Channel*, Stockholm.
Tagg, P. (1977) *Populär/musik och Medierna* (Popular Music and the Media), Gothenburg University, Dept of Musicology.
—— (1979) *Kojak, 50 seconds of Television Music*, Gothenburg University, Department of Musicology.
Taylor, F.W. (1913) *Principles and Methods of Scientific Management*, New York: Harper & Brothers.
Time Magazine (1991) 'A $1 billion Pacific alliance', 11 Nov., p. 50.
Times, The (1990) 'Polygram makes record profit as CD sales climb', 28 March, London.
Trinidad and Tobago Government (1987) *The Establishment of a Telecommunications Authority for the Republic of Trinidad and Tobago*, White Paper by the Task Force on Telecommunications, Office of the Prime Minister, Port of Spain.
Tunstall, J. (1977) *The Media are American*, London: Constable.

—— (1986) *Communications Deregulation, the Unleashing of America's Communications Industry*, Oxford: Basil Blackwell.
Tunstall, J. and Palmer, M. (1991) *Media Moguls*, London: Routledge.
TV3 (1991) *TV3 News* 1, London: TV3-Scansat.
Uddy, S. (1959) *Organization at Work: A Comparative Analysis*, New Haven: HRAF Press.
Ugboajah, F. (1985) 'Media habits of rural and semi-rural (slum) Kenya', in *Gazette* 36: 175–91, Dordrecht, Netherlands.
Unesco (1991) *World Commission on Cultural Development*, draft resolution no. 26 C/COM. IV/DR. 1/Rev. 1, Paris.
Wal, H. van der (1985) *The Impact of New Technologies and the Strategies of the Music Industries*, Report CC–GP 11 (85) 15, Strasbourg: Council of Europe.
Wallis, R. (1990) *Internationalisation and Localisation Trends in the Development of Radio and its Relationship to the Phonogram Industry*, Report 57, Gothenburg University, Unit of Mass Communication.
Wallis, R. and Baran, S. (1990) *The Known World of Broadcast News*, London: Routledge.
Wallis, R. and Malm, K. (1980) *The Interdependency of Broadcasting and the Phonogram Industry*, Document no. 6, Vienna, Mediacult.
—— (1982) 'The interdependency of broadcasting and the phonogram industry: a cast study covering events in Kenya in March 1980', in *Popular Music Perspectives*, IASPM, Dept of Musicology, Gothenburg University, pp. 93–110.
—— (1983) 'The role of the Welsh phonographic industry in the development of a Welsh language pop/rock/folk scene', in *Popular Music Yearbook* 3, Cambridge: Cambridge University Press, pp. 77–105.
—— (1984) *Big Sounds from Small Peoples*, London: Constable.
—— (1986) *The Workings of the Phonogram Industry: Three Analytical Approaches*, Report 86: 1, Stockholm: Musikmuseet.
—— (1987) 'National identity in a changing world of media technology', in K. Blaukopf (ed.) *New Media: A Challenge to Cultural Policy*, Vienna: VWGO, pp. 135–76.
—— (1988) 'Push-pull for the video clip: a systems approach to the relationship between the phonogram/videogram industry and music television', in *Popular Music* 7 (3): 267–85.
—— (1990) 'The implications of structural changes in the music industry for media policy and music activity', in K. Roe and U. Carlsson (eds) *Popular Music Research*, Gothenburg University: Nordicom, pp. 11–20.
Warner, K. (1982) *Kaiso: The Trinidad Calypso, a Study of the Calypso as Oral Literature*, Washington: Three Continents Press.
White, T. (1983) *Catch a Fire: The Life of Bob Marley*, New York: Holt, Rinehart & Winston.
Wicke, P. (1988a) 'Musik und Musikgeschäft in den USA. Nr 4 Los Angeles' *Wochenpost* 12: 15.
—— (1988b) *Musikindustrie in den USA – Eine Analyse*, Informationen beim Komitee für Unterhaltungskunst der DDR, no. 6.88, Berlin.
Williams, C. (1977) 'Non-violence and the history of the Welsh Language Society', in *Welsh History Review* 8 (4): 426–55.
—— (ed.) (1982) *National Separatism*, Cardiff.
Willis, P. (1978) *Profane Culture*, London: Routledge & Kegan Paul.

Index

ABBA 7, 179, 228, 235, 239
Adorno, T.W. 17–18, 214
advertising 30, 31, 45, 65, 110, 126, 137, 157, 158, 164, 173, 176, 201
AIT Records 86
Alarm, The (Welsh group) 153
Alpha Blondy (Ivory Coast group) 89
Amunga, David 98, 100
ANC 109
Anglo-American influence 69–70, 89, 90, 113, 212, 233–4, 237–8, 241
Anhrefn (Welsh group) 133–4
Ar Log (Welsh group) 142
ASCAP (us copyright society) 203, 205, 235, 240
Asher, Dick 206
Asia 212
Association of Jamaican Record Producers 59
audience/listeners 30, 130, 131, 133; fragmentation 13–14, 220–1; patterns 13; statistics 93–4, 161, 165–6; target 137–9; youth 130–1, 140–1
Australia 253

baila music (Sri Lanka) 242
Bangor University 148
Bank of Jamaica 62
Bankole, Anum 76
Banyan TV Production Company 66
BBC 125, 137, 218; television 131, 142; in Wales 126, 127–9, 133
Belafonte, Harry 38, 242
Berlusconi, Silvio 206, 227
Bertelsmann Music Group (BMG) 178, 179, 181, 183–4, 212, 228
Best Village competition (Trinidad) 69
Betaudier, Holly 71

Big Five 11, 26, 29, 40, 167, 178–81, 206, 227–9
Black Systems Youth 117
Blackwell, Chris 46
Blaukopf, K. 15, 32
BMG see Bertelsmann Music Group
Boyd-Barrett, O. 211
Brazil 209
British Musicians' Union 136
Broadcast and Radio Diffusion Act (Jamaica) 60
broadcasting 3, 14, 197, 201–2, 204, 252–5; access 238; explosion in 6; international role 16; public service 230; responsibility for 231
Brooklyn connection network 67
BSB 172
Burning Spear (Jamaican group) 89

C Itoh trading company 7
calypso 69, 74–6, 81, 83, 242
Calypso Monarch Competition 81
Canada 252; music policy 198
Cardiff Community Trust 134–5
Caribbean 213, 221, 248; 'Talking with Whom?' report 254–5
Caribbean Basin Initiative 56
carnival 68, 69, 71, 76, 78, 210; in Jamaica 55
cassette players 109, 110
cassettes 86, 89, 149, 158; analogue 6, 10, 198; audio 66–7; pre-recorded 40, 41; spread 8
CBS 11, 84, 178, 203, 212, 238
CBS Kenya 85, 86, 89, 99
CDs (compact discs) 6, 12, 27, 40, 63, 65, 66, 149, 177, 181, 184, 198–200, 203, 235; spread 10

Celtic Song Festival 153
censorship 123, 234
Chama Cha Mapinduzi (CCM) 114
CHAMUDATA (Musician's Union) Tanzania 115
Charles, Rudolph 74
Charlie's Records 66
Charlie's Roots 81
Chile 211
choral music 193
Chrysalis (EMI) 29, 179, 180, 203
Ciclitira, David 169
Cliff, Jimmy 39, 41, 61
CNN 157, 168, 200
Communications Research journal 16
Composers' Copyright Organization (STIM) 186
Contemporary Hit Radio (CHR) 228
copyright 30–1, 34, 56–7, 59, 94, 175, 184, 201, 235, 243, 247; American 2
Copyright Act (1983) Kenya 87
Copyright Organization of Trinidad and Tobago (COTT) 67–8, 78
Council of Europe 3, 222–6; reports 222–3
Cox, P. 169
CRAI label 147, 150
Crawford Productions 86, 87
Crazy (Calypsonian) 75
Creative Production Training Centre (CPTC) 43, 56
Crisell, A. 218
Criw Byw (Welsh production company) 141
Crookes, P. and Vittet-Philippe, P., 'Local Radio and Regional Development in Europe' 218
Cross, Alric 65
cultural imperialism 210–14
Cultural Policy Bill (1974) Sweden 187
culture/subculture approach 15, 17, 18–19, 28, 224
Cytgord (Welsh publisher etc.) 144, 149, 247

Daily News (Tanzania) 110
Daily and *Sunday Gleaners* (Jamaica) 45, 52, 61
dance bands, in Sweden 242–3
Dannen, F. 228–9, 249
DAT *see* Digital Audio Tape
Davies, Geraint 131

De Fleur, M.L. and Ball-Rokeach, S. 20
Decca 145, 149, 151
demand–reward equilibrium 20, 30
Denisoff, R.S. 16
Denmark 186, 232
deregulation 2, 12–14, 26, 31, 50, 59, 136, 158, 204, 206, 227, 230, 254; and media policy 215–21
Desperadoes steelband 74
Deutsche Welle broadcasting 93
Diamond, Brian 171, 172
Digital Audio Tape (DAT) 27
DiMaggio, D. and Hirsch, P.M. 19
DJs 40, 46, 69, 74, 91, 93, 131, 243, 250
Drupatee 69
Dyson, K. and Humphreys, P. 218

EAR *see* East African Records Ltd
East African Records Ltd (EAR) 84, 86
East Indian Music 68, 69
EC *see* European Community
education, closer links 255; music in 96–7, 100–1, 151–2, 210, 225, 245
Educational Broadcasting System (EBS) 43
Edwards, Trebor 142, 146
Eisteddfod 130, 142, 237
Electra (Sweden) 178
Ellington, Duke 190
EMI 7, 86, 145, 151, 178, 179, 186, 226, 227, 228, 238
entertainment, how viewed 33–4
ethnic groups 68, 73, 87, 98, 110, 111, 115
Europe 218; broadcasting in 203–4
Europe (Swedish group) 196, 239
European Broadcasting Union, World Music Workshop 241
European Commission (Brussels) 223
European Community (EC) 224; audio-visual policy 2; 'Culture for the European Citizen of the Year 2000' 224–5
European Institute for the Media 168
Eurovision Song Contest 54
Evans, Gwynfor, hunger strike 127

Fflach (phonogram company) 136, 148–9

films 105; industry 2, 6; music 90, 113
Finson, Tom 57, 58
Fitchett, Joseph 248
Folk and Dance Music Year (Sweden) 236
folk music 38, 68, 121, 142, 189, 191, 192, 194, 209–10, 215
Forteau, Richard 78
France 215, 216
Frankfurt School 17–18
Frith, S. 18, 214, 239
Fujisankei (Fuji) 11, 227

General Electric 226
Golwg (Welsh arts magazine) 146
Gordon, Barry ('Barry G') 43, 45, 47–50, 247, 250
Gothenburg Symphony Orchestra 191
government policies 218–19, 229–36 *see also under* named countries
Grondal, T. 19
Guadeloupe 209

Häggkvist, Dag 180
hardware/software 8, 10–11, 199, 239; availability 108–9; growth 39–40, 46; innovations 26; manufacture 5–6
Harlech television (HTV) 137
Hensell, Perry 44, 62–3, 64, 240, 251
Higham, N. 218
Hirsch, P.M. 16, 18
Hoddinott, Alun 150
Hoola Bandoola (Swedish group) 18, 184
Horkheimer, M. 17
hurricane Gilbert 58
Hussey, Dermot 50–1

IFPI group 94, 178, 181, 225
ILR Consortia 135
IMF 254
information, dissemination 5
instruments 80, 242, 247; availability 116–17, 152–3, 200; electronic 27–8; in schools 64
International Council for Traditional Music (ICTM) 208–9
International Federation of Phonogram and Videogram Industries (IFPI) 225
International Herald Tribune (USA) 248
International Music Council (IMC) 221

International Music and Media Conference (Amsterdam) 179
Iran 212–13
IRIE 51
Isaacs, Gregory 61
Island (Polygram) 29, 179, 180, 203
Italian Broadcasting Bill 227
Italy 216
Iwan, Dafydd 133, 134, 145, 146–7, 150

Jackson, Michael 206, 249
Jamaica 229, 235, 240, 250, 255; actors, issues, policies 55–64; broadcasting/print media 42–5; economy 4; first CDs in 10; music/media environment 38–42; role of music in 45–55
Jamaica All-Media Surveys 39, 47–50
Jamaica Broadcasting Corporation (JBC) 42–3; JBC2 47, 52; JBC-TV 52, 56, 58; 'Music, Music, Music' 52
Jamaica Cultural Development Commission (JCDC) 54
Jamaican Folk Singers 61
Japan 212–13
jazz 17, 188, 190, 193; Swahili 111, 113, 116, 120, 123, 230
Jones, Aled 149–50
Jones, Huw 138, 145, 153
Jones, Lyn 129, 130
Juwata Jazz Band 121

Kaduma, Godwin 120
Kalanda, Teddy 102, 107
Kalikawe, Justine 116–17
Kamaru, Joseph 87
Kamba, S.F. 121
Kante, Mori 105
KANU (Kenya political party) 85
karaoke 247
Kassav (zouk group) 81
Keita, Salif 105
Kenya 201, 219, 230, 231, 235, 236, 238, 249; actors, issues, policies 92–100; colonial heritage 92; coup 1; data collection in 33; economy 4; investment 84; LPs in 10; music/media environment 84–92, 100–7; tribal languages 89
Kenya Arts Co-operative Society (ARTCO) 94, 98–100

Kenya Association of Record
  Producers (KAPI) 94
Kenya Blue Stars 105
Kenya Institute of Education 85, 97;
  music lessons 91
Kenya Music Festival 91
Kenya Musicians' Union 94
Kenya National Association of
  Phonogram Industries (KRPA) 94
Kenya National Music Organizations'
  Treaty 94
Kenya School of Music 92
Kenyan Presidential Commission on
  Music, Report 8, 95–7, 100, 210,
  231, 232
Kikuyu music 87
Kinnevik company 177
Kivikuru 109
KLAS 51

Ladysmith (South African group) 89
Laird, Christopher 66, 68, 78, 79–80
languages, Lapp 246; minority 201;
  Swahili 111, 113, 114, 209, 230;
  tribal 89; Welsh 125–7, 135–6,
  141–2, 151, 152, 210
Ledin, Thomas 182, 228
Lee, Byron 55
Lee, Neville 41, 43–4, 52, 57
Lili and Sussie 168
Livingstone, Grace 48–9
local music 8, 22, 51, 236–7; changes in
  24–5; cottage industry 25–6;
  decrease 52; effects on 42; increase
  45–54, 70; in Kenya 98–107; low
  priority 76, 78; share of 89–92; in
  Tanzania 120–4; in Trinidad 68,
  69–70
local–international dichotomy 237–9
Lonrho organization 86
Lord Shorty 81
LPs *see* vinyl records
Lull, J., *Popular Music and
  Communication* 16

MACAL Company 65
McBride, S., report 222
McQuail, D. 16
Madonna 249
Makeba, Miriam 105
Makuyu Stars 101
Male Voice Choir (Wales) 129

Manborde, Frank 61
Mandela, Nelson 234
'Mango Tree School of
  Communications' 57, 58, 213
Manley, Michael 45
Marcher Sound 135
Marcuse, H. 17
Marley, Bob 39, 46, 56, 61, 240
mass communication theory 15–16, 20
Matsushita 11
Mattelart, A. 211–12, 213
Matthias, William 150
MCA 11
Mdsanjo, Mr 87
media, access to 133, 223;
  conglomerates 226–7; influence 246;
  music content 240–1
media policies, defined 21–2, 23;
  formulations 25, 26; national level
  229–36 *see also under* named
  countries
Mediacult Research Centre (Vienna)
  221, 223
mediaization process 24, 241–3, 245
Medvik 204
Mercedes 157
Ministry of Information (Kenya) 93
MISC *see* Music Industry in Small
  Countries
Moi, Daniel Arap 89, 93, 231
Mordecai, Martin 57, 60
Motion Picture Association of America
  57, 201, 203
Mowlana, H. 212–13, 222
MTV satellite channel 6, 44–5, 80, 137,
  157, 171–2, 197, 200, 201, 206, 214,
  237
Mulryan, P. 27
multiclone development 202–3
Murdoch, Rupert 157, 168, 226
Mushrooms, The, 'Jambo Bwana' 102
music, academic approaches 15–19;
  access 10–11, 14–15; children's 188;
  competitions 116, 129, 142; foreign
  influence 80–1, 83; globalization 6–8;
  importance 74, 120; live 54–5; major
  and independent producers 12;
  media distribution 24; with a
  message 111, 115; performance
  activity 191, 193, 195; policy changes
  1–2, 3; power of 117; recording 66;
  research project described 3–5;

(semi)recorded 54; skill and knowledge 247; systems approach 19–20; three levels 25–6
music activity, cultural dominance 209–10; exchange 208–9; imperialism 210–14; defined 22–3; transculturation 214–15
Music Advisory Board (Kenya) 98
Music Box TV 167, 169, 171
Music Copyright Society of Kenya 94, 101
Music Industry in Small Countries (MISC) project 24, 208; *Big Sounds from Small Peoples* 2–3; data collection 32–7; origins of research 11–15
music policies 105, 107, 139–44, 214, 256; local 251; national 249–50 *see also under* named countries
Music Scene 85
Mwyn, Rhys 133–4

NAR, White Paper on telecommunications 79
narrowcasting 197
National Action Cultural Committee (NACC, Trinidad) 69, 76
National Alliance for Reconstruction (NAR) 72
National Arts Council (Tanzania) 115
National Broadcasting Service (NBS, Trinidad) 65, 69
National Council for Cultural Affairs (Sweden) 158, 188; 'Five Researchers on Cultural Commercialism' 190; 'The Phonogram in Cultural Policy' 187
National Ngoma Troupe 111, 115
Nationalteatern (Swedish group) 183
NBC TV 226
Neighbourhood Radio (Sweden) 159–60, 164, 204, 216–17, 230, 234, 254
Nepal 246
'Network, The' (US group) 228
ngoma music 111, 115, 121
Nimbus company 149
Nordic Channel tv 157
Nordisk Television 173
Northern Ireland 131
Nyerere, Julius 113, 114
Nylof, G. 190

Okema, Michael 117
Omondi, Washington 95
organizational theory 20; constraints 19, 20, 28–9
Oshin (Japanese 'soap') 212
Owen, Marie 141

P1/2/3 radio stations (Sweden) 161–2, 163
Pan Trinbago 75–6
'pan yards' 75
parang music 68, 69
Peel, John 134, 141
Penillion, Festival 142; Singing Society 151
People's National Movement (PNM) 72
performance/nonperformance, activity 245–8; fees 56–7
Performing Right Society of London (PRS) 94
Peterson, R.A. 19; and Berger, D.G. 16, 18
phonogram industry 5, 6, 63, 203, 229–30; conglomerates 248–9; economic factors 28; environment 16; income 30, 184–5; integration 17, 29–31; interactionist approach 17, 18; in Jamaica 40–1; in Kenya 87–8, 94; legislation 29; marketing 43; ownership 235; research into 15–19; set-up 26; subsidies 188–90; in Sweden 177–84; system constraints 25–9; trends 12–13; in Wales 145–50
Phonogram Performance Ltd (PPL) 147
Pink Floyd, 'Another Brick in the Wall' 228
piracy 11, 41, 67, 68, 87–8, 123
Polar label 179
Polygram 10, 86, 99, 100, 145, 149, 177, 178, 179, 203, 212, 235
popular music 17–19, 214; in Jamaica 42; in Kenya 92–3, 101–2, 104–5, 107; in Sweden 188
press 66, 110, 252; in Jamaica 45; in Kenya 85; in Trinidad 65
punk 18

Raboy, M. 252
radio 6, 27, 30, 31, 65, 217, 232; access 108, 109–10; community 164–6; content/output 55, 60–1; expansion

6, 12–14; importance 91–2; local 55–6, 62, 160–6, 162–4, 218, 251, 254–5; national 158, 160–2; neighbourhood 159–60, 164–6; public 241; satellite 160; selection process 53; spread of 84–5; transborder 223
Radio Atlantic 252 Long Wave 126
Radio Authority 136
Radio Cardiff 218
Radio Caroline 157
Radio Central 43
Radio Cymru 125, 129–34, 137, 140, 153, 230, 237, 249, 254
Radio Delle Donne (Italy) 218
Radio IRIE 43
Radio KLAS 43
Radio Luxembourg 126
radio stations, in Jamaica 40–1, 42–4, 55–6; in Kenya 85; in Sweden 158, 159–6, 251; in Tanzania 109–10; in Trinidad 69, 72, 80; in Wales 125–36, 135–6 *see also under* named stations
Radio Tanzania 93, 94, 109–11, 113, 115, 116, 230, 232, 234; recorded library 113, 122
Radio Trinidad 65, 69
Radio Wales 126, 127–9, 133
Radio Waves 43, 51
rap 40, 46–7
Rasta movement 45
RCA 178
record pressing plants 40, 84, 86, 99, 110, 121, 184, 235, 242
Record Station label 181, 183–4
recording studios 40, 87, 89, 97, 121, 148
Red Dragon Radio 135
reggae 38, 46, 47, 54, 61, 81, 117, 190, 243; Welsh form 147
religion 52, 61, 76, 164
Rikskonserter (concert organization) 187
RJR, Fame (FM) 42, 47; Radio Capital 47; Supreme Sound (AM) 42, 43, 47
Roaring Lion (calypsonian) 81, 83
rock-'n'-roll 18
Rockers Magazine 45
Roe, K. 170
Roland Co-operation 247
Rome Convention 30, 31, 132, 184, 204, 224, 225

Roxette (Swedish group) 238; 'Joyride' 228
Rudder, David 81, 83

S4C (Sianel Pedwar Cymru) 137–44, 153, 230, 231–2; TV 136–9, 249, 254
Safari, Margaret 91, 105
SAIN Records 127, 132, 133, 134, 138, 145, 147–50
Sargeant, Lancelot 66
satellite television 14, 158, 167–77, 200–3, 206, 213, 227, 237; dishes 65; increase 52; influence 44–5; ownership 39–40; tax on 39, 57–8 *see also under* named companies *and* television
Scansat company 172
Schiller, H.I. 211, 213, 214
Schlesinger, P. 32
Schramm, Wilbur, *Mass Media and National Development* 222
Seaga, Edward 38, 57, 59
sing-jay (Jamaica) 247; hybrids 40
SKY television 157, 167, 168–71, 173, 201
soca (soul-calypso) 55, 81; 'chutney' 69; soccer 70; as 'zouk' 81
software *see* hardware/software
Sonet (Sweden) 178–80, 235
Sony 11, 199, 203, 212
Soramäki, M. and Harma, J. 178
South African Gallo Records 86
sponsorship 55, 76, 117, 121, 150–1, 206–8
sport 172, 176, 233
State Bureau of Statistics (SCB) Sweden 160
steelbands 69, 74, 75–6, 210; school competition 80
Stenbeck, Jan 172, 175–7, 204, 226–7
STIM 239, 251
Stockholm Opera 186
Stone, Carl 38, 39, 45, 47–8
Straker's Records 66
Studio Les 148
Sundar Popo 69
Sveriges Radio 157, 159, 160–2, 176–7
Swaggert, Jimmy 52, 76
Swansea Sound 135
Sweden 4, 209, 228, 229, 232–3, 235, 236, 242–3, 246, 250; actors, issues, policies 160–77, 185–95, 251; data

collection 33; government report 186; listening patterns 13; media environment 156–61; Midsummer weekend 1; music income 184–5; trends 210–11; repertoire 181–4
Swedish Association of Popular Music Composers (SKAP) 162, 188, 217
Swedish Broadcasting Corporation 1, 160–2
Swedish Composers' Copyright Society (STIM) 33, 162, 169, 170
Swedish Independent Music Producers (SOM) 180–1, 183
Swedish Music Movement 18
Swedish National Radio 81, 189
Swedish Radio, Audience Research Department (PUB) 160
Swedish TV 166–8

taarab style music 113
Tambu, 'roadmarch' calypso 76
Tanzania 201, 209, 219, 230, 235; actors, issues, policies 114–20; data collection 33; economy 4, 108; music in media 108–14, 120–4; story of musician 243, 245
Tanzania Film Company (TFC) 110, 115, 116, 121
Tanzanian Radio 241
Tanzanites (Tanzanian group) 200
tarab music 90
tax 251
TAXI CONNECTION, concert 54
technology 197, 198, 199, 202, 227, 243; communication 3; digital 10–11; gap 239–40; innovations 26–9; role 248
Tele-X satellite 157, 173, 231
Teledu'r Tir Glas 138
Teleproductions Association 66, 79
teletext system 144
television 6–7, 131, 248; commercial 172–7; franchise 253; growth 109; in Jamaica 52–3; music on 166–77, 166–8; ownership 39; spread of 85–6, 92; in Sweden 157–8, 174–6; transborder 223; in Trinidad 65–6, 71–2, 79; in Wales 136–44 *see also under* named companies *and* satellite television
Tett, Sheila 105
Thiongo, Margaret 100

Thomas, Lyn 142, 144, 152
Time-Life, merger 7
Time-Warner 7, 11, 176, 179, 203
Toshiba 7, 11, 226
tourism 41–2
trade unions 234–5
traditional music 110–11, 115, 246; competitions 116
transculturation 8, 214–15
transnational business 28–9
transplantation process 24
Trinidad 200, 209, 210, 219, 229, 236, 240, 242, 250, 254; economy 4; media environment 65–8; music interaction 72–83; music in media 68–72
Trinidad Express, The 66
Trinidad Guardian 65
Trinidad and Tobago Television (TTT) 65–6, 72
TTT *see* Trinidad and Tobago Television
Tunstall, Jeremy 15, 213, 214, 222
TV3/4 Sweden 157–8, 172–6, 208, 231, 253
TV Plus (vetting committee) 175

U2 (Irish group) 203
Unesco 3, 221–2; in Caribbean 55–6; 'Communication in the Service of Humanity' 222; conferences 8; Declaration on the Mass Media (1979) 221
United Kingdom 216, 253
United States 211–12, 213, 222, 225–6; economy 4; influence of 56; payola scandals 228–9

VCRs 85, 109, 113, 158
Viacom 172
video 6, 24, 27, 43–4, 85, 141, 169, 171, 173, 206, 234; clips 80, 92, 167–8; independent production houses 66; influence on young people 44–5; local 53, 56; as marketing tool 12, 14; rental business 158
Vietnam 234
village musicians 101–2, 104
vinyl records 12, 67, 86, 89, 177, 178, 181–3; decline 10
Virgin Records 11, 79–80, 183, 238

Voice of Kenya (VoK) 1, 85, 89–92, 93, 94, 97–8, 122, 232; TV 92
VoK *see* Voice of Kenya
Volvo 157, 190

Wailer, Bunny 41, 61
Wales (Cymru) 218, 219, 229, 235, 238, 253–4; education 151–2; employment 152; language 152; media environment 125–7; minority culture 4; music attitudes 152–5; policies 127–44, 150–1
Walters, Gareth 150
Wandera, Rose 84–5, 95
Ware, Raymond 145
Weekend Enquirer (Jamaica) 45
Welsh Arts Council 150, 151
Welsh Home Service 126
Welsh Language Society 126, 130, 140, 236
Welsh National Opera 151, 224

Welsh Nationalist party 126
White, Timothy 42
Whylie, Marjorie 44, 53
William, Fadhili, 'Malaika' 101–2
Williams, Eric 69
Williams, Euryn Ogwen 138, 140
Williams, Grace 150
Williams, Hugh Tregellis 197
Williams, Winston 50
WIPO *see* World Intellectual Property Organization
women, in bands 80; and music 104–5
World Bank 254
World Commission on Culture and Development 221–2
World Intellectual Property Organization (WIPO) 3; Tunis Model Law 59
World Music/World Beat 215

Y Jecsyn Ffeif (J5) 147